STUDIES IN AMERICAN LITERATURE

Volume I

☆☆☆☆☆☆☆☆☆☆☆☆☆☆☆☆☆☆☆☆☆☆☆☆☆☆☆☆☆☆☆☆☆☆☆

PACIFISM AND REBELLION
IN THE WRITINGS OF
HERMAN MELVILLE

by

JOHN BERNSTEIN

Princeton

FOLCROFT LIBRARY EDITIONS / 1974

Library of Congress Cataloging in Publication Data

Bernstein, John.
    Pacifism and rebellion in the writings of Herman Melville.

    Reprint of the 1964 ed. published by Mouton, Hague, which was issued as V. 1 of Studies in American literature.
    Bibliography: p.
    Includes index.
    1. Melville, Herman, 1819-1891–Philosophy. 2. Pacifism in literature. I. Title.
PS2388.P5B4 1974   813'.3   74-16813
ISBN 0-8414-3295-3   Limited 100 Copies

Limited 100 Copies

Manufactured in the United States of America

Folcroft Library Editions
Box 182
Folcroft, Pa. 19032

PACIFISM AND REBELLION
IN THE WRITINGS OF
HERMAN MELVILLE

by

JOHN BERNSTEIN

Princeton

1964
MOUTON & CO.
LONDON · THE HAGUE · PARIS

© Copyright 1964 Mouton & Co., Publishers, The Hague, The Netherlands.

No part of this book may be translated or reproduced in any form, by print, photoprint, microfilm, or any other means, without written permission from the publishers.

Printed in The Netherlands

TO MY PARENTS

ACKNOWLEDGEMENTS

It is a pleasure to acknowledge the kindness of those who have helped me in various ways in my work on this study. Joan M. Vizard, John Dickens Norstedt, and Professor James Missey of Beloit College have read the manuscript and offered perceptive suggestions. Several professors of American literature at both Haverford College and the University of Pennsylvania – Gerhard Friedrich, Max Bluestone, and R. W. B. Lewis – have helped to kindle my interest in Melville. Professor Arthur Scouten has given me all sorts of aid and encouragement. Special thanks are due to Professor Robert E. Spiller, whose level-headed advice saved me from numerous dubious positions in my interpretations. Most of all, I wish to thank Professor Charles Boewe, who first suggested that I work on some aspect of pacifism in Melville's writings, for his incisive criticism and good-humored assistance while I was working on this volume.

A grant from the Princeton University Research Committee helped make publication of this book possible.

J. B.

TABLE OF CONTENTS

Acknowledgements 7
Introduction 11
   I. *Typee* and *Omoo:* The Noble Savage and the Corrupted Savage 15
   II. *Mardi:* The Metaphysical Leap 31
   III. *Redburn:* Innocence and Experience 57
   IV. *White-Jacket:* The Philosophy of Pacifism . . . 68
   V. *Moby-Dick* 82
   VI. *Pierre:* The Fool of Virtue 126
   VII. *Israel Potter* and *The Confidence Man* 146
   VIII. The Short Stories: A Partial Reconciliation of Differences 165
   IX. The Poetry: A Workable Philosophy of Rebellion . 180
   X. *Billy Budd:* The Testament of Rebellion 202
   XI. Summary and Conclusion 214
Bibliography 222
Index 231

INTRODUCTION

In this study, which deals with all of Melville's fiction and poetry, I hope to show that pacifism or rebellion appear as themes in virtually all of the author's writings, that they emerge as polarities in Melville's major works, and that an understanding of the issues involved in the conflict between these two themes is essential to an understanding of Melville as a thinker and as an artist.

Often, however, pacifism and rebellion, far from being antithetical, are complementary. For example, the two most devout pacifists of all time – Christ and Gandhi – rank also in the forefront of history's greatest revolutionists. Nor do we find in the early writings of Herman Melville that the themes of pacifism and rebellion come into conflict. Indeed in *White-Jacket* (1850), they go hand in hand. This book, though decidedly anti-war and stressing much of the "turn the other cheek" attitude of Christ, contains strong social protest, being in particular a vigorous rebellion against the practice of flogging American sailors and in general a profound criticism of the corruptions of democracy. Yet in Melville's next novel, *Moby-Dick* (1851), the two themes are violently in conflict. The struggle between Starbuck and Ahab, as I hope to explain later, is at its very basis the struggle between a pacifist and a rebel. And this same central tension is to be found in the rest of the major works following *Moby-Dick:* in the conflicting attitudes revealed by a comparison of poems like "Stonewall Jackson" and "Shiloh" in *Battle-Pieces,* in the philosophical debates between such diametrically opposed characters as Derwent and Ungar in *Clarel,* and in the alternate philosophies of life represented by the Christian resignation of Billy Budd to his unjust fate and by the rebellious spirit of the French Revolution as symbolized by the warship, the *Athéiste*.

Pacifism and rebellion, as I have suggested, appear as polarities in most of Melville's major works, such as *Moby-Dick, Clarel,* and *Billy Budd*. But even in such early novels as *Typee* and *Omoo,* in which these two themes are not placed in opposition, some aspects of pacifism and rebellion are raised. It can be safely said that all but the most minor of Melville's works deal with pacifism and/or rebellion, though these two themes may appear either individually or together, and if the latter is the case, they may be either complementary or antithetical. One of the things that I will attempt to do in this analysis is to trace chronologically Melville's handling of these two themes from work to work, for this seems to me to be one of the best ways to study the changes and development in Melville's thought and craft. What a world of difference there is between the simple physical revolt of Tommo in *Typee* and the Promethean, metaphysical, and intellectual rebellion of Ahab in *Moby-Dick*!

The most important reason for choosing pacifism and rebellion as vehicles by which to analyze the works of Melville, however, is that these two themes lead us directly to the center of the author's philosophy. Pacifism and rebellion are tightly interwoven with Melville's concept of natural law and the ethical structure of the universe, with his attitude towards Christ and Christianity, and with the enigma of evil, both human and universal. Let me illustrate this briefly. To vastly oversimplify, one can say that Melville's pacifist is a man who sees some sort of moral order in the universe – whether it be the *natural* dignity and goodness of the Typees or a form of ultimate judgment and justice, a "last Assizes" to use Captain Vere's words. The prototype of the Melvillean pacifist-hero would be the gentle Quaker Starbuck. Melville's rebel-hero, on the other hand, views the universe as being essentially chaotic. For men such as Ungar or Ahab, the world, if not downright evil, is at best amoral. It is the duty of the rebel-hero to fight against the forces of injustice and chaos, and to attempt to insert some sort of man-made value into the cosmos. Melville's pacifist is a man who accepts Christ. His rebel feels that Christ offers a false answer, that Jesus, by stressing submissiveness, betrays the cause of justice. Another goal of this study, then, will be to suggest that in the long run, a study of Melville's attitudes towards pacifism and rebellion is a key to understanding Melville's concept of the universe.

As this analysis is a study of pacifism and rebellion in the writings of Herman Melville, some sort of definition of the words *pacifism* and *rebellion* is necessary. Since part of my concern, however, is with the development of Melville's concepts of both pacifism and rebellion, a narrow definition of either term would be self-defeating. Broadly speaking, by *pacifism* I mean that attitude towards life which rejects the use of physical violence as a way to solve differences that may exist either between individuals or between nations. Moreover, pacifism is traditionally associated with some form of religious values. With the exception of Bartleby, this is also true of Melville's pacifists, who are either strongly Christian in their outlook or, though professing no formal religious beliefs, are presented as Christ-like, such as Billy Budd. *Rebellion* will be defined as it appears in *The American College Dictionary:* "Resistance against or defiance of any authority or control." This definition is general enough to include both the mutiny of the slaves aboard the *San Dominick* and Ahab's Promethean defiance of the gods. In addition, it should be pointed out that for the greater part, Melville's pacifists are concerned more with man's relationship to his fellow men than they are with man's relationship to the universe. The converse is true of Melville's rebel-hero. The rebel's primary interest is in the individual's position in the universe, his status in the eyes of the gods, and his assertation of human dignity against the black face of chaos. For Ahab and the other rebel-heroes, contact with human beings is secondary to man's struggle against the hostility of the cosmos.

The need for a study of the Melville canon similar to the approach I propose has long been recognized by Melville scholars. Recently, in his review of Merlin Bowen's *The Long Encounter: Self and Experience in the Writings of Herman Melville*, Harry Moore wrote in the July 17, 1961, issue of *The New York Times Book Review:*

Mr. Bowen is right in saying that the line between active and passive resistance is hard to draw, but it should be remembered that although Prometheus when bound is passive, he had once engaged in emphatically successful action. Perhaps, instead of putting Bartleby with Ahab, Mr. Bowen should have devised another category for passive resisters . . .

My analysis, I hope, will do this.

CHAPTER I

TYPEE AND *OMOO:* THE NOBLE SAVAGE
AND THE CORRUPTED SAVAGE

> "Whitman we have called our greatest voice because he gave us hope. Melville is the truer man."
> Charles Olson, *Call Me Ishmael*

Some time during the month of July in 1842, a young American mariner became disgusted with life aboard the whaler *Acushnet,* jumped ship at Nukuhiva, one of the most beautiful of the Marquesan Islands, and lived with a tribe of cannibals called the Taipis for no more than a few weeks. The exact explanation of why and how he fled from the land of the Taipis is not quite clear, but it can now be stated with certainty that Herman Melville signed as an able seaman aboard the Australian whaler the *Lucy Ann* – the ship which carried him away from Nukuhiva – on August 9, 1842.[1] After a rather ill-fated cruise, the *Lucy Ann* reached Tahiti, where Melville was imprisoned along with most of the ship's crew on the charge of mutiny. The open air calaboose which served as a prison was in reality more like a boarding house, and Melville and a companion soon easily escaped, afterwards living like beachcombers for several weeks. The experiences of these few months provided raw material for two books, and exerted a strong influence on Melville's thought for the rest of his life.

The two books produced as a direct result of this period were *Typee* (1846) and *Omoo* (1847). Both works are novels of adventure, presented through the eyes of a first-person narrator, and in both books it is impossible to separate fact (Melville's actual experiences in the South Seas) from fiction (incidents and em-

---

[1] Leon Howard, *Herman Melville* (Berkeley and Los Angeles, 1958), p. 54.

broiderings which are strictly the products of the budding artistic imagination of the fledgling author). Though the imagery in both works is for the most part quite carefully controlled, *Typee* and *Omoo* differ from the rest of Melville's writing in that they are neither symbolic nor allegorical. Nevertheless, both creations are far richer than most travel journals or novels of pure adventure. One reason for this is that even the young Melville is a far better craftsman than is Henry Rider Haggard, for example. More important, though *Typee* and *Omoo* lack the intense metaphysical probing to be found in the author's later work, it is quite apparent that Melville did much more in the South Pacific than lie on the warm sands and munch breadfruit; he did a great deal of thinking about the differences between "primitive" and "civilized" man and about the nature of evil, and his speculation upon this subject may readily be seen in his first two novels.

As had been indicated in the introduction, Melville's attitude towards both pacifism and rebellion is closely tied up with his views on natural law. Hence, any exploration of pacifism and rebellion in Melville's writings must begin with an assessment of the impact of the Typees – surely a race of people as similar to Rousseau's "Natural Man" as is humanly possible – upon the mind of Tommo, the chief protagonist of *Typee*.

When the *Dolly,* an American whaler, arrives at the bay of Nukuhiva after having been at sea for six months, it is boarded by an uninhibited horde of lovely Marquesan maidens, whose "free unstudied action"[2] is in sharp contrast to the narrow confines and rigorous discipline of the ship. This comparison is not lost upon Tommo, the narrator of *Typee,* who shortly thereafter decides to jump ship. In addition to his personal desire to elude the hardships of the sailors' lot and to enjoy the unrestricted freedom of life on shore, Tommo gives a more general and philosophical explanation for his desire to escape – the injustice of the captain. The narrator rhetorically asks himself whether a person is bound to a contract (i.e. the signing of the ship's articles) if the other party (the captain) violates it. The answer, according to Tommo, obviously is no.

[2] Milton Stern (ed.), *Typee and Billy Budd* (New York, 1958), p. 13.

Having settled the principle, then, let me apply it to the particular case in question. In numberless instances had not only the implied but the specified conditions of the articles been violated on the part of the ship in which I served. The usage on board of her was tyrannical; the sick had been inhumanly neglected; the provisions had been doled out in scanty allowance; and her cruizes were unreasonably protracted. The captain was the author of these abuses; it was in vain to think that he would either remedy them, or alter his conduct, which was arbitrary and violent in the extreme.[3]

Tommo's cry of defiance is in a minor key, and his reaction to unjust authority is merely an attempt to remove himself from the jurisdictions of that injustice, not an attempt to fight against the source of this evil. It is important to note that not only is Tommo's response to injustice altogether at odds with the reactions of the more mature Melvillean rebel-hero, but that the presentation of this situation in *Typee* differs entirely from the handling of similar events in the author's later works. Unlike the ship in *White-Jacket*, the *Dolly* is not symbolic of the whole world, nor do the signing of the ship's articles in *Typee* imply some sort of more universal compact on a Lockean scale concerning the rights of man, as they do in *Billy Budd*.

Tommo successfully escapes from the *Dolly* with one of his shipmates, an agile youth named Toby, and the two make their way into the mountains, hopeful of falling in with the friendly Happars. But such is not their fate, for the first natives they encounter are the feared Typees, noted for their cannibalism. The two young sailors are led to a native village where they are treated with kindness, but are informed in no uncertain terms that they are not to attempt to leave the valley of the Typees.

Since there is virtually no work to be done in the valley and since Tommo is incapacitated by a badly infected leg anyway, he spends all of his time observing the life about him and meditating upon these observations. Tommo's train of thought moves through several phases, from the particular to the general, and it is through a study of his musings that we first get a hint of Melville's concept of the natural state of man, an understanding of which is essential

---

[3] *Ibid.*, p. 18.

in tracing the development of pacifism and rebellion as concepts in Melville's thinking.

Tommo's first observations are simple enough, the type of observations that any traveler makes the first few days in a foreign land, how things differ from home. Tommo contrasts the customs of the Typees to those of the Europeans and Americans. The first direct comparison which he makes is a humorous one. After watching the strenuous contortions of Kory-Kory as he attempts to start a fire, Tommo comments:

> What a striking evidence does this operation furnish of the wide difference between the extreme of savage and civilized life. A gentleman of Typee can bring up a numerous family of children and give them all a highly respectable cannibal education, with infinitely less toil and anxiety than he expends in the simple process of striking a light; whilst a poor European artisan, who through the instrumentality of a lucifer performs the same operation in one second, is put to his wit's end to provide for his starving offspring that food which the children of a Polynesian father, without troubling their parent, pluck from the branches of every tree around them.[4]

But after Tommo has become better acquainted with the Typees and his fear of being devoured by the natives has ceased for the time being, he begins to make more profound commentaries about the inhabitants of the valley. His major concern is now not so much with the physical life of the people as it is with the nature of their characters. This shift in approach is almost inevitable, but it is important. It is similar to the change in outlook of an American, who might remark after two days in Paris that French food is considerably more exciting than American food, and the more penetrating observation of the same American after several years in France that the French are more concerned with the art of living than are their American counterparts.

The longer Tommo stays in the valley, the more he is impressed with the kindness and friendliness of the Typees. The natives live in complete harmony with each other. "Never was there exhibited the least sign of strife or contention among them."[5] In addition

---

[4] *Ibid.*, p. 110.
[5] *Ibid.*, p. 124.

An unbounded liberty of conscience seemed to prevail. Those who pleased to do so were allowed to repose implicit faith in an ill-favoured god with a large bottle nose and fat shapeless arms crossed upon his breast ... the islanders always maintained a discreet reserve with regard to my own peculiar views on religion.[6]

The inherent nobility of the savages can be seen in almost any of their activities. The following is a description of the Feast of the Calabashes.

During the festival I had not failed to remark the simplicity of manner, the freedom from all restraint, and, to a certain degree, the equality of condition manifested by the natives in general. No one appeared to assume any arrogant pretentions. There was little more than a slight difference in costume to distinguish the chiefs from the other natives. All appeared to mix together freely, and without any reserve ...[7]

The only explanation which Tommo is as yet ready to offer for the elevated state of the Typees is a rather simple one, even though Rousseau is cited. "But the continual happiness, which so far as I was able to judge appeared to prevail in the valley, sprung principally from that all-pervading sensation which Rousseau has told us that he at one time experienced, the mere buoyant sense of a healthful physical existence."[8]

But soon, Tommo begins to make generalizations about primitive man based upon his observations of the Typees. The central section concerned with the development of Melville's concept of natural law and the nature of uncorrupted man is Chapter XXVII of *Typee,* entitled "The social Condition and general Character of the Typees".

In short, there were no legal provisions whatever for the well-being and conservation of society, the enlightened end of civilized legislation. And yet everything went on in the valley with a harmony and smoothness unparalleled, I will venture to assert, in the most select, refined, and pious associations of mortals in Christendom. How are we to explain this enigma? These islanders were heathens! savages!

[6] *Ibid.,* p. 168.
[7] *Ibid.,* p. 183.
[8] *Ibid.,* p. 125.

20   "TYPEE" AND "OMOO"

ay, cannibals! and how came they, without the aid of established law, to exhibit, in so eminent a degree, that social order which is the greatest blessing and highest pride of the social state?

It may reasonably be inquired, how were these people governed? how were their passions controlled in their everyday transactions? *It must have been an inherent principle of honesty and charity towards each other. They seemed to be governed by that sort of tacit common-sense law which, say what they will of the inborn lawlessness of the human race, has its precepts graven on every breast. The grand principles of virtue and honour, however they may be distorted by arbitrary codes, are the same all the world over: and where these principles are concerned, the right or wrong of any action appears the same to the uncultivated as to the enlightened mind. It is to this indwelling, this universally diffused perception of what is just and noble, that the integrity of the Marquesans in their intercourse with each other is to be attributed.*[9] [Italics my own.]

This position is elaborated upon several pages later.

Civilization does not engross all the virtues of humanity: she has not even her full share of them. They flourish in greater abundance and attain greater strength among many barbarous people. The hospitality of the wild Arab, the courage of the North American Indian, and the faithful friendships of some of the Polynesian nations, far surpass any thing of similar kind among the polished communities of Europe. If truth and justice, and the better principles of our nature, cannot exist unless enforced by the statute-book, how are we to account for the social condition of the Typees? So pure and upright were they in all the relations of life, that entering their valley, as I did, under the most erroneous impressions of their character, I was soon led to exclaim in amazement: "Are these the ferocious savages, the blood-thirsty cannibals of whom I have heard such frightful tales! They deal more kindly with each other, and are more humane, than many who study essays on virtue and benevolence, and who repeat every night that beautiful prayer breathed first by the lips of the divine and gentle Jesus." I will frankly declare, that after passing a few weeks in this valley of the Marquesas, I formed a higher estimate of human nature than I had ever before entertained.[10]

Primitive man, then, as viewed by Melville, is happy, kind, dignified, friendly, and able to live in harmony with his fellows. And he is this way because he follows closely natural law or principles

[9] *Ibid.*, p. 198.
[10] *Ibid.*, p. 200.

inherent in the universe. To state this somewhat differently, the natural state of man is a good state, and there is more truth in "the dark wisdom of the blood" (to borrow a phrase from D. H. Lawrence) than there is in all of the accomplishments and accouterments of civilization. Though there are instances of evil in *Typee*, this evil is neither beyond the control of man nor an underlying aspect of human nature, but it is rather a result of the corruption of natural law by the white man's civilization.

Melville's attitude about the nature of evil changes radically in his later works. In his writings after *Omoo*, he sees evil as being a primarily metaphysical problem, a basic part of the universe with which all men, whether civilized or savage, must come to grips. But though the burden of guilt for most of the world's evils no longer falls upon the white man's shoulder, Melville still remains an intense critic of civilization, and his sympathies in all of his works with the possible exception of "Benito Cereno" are inevitably with the uncivilized and dusty-skinned races. There may be a world of difference philosophically between the contented cannibals of the Typee valley and the dark heathens such as Fedallah or Queequeq, who are highly sympathetic to Ahab's defiance of the universe; but nonetheless, Melville's savages are virtually always closer to a true understanding of the universe than is the white man, with the occasional exception of a Captain Ahab, who in some ways out-primitives the primitives.

It would also follow from the above discussion that so long as Melville regards evil as a man-made rather than a God-made phenomenon, the Melvillean rebel would be more of a social reformer than a man whose rebellion is on an intense metaphysical plane, as is the case with Ungar or Ahab.

The land of the Typees, however, is a "Happy Valley" in which there is neither metaphysical evil nor a need for social reformers. It is, as Melville suggests, quite similar to the Garden of Eden. If this is the case, why does Tommo quit his South Sea paradise? The major artistic and thematic weakness of *Typee* is that Melville never really deals honestly with this question. To be sure, Tommo talks of his horror of being tattooed and of his renewed fears of becoming the chief course of a Typee banquet. But these reasons for Tommo's flight do not seem to be sufficient for they are not convincingly presented. After an extremely humorous description of native tattooing and of the desire of the great Karky to practice his art on the young American, Tommo suddenly comments that because of the natives' plans to have him tattooed, "my existence became a burden to me; the pleasures I had previously enjoyed no longer afforded me delight, and all my former desire to escape from the valley now revived with additional force".[11] Since there is no evidence at all to support Richard Chase's hypothesis that tattooing in this instance can be equated with castration,[12] Tommo's reaction to the situation appears greatly exaggerated. In addition, Tommo's renewed fears concerning the Typees' cannibalism also seems somewhat dubious, for he himself had not too long ago observed that "I was much inclined to believe that such shocking festivals must occur very rarely among the islanders, if, indeed, they ever take place".[13] Hence, these reasons for Tommo's escape back to civilization are not psychologically convincing for they represent too abrupt a shift away from his previous attitudes.

A more profound explanation – albeit rather rhapsodical and lacking textual support – is that found in D. H. Lawrence's *Studies in Classic American Literature*. The gist of Lawrence's argument is that a place such as the valley of the Typees can never be the answer to the problems of an intelligent person who had formerly dwelt in the white man's world. For such a person had already lost his innocence, and is aware of evil. A brief sojourn in a primitive land might be pleasant and renew one's faith in man, perhaps even become a symbol of all that is good in the world. But to live there for the rest of one's life and pretend to ignore the evil which exists almost everywhere else would be an act of cowardice.

We can't go back. We can't go back to the savages: not a stride. We can be in sympathy with them. We can take a great curve in their direction, onwards. But we cannot turn the current of our lives backwards, back towards their soft warm twilight and uncreate mud. Not for a moment. If we do it for a moment, it makes us sick.

[11] *Ibid.*, p. 217.
[12] See *Herman Melville* (New York, 1949).
[13] *Typee*, p. 128.

... Try to go back to the savages, and you feel as if your very soul was decomposing inside you. That is what you feel in the South Seas, anyhow: as if your soul was decomposing inside of you. And with any savages the same if you try to go their way, take their current of sympathy.[14]

It is not that the white man's way is better than that of the savages. The opposite is true. But a white and civilized man cannot hide from either his whiteness or his civilization. Lawrence continues:

The very freedom of his Typee was a torture to him. Its ease was slowly horrible to him. This time *he* was the fly in the odorous tropical ointment.

He needed to fight. It was no good to him, the relaxation of the non-moral tropics. He didn't really want Eden. He wanted to fight. Like every American. To fight. But with the weapons of the spirit, not the flesh.

That was the top and bottom of it. *His soul was in revolt, writhing forever in revolt. When he had something definite to rebel against — like the bad conditions on a whaling ship — then he was much happier in his miseries.* The mills of God were grinding inside him, and they needed something to grind on.

When they could grind on the injustice and folly of missionaries, or of brutal sea-captains, or of governments, he was easier.[15] [Italics in the last two paragraphs my own.]

If we accept Lawrence's interpretation, a writer from whom I have quoted so extensively not only because he is a top-flight critic, but more important because his mind and outlook towards life are almost identical with those of Melville, Tommo quits the Happy Valley of the Typees in order that he may lead the life of a rebel and fight against the forces of injustice.

Perhaps the most important scene in terms of pacifism and rebellion occurs at the close of *Typee*. As the boat carrying Tommo towards freedom flees from the angered savages, the hero notices that Mow-Mow, a native chief, has swum out into the water and is about to seize one of the oars. Tommo notes that "Even at the moment I felt horror at the act I was about to commit; but it was no time for pity or compunction, and with a true aim, and exerting all my strength, I dashed the boat-hook at him.

[14] New York, 1955, pp. 149-50.
[15] *Ibid.*, pp. 150-1.

It struck him just below the throat and forced him downwards."[16] This scene is almost identical to the one in *Mardi* in which Taji is forced to kill the old priest in order to free Yillah, though Melville's handling of this incident in the later novel in on an entirely symbolic level. Also, as F. O. Matthiessen suggests, Starbuck in *Moby-Dick* is in the same position as is Tommo in *Typee,* but the Quaker first mate refuses to resort to violence.[17]

Thus, though Tommo's action in maiming the cannibal chief is not deeply explored in *Typee* itself, this particular scene recurs in varying forms throughout Melville's work, much like a leitmotif. Even on the simplest level, however, it should be noted that Tommo's first action upon returning to the white man's world is one of violence. Tommo's boat-hook is raised not only against Mow-Mow, but also in effect against the very type of existence to be found in the valley of Typees. As Ronald Mason says, 'Tommo escaped, killing a Typee warrior in the struggle. In violence he discarded immature innocence and returned to the shoddy sophistication which he loathed".[18]

Omoo is a continuation of the narrative of *Typee,* concerning the further adventures of Tommo aboard the Australian ship, the *Little Jule,* his life as a beachcomber in Tahiti, and his various expeditions with Doctor Long Ghost, one of Melville's most successful character creations. There is some difference in tone between the two books however. Though *Typee* is written with a good deal of wit, it is not primarily a humorous book. *Omoo* is. It seems safe to say that *Omoo* is the most sustained piece of comic writing in the Melville canon. Again, it is valuable to turn to the commentary of D. H. Lawrence. "Perhaps Melville is at his best, his happiest, in *Omoo*. For once he is really reckless. For once he takes life as it comes. For once he is the gallant rascally epicurean, eating the world like a snipe, dirt and all baked into one *bonne bouche*".[19]

Although *Omoo* may well be Melville's "happiest" creation, it is also the work which contains the highest ratio of adventure to

---

[16] *Typee*, p. 247.
[17] *American Renaissance* (New York, 1941).
[18] *The Spirit Above the Dust* (London, 1951), p. 29.
[19] Lawrence, p. 152.

contemplation, and of all of Melville's compositions, it is the one with the least amount of philosophical or intellectual content. And, along with *White-Jacket, Omoo* is the only work of Melville's in which pacifism is used as a means by which to further rebellion.

When the *Little Jule* finally reaches Tahiti, the invalid captain is taken ashore, but the crew is forced to remain on board. Coupled with their previous harsh treatment at sea, this confinement to the ship breeds a murderous attitude in the men, which the protagonist attempts to channel in a constructive direction.

Meanwhile, Long Ghost and I laboured hard to diffuse the right spirit among the crew; *impressing upon them that a little patience and management would, in the end, accomplish all that their violence could; and that, too, without making a serious matter out of it.*

For my own part, I felt that I was under a foreign flag: that an English consul was close at hand, and that sailors seldom obtain justice. *It was best to be prudent. Still, so much did I sympathize with the men, so far, at least, as their real grievances were concerned; and so convinced was I of the cruelty and injustice of what Captain Guy seemed bent upon, that if need were, I stood ready to raise a hand.*[20] [Italics my own.]

The narrator (he is not given any official name in *Omoo*, though for brief periods he is dubbed either Typee or Paul, and it would be a misinterpretation to completely identify him with Melville) forestalls any immediate violence by suggesting that the crew send a "Round Robin" – a document whose signatures are arranged in such a way that no man can be picked out as leader – listing their grievances to the English consul in Tahiti. The results of this "Round-Robin" are not very fruitful, however. Wilson, the consul, comes aboard the *Little Jule* and tells the crew as bluntly as possible that the ship is supposed to go out to sea at once under the command of the usually inebriated first mate Jermin, and that none of the men will be allowed to go ashore. Armed rebellion at this point seems almost inevitable. The narrator explains his own attitude as follows:

All we wanted was to have the ship snugly anchored in Papeetee Bay: entertaining no doubt that, could this be done, it would in some way

---

[20] *The Romances of Herman Melville* (New York, 1931), p. 231.

or other peaceably lead to our emancipation. *Without a downright mutiny, there was but one way to accomplish this: to induce the men to refuse all further duty, unless it were to work the vessel in.* The only difficulty lay in restraining them within proper bounds. Nor was it without certain misgivings, that I found myself so situated, that I must necessarily link myself, however guardedly, with such a desperate company; and in an enterprise too, of which it was hard to conjecture what might be the result. But anything like neutrality was out of the question; and unconditional submission was equally so.

On going foreward, we found them ten times more tumultuous than ever. *After again restoring some degree of tranquility, we once more urged our plan of quietly refusing duty, and awaiting the result. At first, few would hear of it; but in the end, a good number were convinced by our representations.*[21] [Italics my own.]

The young sailor and Long Ghost are ultimately successful in getting the crew to accept their policy of non-violent resistance, but the long-run efficacy of this pacifism is not clear cut. In terms of any abstract rectifying of injustice, the pacifism practiced by the crew of the *Little Jule* is a total failure. The men are tried as mutineers, found guilty, and sent to jail. Neither the captain nor the first mate are ever officially reprimanded for their maltreatment of the crew. But in terms of the practical result of getting the men off the ship and into the more pleasant surroundings of Tahiti proper, no policy could have been more effective. Though the men are theoretically in prison, they have almost complete freedom of movement, for the "Calabooza Beretanee" is probably the least jail-like jail in the history of literature, being in most ways similar to a highly dilapidated but extremely hospitable boarding house.

It is impossible to ascertain Melville's attitude towards pacifism and rebellion as seen in *Omoo*. It is true that we have in this novel non-violence used as a tool of rebellion. But the union of the two forces of pacifism and rebellion, which ultimately emerge as antitheses in Melville's later works, is presented not as a moral or philosophical issue, but solely in terms of what would work best. Though there seems to be no question that the resort to non-violent revolt is by far the most effective solution for the sailors

---

[21] *Ibid.*, p. 237.

aboard the *Little Jule* in their *particular* case, there is nothing in the novel to indicate that Melville feels that non-violence is generally the most effective form of rebellion. A further complication is that virtually nothing is treated with seriousness in *Omoo* except the unhappy condition of the natives of Tahiti.

In *Typee,* Melville presented a delightful picture of primitive man in his natural surroundings, happy and dignified, a noble savage governed by natural law. As one commentator has noted, the crux of the relationship between *Typee* and *Omoo* is "the contrast, not between native and white man, but between one kind of native and another".[22] If the valley of the Typees had been a Garden of Eden, Tahiti was a Paradise Lost, though the fallen state of the Tahitians was not because of any moral breakdown from within, but was rather the direct influence of the white man. What Alan Paton has so penetratingly observed about Africa in *Cry, the Beloved Country* casts a great deal of light upon the situation Melville found in Tahiti.

The old tribal system was, for all its violence and savagery, for all its superstition and witchcraft, a moral system. Our natives today produce criminals and prostitutes and drunkards, not because it is their nature to do so, but because their simple system of order and tradition has been destroyed. It was destroyed by the impact of our own civilization.[23]

The sheerly physical evils introduced by civilization into the South Seas are horrifying enough. When the white man came into Tahiti, he brought with him not only the scourge of venereal disease, but also the mosquito. As a direct result of his influence, the production of breadfruit, the staple food of the Tahitian diet, was sharply curtailed. But it is best to let Melville speak for himself.

About the year 1777, Captain Cook estimated the population of Tahiti at about two hundred thousand. By a regular census, taken some four or five years ago, it was found to be only nine thousand. This amazing decrease, not only shows the malignancy of the evils necessary to produce it; but, from the fact, the inference unavoidably follows, that all the wars, child murders, and other depopulating causes, alleged to have existed in former times, were nothing in comparison to them.

[22] Mason, p. 34.
[23] New York, 1948, p. 146.

These evils, of course, are solely of foreign origin. To say nothing of the effects of drunkenness, the occasional inroads of the small-pox, and other things, which might be mentioned, it is sufficient to allude to a virulent disease, which now taints the blood of at least two-thirds of the common people of the island; and in some form or other, is transmitted from father to son.[24]

Though Melville was highly critical of civilization's influence on Tahiti in general, his most vehement attack was on the missionaries in particular, for it was they who were most responsible for the breakdown of the ancient native culture, and hence were largely responsible for the psychological and moral collapse of the people. All sorts of evils were perpetrated under the guise of furthering the cause of Christianity. Native policemen literally beat unwilling islanders into the churches on Sundays. The Tahitians were taught about the equality of all men in the eyes of God and then confronted with such manifestations of brotherly love as segregated schools for missionary children, surrounded by fences to keep them away from the "corrupting" influences of the natives. Harmless diversions such as the traditional athletic contest were banned.

After alluding to the manifold evils entailed upon the natives by foreigners, and their singularly inert condition; and after somewhat too severely denouncing the undeniable errors of the mission, Kotzebue, the Russian navigator, says, "A religion like this, which forbids every innocent pleasure, and cramps or annihilates every mental power, is a libel on the divine founder of Christianity. It is true, that the religion of the missionaries has, with a great deal of evil, effected some good. It has restrained the vices of theft and incontinence; but it has given birth to ignorance, hypocrisy, and a hatred of all other modes of faith, which was once foreign to the open and benevolent character of the Tahitians."[25]

(It should be here strongly emphasized that Melville's attack upon the missionaries in *Omoo* is in no ways to be construed as an attack upon Christianity itself, though in his later works, he finds himself at odds with the philosophical basis of the religion.)

This picture of the unfortunate plight of the Tahitians is further

[24] *Romances*, p. 297.
[25] *Ibid.*, p. 294.

heightened by Melville's skillful counterpointing of their condition with that of the Typees. A living embodiment of this comparison is the noble Marbonna, a Marquesan who physically and ethically towers above all others in the palace of the Tahitian Queen Pomaree, and "a wild heathen, moralizing upon the vices and follies of the Christian court of Tahiti – a savage, scorning the degeneracy of the people among whom fortune had thrown him".[26]

Omoo is in some ways a work of social protest similar to *Redburn* and *White-Jacket,* an expression of the author's rebellion against man's inhumanity to man. But unlike *White-Jacket,* which can positively suggest that flogging should be abolished, *Omoo* can do nothing but expose evil, for Melville feels that nothing can be done to improve the plight of the Tahitians.

Their prospects are hopeless. Nor can the most devoted efforts, now exempt them from furnishing a marked illustration of a principle, which history has always exemplified. Years ago brought to a stand, where all that is corrupt in barbarism and civilization unite, to the exclusion of the virtues of either state; like other uncivilized beings, brought into contact with Europeans, they must here remain stationary until utterly extinct.[27]

In this chapter, I have attempted to show that though neither pacifism nor rebellion are treated with much profundity in Melville's first two novels, *Typee* and *Omoo* do set the background for the later development of these two themes. Tommo, the narrator of *Typee,* initially reacts against the injustice aboard his ship by fleeing to the valley of the Typees. But despite the fact that he finds happiness among the Typees and comes to think that these so-called savages have more dignity, kindness, and honor than does civilized man, Tommo nevertheless eventually escapes back to the world of the white man. As I have earlier suggested, neither his fear of cannibalism nor of tattooing are sufficient explanations for Tommo's action. A much better reason, though one that can not be conclusively established, is that Tommo, a creature of civilization, must leave the Typees if he is to retain his integrity. Civilized man cannot ignore the evil that exists in his own world,

[26] *Ibid.,* p. 361.
[27] *Ibid.,* p. 297.

he cannot dodge his duty by hiding in a primitive and unfallen society. To do so is cowardice, to do so spells damnation. Tommo returns to the world of the white man because he wishes to wage an active rebellion against injustice. But in the very act of escaping from the valley so that he might more aggressively combat evil, he maims a native chief who is pursuing him. In this incident, we have presented the initial clash of pacifism and rebellion in Melville's writings. In *Omoo,* on the other hand, the protagonist champions the cause of non-violence as the most effective means of rebellion. No kind of rebellion, whether violent or pacifistic, however, will help the Tahitians, for though the hero of *Omoo* is horrified by the white man's maltreatment of the natives, he is unable to do more than expose this evil, as he feels that their plight is hopeless.

A study of *Typee* and *Omoo* also tells us a good deal about Melville's early concept of the nature of the universe. Generalizing upon the condition of the Typees, Tommo suggests that primitive man is basically good, and he is good because he obeys *inherent* principles of decency and because his conduct is governed by *natural* law. Evil, as presented in Melville's first two novels, is essential a negative quality, a perversion of natural law. The injustices portrayed in *Typee* and *Omoo* are presented in terms of man's inhumanity to man (in particular, the white man's inhumanity to primitive man) not in terms of man as being at the mercy of the elements or as being the victim of unjust fate or of the whim of the gods, as is the case of *Oedipus Rex,* let us say. So long as Melville views evil as a man-made creation rather than an inherent part of the nature of things, rebellion can at best be a tool of social reform. Only when Melville comes to see evil as an *active agent,* as in *Moby-Dick,* does rebellion emerge as a full-fledged philosophy in itself, an approach to life which is as all-encompassing as is pacifism.

CHAPTER II

MARDI: THE METAPHYSICAL LEAP

> I raised my head. The offing was barred by a black bank of clouds, and the tranquil waterway leading to the uttermost ends of the earth flowed somber under an overcast sky – seemed to lead into the heart of an immense darkness.
>
> Joseph Conrad, *The Heart of Darkness*

Along with such works as Shakespeare's *Love's Labour's Lost* and Ernest Hemingway's *Across the River and Into the Trees*, *Mardi* (1849) ranks as one of the very worst compositions produced by one of the greatest writers of the English language. Even the novel's foremost champion, Merrell Davis, is forced to admit that "as art *Mardi* leaves much to be desired".[1] There are three major reasons why *Mardi* is an artistic failure. First, Melville bit off more than he or any other writer could chew. Mardi is symbolic of the entire world, and the book itself ranks as perhaps the most ambitious attempt in the history of Western literature. As Jean-Jacques Mayoux has so astutely commented in his book, *Melville,* "It seems as though he wanted to cram all the speculations on time and eternity, the finite and infinite, mind and matter, as well as those concerning human societies into this fat work, on which he lavished humor, verve, imagination, irony, and eloquence, without however succeeding in making the heavy dough rise".[2] The second reasons for *Mardi's* failure, and a reason which cannot be entirely divorced from the first, is that Melville uses four different levels or techniques of presentation. (1) Initially, we have the level of

---

[1] *Melville's Mardi: A Chartless Voyage* (New Haven, 1952), p. 200.
[2] New York, 1960, Translated by John Ashbery, p. 52.

straight South Sea romance, much in the tradition of *Typee* and *Omoo*. (2) With the appearance of Yillah and Aleema, however, Melville takes a metaphysical leap, and the book becomes a sort of mythopoetic search, similar in some ways to Shelley's "Alastor". (3) The greater part of the novel concerns itself not so much with dramatic presentation as with intellectual discussions. The sections of *Mardi* dealing with the philosophical debates among Babbalanja the philosopher, Yoomy the poet, Mohi the historian, and Media the king are reminiscent of Plato's *Republic* or Hume's *Dialogues Concerning Natural Religion*. (4) In the depictions of Vivenza, Maramma, Diranda, etc., Melville makes use of the same type of satire as is found in *Gulliver's Travels*.[3] As I have suggested, one of the great weaknesses of *Mardi* is that the different levels of the book are not well integrated, and the transitions from romance to discourse to satire are somewhat nebulous. Moreover, not only are these four strands not well meshed, but there are contradictions even within the individual portions of the work. For example, the philosophy of Mohi switches from speech to speech. A final reason for *Mardi's* lack of success is that the major symbols, the lovely Yillah and the dark Queen Hautia, are presented in such murky and unspecific terms that any sort of definite evaluation of what they stand for is virtually impossible.

But to criticize *Mardi* as a work of art is to tell only half of the story. In some ways, it is the most significant book Melville ever wrote, the key to understanding his development as an artist and as a thinker. James Baird has observed in *Ishmael* that Melville's novel "is the most important of all American experimental literary works documenting the development of the symbolistic imagination".[4] We find in *Mardi* the sudden metamorphosis of Melville from a writer of comparatively simple and straightforward travel adventures to an author deeply committed to symbolism as a technique whose major concern is with the most profound and pressing issues facing mankind. Most important, no matter what the artistic

---

[3] Most critics of *Mardi* make vague reference to *Gulliver's Travels*. I suspect that a close comparison of Book 3 of Swift's work with such chapters as "They Land at Hooloomooloo" would reveal a more specific debt.
[4] Baltimore, 1956, p. 192.

merits or defects of *Mardi,* there is a tremendous amount of wisdom in the book. Melville's evaluation of Vivenza (America) and its future problems, for instance, has been substantiated by the course of history.[5]

Because of *Mardi's* uneven and at times self-contradictory nature, however, it is not surprising that no consistent or all-encompassing philosophy of either pacifism or rebellion is evolved in the novel. But for the first time in his writings, Melville probes deeply into these two attitudes, and into such other closely related issues as the acceptability of Christianity as a way of life, etc. In terms of the development of the themes of pacifism and rebellion, the following are the most significant sections of *Mardi:* Taji's freeing of Yillah at the cost of slaying the old priest Aleema, various discourses by Babbalanja on the nature of the universe, the satirical sections dealing with the war games in Diranda, the revolutions in Europe and slavery in America, and finally, the end of the novel, where Taji rejects Serenia and sails out "over an endless sea".[6] Since *Mardi* has little internal consistency, our approach will deal with pacifism and rebellion, not necessarily in the order that events occur in the novel, but through a systematic study of the different structural levels of the novel previously discussed, with particular attention being paid to the last few chapters, in which Melville tries to fuse together the various strands running throughout the book.

Part way through *Mardi,* after Taji and Jarl have escaped from their whaling ship the *Arcturian* and have experienced numerous other adventures, we find them aboard the *Chamois* on the open sea with their new companion, the native Samoa. They are at long last drawing close to land when they encounter a huge craft "consisting of a pair of parallel canoes".[7] Taji wishes to have a meeting with the strangers, but as the *Chamois* draws near to them, they

---

[5] It should be pointed out, also, that in many ways *Mardi* is a dry run for *Moby-Dick.* Ahab's pursuit of the whale is similar to the pursuer-pursued theme in *Mardi.* Also compare the sections dealing with the Christianizing of the sharks to the Cook's sermon in *Moby-Dick* and note that we find in *Mardi* a linking of monomania with the loss of a limb (in the person of Donjalolo).

[6] *Mardi* (in *The Romances of Herman Melville*) (New York, 1931), p. 742.

[7] *Ibid.,* p. 447.

make threatening gestures. "Upon this hostile display, Samoa dropped his oar, and brought his piece to bear upon the old man, who, by his attitude, seemed to menace us with the fate of the great braggart of Gath. But I quickly knocked down the muzzle of his musket, and forbade the slightest token of hostility".[8] Instead of violence, Taji offers gifts to the strangers, and soon he discovers that the mysterious tent on their vessel contains a beautiful maiden, who is being carried to the island of Amma, where she is to be offered as a sacrifice to the gods.

Now, hearing of the maiden, I waited for no more. Need I add, how stirred was my soul toward this invisible victim; and how hotly I swore, that precious blood of hers should never smoke upon an altar. If we drowned for it, I was bent upon rescuing the captive. But as yet, no gentle signal of distress had been waved to us from the tent. Thence, no sound could be heard, but an occasional rustle of the matting. Was it possible, that one about to be immolated could proceed thus tranquilly to her fate?

But desperately as I resolved to accomplish the deliverance of the maiden, it was best to set heedfully about it. I desired no shedding of blood: though the odds were against us.[9]

But an avoidance of bloodshed is impossible, for Taji and Samoa are suddenly assailed by the old priest Aleema and his sons, and before he knows what he is doing, Taji has slain the old man. Yillah is quickly rescued, and Taji and his friends flee from the priest's avenging offspring.

Obviously, numerous complex issues are involved here. The most overt one in terms of our topic is whether or not violence is justified as a means by which to further the cause of liberty. The narrator had originally shunned violence, knocking aside Samoa's musket. But the moment he decides to free the maiden, physical force is inevitable. If Taji had not resorted to arms, he would have committed no evil, but Yillah would have been destroyed. As the result of his use of violence, Taji succeeds in liberating Yillah, but only at the cost of killing Aleema, which is a crime, as the narrator himself readily admits ("Am I a murderer, stars?").[10] To rephrase

[8] *Ibid.*, p. 448.
[9] *Ibid.*, p. 450.
[10] *Ibid.*, p. 476.

this, the question seems to be whether it is better to be pacifistic and not to sacrifice one life for another, or to act violently, which is evil, to be sure, but which also results in a great good – the freeing of Yillah and all that she represents.

For Yillah is no earthly being but an extremely complex symbol, one far from successfully or clearly developed in terms of the novel. She is an ethereal creature who believes that her lineage is more than mortal, a member of the Pacific Tullas who "pertain to some distant sphere, and only through irregularities in the providence of the gods, come to make their appearance upon earth: whence, the oversight discovered, they are hastily snatched".[11] Her name is a play upon the word "lily"[12] which refers not only to the flower, but also means "delicately fair" and "pure; unsullied". I would not disagree with any of the critics who say that Yillah is a symbol of happiness, ultimate truth, and innocence. But I think it is a mistake to speak of Yillah only on a spiritual level, for the sexual symbolism of the following passage needs no explanation. "Was not Yillah my shore and grove? my meadow, my mead, my soft shady vine, and my arbor? Of all things desirable and delightful, the full-plumed sheaf, and my own right arm the band?"[13] Whatever Yillah represents, she is totally satisfying on all levels of human experience, an earthly embodiment of the physical and spiritual dreams of every man. "And true it was to say so; and right it was to swear it, upon her white arms crossed. For oh, Yillah; were you not the earthly semblance of that very sweet vision that haunted my earliest thoughts?"[14]

A foil to Yillah is the mysterious Queen Hautia.[15] Whereas Yillah is blond, blue-eyed, and pale, Hautia when she first appears is "enveloped in a dark robe of tappa"[16] and her three attendants

---

[11] *Ibid.*, p. 462.

[12] See Merrell Davis' excellent article, "The Flower Symbolism in *Mardi*", *MLQ*, II (December, 1941), 625-38.

[13] *Romances*, p. 457.

[14] *Ibid.*, p. 465.

[15] A fuller exploration of the differences between Hautia and Yillah may be found in F. I. Carpenter's "Puritans Preferred Blondes: The Heroines of Melville and Hawthorne", *NEQ*, IX (June, 1936), 253-72.

[16] *Romances*, p. 479.

are "black-eyed damsels, deep brunettes".[17] Yillah must be pursued and liberated. Hautia pursues and must be escaped from. Broadly speaking, Yillah stands for truth, innocence, purity and goodness. Hautia represents falsehood, experience, seduction and evil. Though the sinister Queen promises to deliver "Beauty, Health, Wealth, Long Life, and the Last Lost Hope of man",[18] she in reality offers sin and eternal damnation.

The major critical point to be made in a discussion of Yillah and Hautia is not so much an exact definition of what they symbolize, for this, in my opinion, is impossible, but to show that Yillah and Hautia are in the long run inseparable, different sides of the same coin, so to speak. The concept of hemispheres is a recurrent one in Melville's writings: Ahab is divided in half by a scar which runs the length of his body, the tortoises in "The Encantadas" have melancholy, dark backs and bright, gold-hued breast plates, etc. The dual aspect of life is first symbolized in *Mardi* by the "pair of parallel canoes" which are the foundation of Aleema's vessel, but this dichotomy is also reflected in the good and evil aspects of the slaying of the old priest and the Yillah-Hautia antithesis. Yillah disappears shortly after Hautia makes her appearance on the island of Odo as an incognita, and among the first visitors to reach Taji after her disappearance are Hautia's heralds. Towards the end of the novel, Taji and his companions draw near Flosella-a-Nina, the isle of Hautia.

Approaching the dominions of one who so long had haunted me, conflicting emotions tore up my soul in tornadoes. Yet Hautia had held out some prospect of crowning my yearnings. *But how connected were Hautia and Yillah?* Something I hoped; yet more I feared. ... *Nevertheless, in some mysterious way seemed Hautia and Yillah connected.* But Yillah was all beauty, and innocence; my crown of felicity; my heaven below; – and Hautia, my whole heart abhorred. Yillah I sought; Hautia sought me. One, openly beckoned me here; the other dimly allured me there. *Yet now I was wildly dreaming to find them together.*[19] [Italics my own.]

[17] *Ibid.*, p. 480.
[18] *Ibid.*, p. 740.
[19] *Ibid.*, pp. 735-6.

Taji and his friends enter Hautia's bower, where the beautiful seductress approaches them.

My soul ebbed out; Yillah there was none! but as I turned around open-armed, Hautia vanished.
"She is deeper than the sea," said Media.
"Her bow is bent," said Yoomy.
"I could tell wonders of Hautia and her damsels," said Mohi.
"What wonders?"
"Listen; and in his own words will I recount the adventure of the youth Ozonna. *It will show thee, Taji, that the maidens of Hautia are all Yillahs, held captive, unknown to themselves*; and that Hautia, their enchantress, is the most treacherous of queens."[20] [Italics my own.]

Mohi then proceeds to tell the story of Ozonna – a tale which parallels Taji's own quest – who pursued a beautiful maid called Ady, and discovered her transformed in the shape of Rea, one of Hautia's maids, only to lose her again through the machinations of the evil Queen. Taji remarks: "This recital sank deep into my soul. In some wild way, Hautia had made a captive of Yillah; in some one of her black-eyed maids, the blue-eyed One was transformed".[21] It is Hautia who has enslaved Yillah and taken her away from Taji. But also, because Taji retains his vision of Yillah, he is strong enough to resist the queen and tell her, "'Better to me, oh Hautia, all the bitterness of my buried dead, than all the sweets of the life thou canst bestow; even, were it eternal'".[22]

Taji's slaying of the old priest results in something resembling the opening of a "mixed" Pandora's box; the good Yillah is freed as a result of this action, but inexorably hand in hand with her comes the evil Hautia. Taji's use of violence introduces other dualistic motifs into *Mardi*, notably the pursuer-pursued theme. As Taji pursues Yillah, so too is he pursued by three pale specters, avenging sons of the dead Aleema. But just as Taji's pursuit of Yillah is hopeless, so too is the specters' chase after him. They can kill Jarl and Samoa, but so long as Taji follows Yillah, his life seems to be safeguarded from them. Finally, throughout most of

[20] *Ibid.*, p. 738.
[21] *Ibid.*, p. 739.
[22] *Ibid.*, p. 740.

the novel, immediately after Taji has encountered the three sons of the old priest, he the next instant meets the three black-eyed messengers of Hautia. One canoe comes with hate, the other with messages of love, hidden in a floral code.

What is being suggested by these dichotomies is obvious. There is no such thing as absolute good or absolute evil, total innocence or total experience. Qualities exist in this world, not in absolute states, but in relative conditions. As Melville later wrote in *Clarel*

> Evil and good they braided play
> Into one cord.

But even though it may be indisputably clear that this world is a world of relative values and not of absolute standards, nevertheless this distinction is not necessarily accepted by the Melvillean rebel hero, as we shall see later on in our discussion of Taji's rejection of Serenia.

After Yillah mysteriously disappears from the island of Odo, Taji decides to search for her throughout Mardi, and tells his plan to King Media. Media, much to the former's delight, decides to accompany him, and further proposes that they take along three of the king's companions, Yoomy the poet, Mohi the historian, and Babbalanja the philosopher. Once the cruise is under way, Taji for all practical purposes drops out of the novel until the last few chapters. It seems probable that Melville intended this section of *Mardi* to be a debate on roughly equal terms among Media, who, as his name indicates, represents the middle way, and his three friends. Such does not turn out to be the case however, for Babbalanja completely dominates these discussions, so much so that at times they become monologues by the philosopher with occasional questions or comments thrown in by the others. It is perhaps because Melvillle doesn't wish Babbalanja to completely run away with the novel that he has given him three masks through which to speak – the wise philosopher, the man whose speech consists solely of quotations from the ancient sage Bardianna, and, finally, a creature whose mind has been temporarily seized by a devil called Azzageddi. But no matter which mask he is wearing, he talks like Ahab – " 'To scale great heights, we must come out of lowermost depths. The way to heaven is through hell. We need fiery baptisms in the fiercest flames of our own bosoms. We must feel our hearts hot-hissing in us. And ere their fire is revealed, it must burn its way out of us; though it consume us and itself' ".[23] It would not be too much of an oversimplification to say that throughout the early part of the novel, Taji has been a rebel on the physical level, and that in the person of Babbalanja, this rebellion is carried into a more intellectual or philosophical sphere, nor would it be a great misinterpretation to suggest that the penultimate Melvillean rebel-hero Ahab combines the man-of-action aspects of Taji with the initial intellectual skepticism of the brilliant Babbalanja.

As we have previously seen, though Melville does not suggest in *Typee* and *Omoo* that this is the best of all possible worlds, and though he is quite critical of civilization and the white man, we still find in these novels a belief in the essential goodness and order of the universe. Babbalanja, however, bitterly challenges these assumptions. His attack is at first somewhat cautious. He sees the universe not as evil, but as neutral. The four friends are discussing the implications of the development of the silkworm.

Said Yoomy, "Then, Babbalanja, you account that a fit illustration of the miraculous change to be wrought in man after death?"

"No; for the analogy has an unsatisfactory end. From its chrysalis state, the silkworm but becomes a moth, that very quickly expires. Its longest existence is as a worm. *All vanity, vanity, Yoomy, to seek in nature for positive warranty to these aspirations of ours. Through all her provinces, nature seems to promise immortality to life, but destruction to beings. Or, as old Bardianna has it, if not against us, nature is not for us.*"[24] [Italics my own.]

It is also vanity to think of this earth in terms of some sort of abiding life-force. Notice here in Babbalanja's speech, that though what he is saying is antithetical, the phrases he uses are almost word for word from *Ecclesiastes*.[25]

[23] *Ibid.*, p. 706.
[24] *Ibid.*, p. 492.
[25] Surprisingly, this parallel was not pointed out until 1949. See Nathalia Wright, *Melville's Use of the Bible*, Durham, 1949, pp. 97-8. *Ecclesiastes* reads: "One generation passeth away, and another generation cometh:

"Nothing abideth; the river of yesterday floweth not to-day; the sun's rising is a setting; living is dying; the very mountains melt; and all revolve: — systems and asteroids; the sun wheels through the zodiac, and the zodiac is a revolution. Ah gods! in all this universal stir, am *I* to prove one stable thing?"[26]

As the novel progresses, Babbalanja's attacks become sharper. Mohi pokes fun at the inhabitants of the island of Quelquo for believing in small invisible spirits called the Plujii, who are directly responsible for the little evils that plague man.

"Magnanimous Plujii!" cried Media. "But Babbalanja, do you, who run a tilt at all things suffer this silly conceit to be uttered with impunity in your presence? Why so silent?"

"I have been thinking, my lord," said Babbalanja, "that though the people of that island may at time err, in imputing their calamities to the Plujii, that, nevertheless, upon the whole, they indulge in a reasonable belief. For, Plujii or no Plujii, it is undeniable, that in ten thousand ways, as if by a malicious agency we mortals are woefully put out and tormented..."[27]

Babbalanja elaborates upon this philosophy when little Vee-Vee falls and almost breaks his arm.

Minus human inducement from without, and minus volition from within, Vee-Vee has met an accident, which has almost maimed him for life. Is it not terrifying to think of? Are not all mortals exposed to similar, nay, worse calamities, ineffably unavoidable? Woe, woe, I say, to us Mardians.[28]

The philosopher expands this argument into a discussion with Media concerning the nature of Oro (God).

"Is not Oro omnipresent — absolutely every where?"
"So you mortals teach, Babbalanja."
"But so do they *mean*, my lord. Often do we Mardians stick to terms for ages, yet truly apply not their meanings."

---

but the earth abideth forever. The sun also ariseth, and the sun goeth down, and hasteth to his place where he arose. The wind goeth toward the south, and turneth about unto the north; it whirleth about continually, and the wind returneth again according to his circuits. All the rivers run into the sea; yet the sea is not full; unto the place from whence the rivers come, thither they return again."

[26] *Romances*, p. 508.
[27] *Ibid.*, p. 523.
[28] *Ibid.*, p. 609.

"Well, Oro is every where. What now?"

"Then, if that be absolutely so, Oro is not merely a universal onlooker, but occupies and fills all space; and no vacancy is left for any being, or any thing but Oro. Hence Oro is *in* all things, and himself *is* all things – the time-old creed. But since evil abounds, and Oro is all things, then he can not be perfectly good; wherefore Oro's omnipresence and moral perfection seem incompatible. Furthermore, my lord, those orthodox systems which ascribe to Oro almighty and universal attributes every way, those systems, I say, destroy all intellectual individualities but Oro, and resolve the universe into him."[29]

With this statement, largely a rephrasing of the age-old Epicurean argument,[30] any simple or pat acceptance of the universe as being either essentially moral or orderly disappears from Melville's writings.

The portions of the novel dealing with the discussions among Babbalanja, Yoomy, Mohi, and Media and with the philosophical development of the philosopher's skepticism are interwoven, though not particularly skillfully, with satirical sections consisting of visits to lands both real and imaginary. In terms of our topic, the most significant of these visits are those to Maramma (institutionalized and false Christianity), Diranda (home of the war games), Dominora (Great Britain), Franko (France), and Vivenza (the United States).

On the isle of Maramma, domicile of the High Pontiff, is the famous Peak of Ofo, which is inaccessible to man. But shortly

---

[29] *Ibid.*, p. 611.

[30] It is interesting to compare Babbalanja's speech with the rephrasing of Epicurus found in David Hume's *Dialogues Concerning Natural Religion.* "And is it possible, Cleanthes, said Philo, that after all these reflections, and infinitely more which might be suggested, you can still persevere in your anthropomorphism, and assert the moral attributes of the Deity, his justice, benevolence, mercy, and rectitude, to be of the same nature with these virtues in human creatures? His power, we allow, is infinite: whatever he wills is executed; but neither man nor any other animal is happy: therefore, he does not will their happiness. His wisdom is infinite; he is never mistaken in choosing the means to any end; but the course of nature tends not to human or animal felicity; therefore, it is not established for that purpose. Through the whole compass of human knowledge there are no inferences more certain and infallible than these... Epicurus' old questions are yet unanswered. Is he willing to prevent evil, but not able? then is he impotent. Is he able, but not willing? then is he malevolent. Is he both able and willing? whence then is evil?"

after Babbalanja and his fellow travellers land, an old blind man named Pani offers, for an exorbitant price, to guide them around the island and to the top of Ofo itself. The voyagers reject this, for Mohi advises Media that " 'the great prophet Alma (Christ) always declared that, without charge, this island was free to all' "[31] and that furthermore, though he could not lead the travellers to the top of Ofo, he, Mohi, could guide them around the island because at least he had eyes.

The historian leads them to the Morai of Mohramma, burial-place of the Pontiffs, where they again encounter old Pani, who is now showing a group of pilgrims through the island. The blind man stops before a stone image, thinking it is a tree. As he is discoursing, a willful boy, who had also previously rejected Pani's services as a guide enters, and says:

"This must be the image of Doleema; but I am not sure."

"Nay," cried the blind pilgrim, "it is the holy tree Ananna, thou wayward boy."

"A tree? whatever it may be, it is not that; thou art blind, old man."

Then said Pani, turning upon the boy, "Depart from the holy Morai, and corrupt not the hearts of these pilgrims. Depart, I say; and, in the sacred name of Alma, perish in thy endeavors to climb the Peak."

"I may perish there in truth," said the boy, with sadness; "but it shall be in the path revealed to me in my dream. And think not, oh guide, that I perfectly rely upon gaining that lofty summit. *I will climb Ofo with hope, not faith;* Oh, mighty Oro, help me!"

"Be not impious," said Pani; "pronounce not sacred Oro's name too lightly."

"Oro is but a sound," said the boy. "They call the supreme god, Ati, in my native isle; it is *the soundless thought of him, o guide, that is in me.*"[32] [Italics my own.]

This same willful boy is later offered up as a blood sacrifice by the attendants of the temple of Oro (God) when he is so blasphemous as to say that he is not vile in the eyes of Oro. This causes Babbalanja to comment: " 'Just Oro! it was done in the name of Alma, – what wonder then, that, at times, I almost hate that sound. And from those flames, they devoutly swore he went to

[31] *Romances*, p. 554.
[32] *Ibid.*, p. 560.

others, – horrible fable!... But better we were all annihilated, than that one man be damned' ".[33]

After the death of the unfortunate youth, Mohi tells the group about the life of Alma and how he gave lessons to improve the condition of mankind. To this, Babbalanja replies:

The prophet came to dissipate errors, you say; but superadded to many that have survived the past, ten thousand others have originated in various constructions of the principles of Alma himself. The prophet came to do away all gods but one; but since the days of Alma, the idols of Maramma have more than quadrupled. ... The prophet came to guarantee our eternal felicity; but according to what is held in Maramma, that felicity rests on so hard a proviso, that to a thinking mind, but very few of our sinful race may secure it. For one, then, I wholly reject your Alma; not so much, because of all that is hard to be understood in his histories; as because of obvious and undeniable things all round us; which, to me, seem at war with an unreserved faith in his doctrines as promulgated here in Maramma. Besides; every thing in this isle strengthens my incredulity; I never was so thorough a disbeliever as now.[34]

Before the voyagers quit Maramma, they make two final visits, one to the noted artisan Hevaneva and the other to Hivohitee the Pontiff. Hevaneva, who makes religious articles, tells them that when he cuts down trees to make idols, they are nothing but logs, "when the chisel is applied, logs they are still; and when all complete, I at last stand them up in my studio, even then they are logs. Nevertheless, when I handle the pay, they are as prime gods, as ever were turned out in Maramma".[35] Hivohitee they finally locate in a dark glen, and Yoomy enters into the black pagoda where the great Pontiff dwells. After a period of silence, Hivohitee asks Yoomy what he sees.

"The dim gleaming of thy gorget."
"But that is not me. What else dost thou see?"
"Nothing."
"Then thou hast found me out, and seen all! Descend." [36]

[33] *Ibid.*, pp. 566-7.
[34] *Ibid.*, p. 566.
[35] *Ibid.*, p. 569.
[36] *Ibid.*, p. 573.

The satire of the Maramma section is obvious. Christianity has been perverted by the Church, both Catholic and Protestant, though the chapters concerning Hivohitee (the Pope) are mostly directed against Catholicism. Melville makes several specific charges against institutionalized Christianity. First, religion, instead of being a way to salvation, has become a business (the blind guide Pani, the maker of relics Hevaneva). Second, it promises things to man that are impossible (the ascension of the Peak of Ofo). Worst of all, numerous crimes are committed in the name of piety, and often, the people who suffer most are the true believers (the sacrificing of the willful but sincere and idealistic youth). It should be made clear, however, that even in spite of Babbalanja's speech, which to some degree challenges the concept of Alma, Melville's guns are here leveled not so much at *real* Christianity as at the corruption of spiritual value by its secular trappings.

Shortly after Taji and his companions leave Maramma, they come to the island of Diranda, home of the war games. This island is divided into two parts, East and West, ruled by the kings Piko and Hello. The monarchs had always been on friendly terms, but both kingdoms were in danger of overpopulation, and a war between them seemed as if it might be the best possible solution to this problem. Yet King Piko did not wish to start a conflict because it was too much trouble, and furthermore, one of his courtiers suggested that if the ruler were patient, a provident plague might decimate the population. But no such plague came and conflict appeared imminent, until another of Piko's advisers suggested that a series of war games should be inaugurated between the two realms. This plan is communicated to King Hello, who agrees wholeheartedly with it, and the proposal becomes a reality. The games work out to everyone's satisfaction. The two kings take turns entertaining each other, even sharing their crowns, while periodically the population systematically destroys itself because "of the true object of the games, they had not the faintest conception; but hammered away at each other, and fought and died together, like jolly good fellows".[37]

In honor of the voyagers, a special series of games is staged. If

[37] *Ibid.*, p. 619.

a group of warriors fight and survive, the two kings berate them as cowards. But if the gladiators seem on the verge of destroying each other, one of the rulers shouts " 'Die and be glorified!' "[38] This particular set of games comes to an unhappy end, though, for in the middle of them, a haggard figure known as "the Despairer", a man who has had three sons killed in recent contests, rushes into the crowd. Waving a club over his head, he puts everyone to flight.

The Diranda chapters of *Mardi* rank as one of Melville's bitterest anti-war statements, and the satire here concerning battle as a tool merely to satisfy the needs of the ruling elite is so explicit as to need no explanation.

The lands so far visited by the voyagers, with the exception of Ohonoo (in reality Oahu) have been satirical presentations of certain human follies, not satires directed at actual nations. But not long after they quit Diranda, Taji and his friends arrive at a group of lands which symbolize most of the countries of the world. The visits most important for our purposes are the ones made to Dominora (England), Franko (France), and Vivenza (the United States). Merrell Davis has stated in his study on *Mardi* that many incidents in this section are based on historical fact.

... first, the chapter about Franko (France) and Porpheero (Europe) which describes the effects of the 1848 revolutions; second, the chapter on Dominora (England) which describes the Chartists' abortive march on Parliament in 1848; third, the chapter concerned with the reception in Vivenza (the United States) of the news of the 1848 revolutions...[39]

Thus we find in these chapters an analysis not so much of rebellion in the abstract, but of actual social and political revolution.

Melville vehemently satirizes the betrayal of the Chartist movement in no uncertain terms. As the voyagers wander through Dominora, they see a crowd waving a banner which reads "Since we are born, we will live!" and shouting " 'Mardi is man's!' " and " 'Up rights! Down wrongs!' "

[38] *Ibid.*, p. 623.
[39] *Melville's Mardi*, pp. 81-2. I am also indebted to Mr. Davis' study for the more specific interpretations of these historical facts.

Waving their banners, and flourishing aloft clubs, hammers, and sickles, with fierce yells the crowd ran on toward the palace of Bello [the king of England]. Foremost, and inciting the rest by mad outcries and gestures, were six masks; "This way! This way!" –they cried – "by the wood; by the dark wood!" Whereupon all darted in the groves; when of a sudden, the masks leaped forward, clearing a long covered trench, into which fell many of those they led. But on raced the masks; and gaining Bello's palace, and raising the alarm, there sallied from thence a woodland of spears, which charged upon the disordered ranks in the grove. A crash as of icicles against icebergs round Zembla, and down went the hammers and sickles. The host fled, hotly pursued. Meanwhile brave heralds from Bello advanced, and with chaplets crowned the six masks. – "Welcome, heroes! worthy and valiant!" they cried. Thus our lord Bello rewards all those, who to do him a service, for hire betray their kith and their kin.[40]

This elicits no comments from the wayfarers, but another aspect of the British political situation does. As they pass Verdanna (Ireland), Yoomy notes the sad condition of the island, and says that the inhabitants should rebel against the tyrants who rule them. But Babbalanja, surprisingly enough, disagrees.

Verdanna's worst evils are her own, not of another's giving. Her own hand is her own undoer. She stabs herself with bigotry, superstition, divided councils, domestic feuds, ignorance, temerity; she wills, but does not: her East is one black storm-cloud, that never bursts; her utmost fight is a defiance; she showers reproaches, where she should rain down blows. She stands a mastiff baying at the moon.[41]

Babbalanja is in sympathy with the French Revolution of 1848, however. As they pass the coast of Franko, the heavens become black and clamorous sounds are heard. A meteor suddenly lights the sky, showing "Franko's multitudes, as they storm the summit where their monarch's palace blazed, fast by the burning mountain".[42] Since Media is a king, he is horrified by this sight, and even Mohi suggests that actions such as these will make a desert of the land. But the philosopher disagrees.

"... prairies are purified by fire. Ashes breed loam. Nor can any

---

[40] *Romances*, p. 640.
[41] *Ibid.*, p. 648.
[42] *Ibid.*, p. 650.

skill make the same surface forever fruitful. In all times past, things have been overlaid; and though the first fruits of the marl are wild and poisonous, the palms at last spring forth; and once again the tribes repose in shade. My lord, if calm breed storms, so storms calms; and all this dire commotion must eventuate in peace. It may be, that Porpheero's future has been cheaply won."[43]

We find in Babbalanja's speech almost the identical attitude that is expressed towards the French Revolution in the Preface to *Billy Budd,* though the viewpoint here is presented in allegorical language. The philosopher's words are a revolutionary manifesto, not only endorsing rebellion as a justifiable means which to fight tyranny, but also even going so far as to imply that occasional violent upheavals are good things in themselves.

Media naturally does not wish to visit Porpheero at this time of tumult, so they decide to go to Vivenza instead. As they draw close to land, the voyagers see the statue of a helmeted female (the allegorical Columbia). On the temple on which this figure rests are inscribed the words "In-this-republi-can-land-all-men-are-born-free-and-equal", but lower down, written in minute letters, the words "Except-the-tribe-of-Hamo".[44] The free men of Vivenza are quite interested in the revolutions taking place across the sea. Every day

... great crowds ran down to the beach, in wait for canoes periodically bringing further intelligence. Every hour new cries startled the air. "Hurrah! another kingdom is burnt down to the earth's edge; another demi-god is unhelmed; another republic is dawning. Shake hands, freemen, shake hands! Soon will we hear of Dominora down in the dust: of hapless Verdanna free as ourselves; all Porpheero's volcanoes are bursting! The times tell terrible tales to tyrants! Ere we die, freemen, all Mardi will be free."[45]

During the uproar, both Babbalanja and Media steal away, and shortly thereafter, another crowd of Vivenzans finds an anonymous document, written either by the philosopher or more probably, the king. Most of this declaration, which is certainly one of the most

---

[43] *Ibid.,* p. 651.
[44] *Ibid.,* p. 659.
[45] *Ibid.,* p. 664.

penetrating critiques of America and democracy ever written, lies beyond the scope of this study. But some of it is concerned with non-violence and rebellion. Vivenza is contrasted to a fiery young boy.

> But years elapse, and this bold boy is transformed. His eyes open not as of yore; his heart is shut up as a vice. He yields not a groat; and seeking no more acquisitions, is only bent on preserving his hoard. The maxims once trampled under foot, are now printed on his front; and he who hated oppressors, is become an oppressor himself.
> Thus, often with men; thus, often, with nations. Then marvel not, sovereign-kings! that old states are different from yours; and think not, your own must forever remain liberal as now.
> . . . .
> Now, though far and wide, to keep equal pace with the times, great reforms, of a verity, be needed; nowhere are bloody revolutions required. Though it be the most certain of remedies, no prudent invalid opens his veins, to let out his disease with his life. And though all evils may be assuaged; all evils can not be done away. For evil is the chronic malady of the universe; and checked in one place, breaks forth in another.[46]

It is important for America to keep its liberal spirit, but actual revolution must be condemned, for violence is worse than the evil which it seeks to destroy, and moreover, it is vanity for man to think that he can drive evil from this world, for evil is an inherent part of the human condition.

This attitude towards political revolution is challenged by Yoomy, however, when the travellers arrive in Southern Vivenza. Even Media the king is shocked by the collared slaves he finds there.

> "Pray, heaven!" cried Yoomy; "they may yet find a way to loose their bonds without one drop of blood. But hear me, Oro! were there no other way, and should their masters not relent, all honest hearts must cheer this tribe of Hamo on; though they cut their chains with blades thrice edged, and gory to the haft! 'Tis right to fight for freedom, whoever be the thrall."
> "These South Savannahs may yet prove battle-fields," said Mohi, gloomily, as we retraced our steps.
> "Be it," said Yoomy. "Oro will van the right."

[46] *Ibid.*, pp. 666 and 668. Note how closely this resembles Blake's Orc cycle.

"Not always has it proved so," said Babbalanja. "Oft-times, the right fights single-handed against the world; and Oro champions none. In all things, man's own battles, man himself must fight. *Yoomy: so far as feeling goes, your sympathies are not more hot than mine; but for these serfs you would cross spears; yet, I would not.* Better present woes for some, than future woes for all." [47] [Italics my own.]

This divided feeling towards how to bring about the abolition of slavery is also reflected in *Battle-Pieces* (1866), and the issues involved here are more complicated than one might at first suspect. Media, Mohi, Babbalanja and Yoomy all are vehemently opposed to slavery. But the poet's emotional reaction is sharply contrasted to the intellectual response of the philosopher. Yoomy is the most militantly rebellious of the four on the issue of slavery, and his outlook is buttressed by his faith that God will aid the righteous. Babbalanja, skeptical as usual, disagrees that God necessarily sides with justice. His skepticism towards violent revolt echoes the attitude to "bloody revolutions" expressed in the previously discussed anonymous document, but is at odds with the philosopher's former doctrine justifying the French Revolution of 1848. In this particular issue of slavery, *Mardi* expresses a viewpoint which we find in no other of Melville's works. For here, skepticism is aligned, not with rebellion, but with pacifism, and rebellion is linked, not with a defiance of the universe, but with a belief in God.

As may be seen from the above discussion, no consistent viewpoint towards violent revolution as a means to economic and political freedom is developed in *Mardi*. The French and the American Revolutions and the abortive Chartist uprising are regarded sympathetically. But Babbalanja questions violent revolution as a tool to further freedom in Ireland or to liberate the slaves, towards whom he is deeply sympathetic, in the United States. And the anonymous pamphlet, written either by Media or the philosopher, decries the use of violence as a liberating force. Yoomy is the foremost champion of physical rebellion in *Mardi,* though his zeal for freedom, unlike Babbalanja's, seldom carries over into an intellectual revolt against the nature of the universe. Mohi and partic-

[47] *Ibid.*, p. 671.

ularly Media are, broadly speaking, political and philosophical conservatives. To generalize briefly, political revolution is usually looked upon favorably in *Mardi,* though with numerous and profound reservations.

But political revolution is only a small part of the philosophy of rebellion. The crux of the conflict between pacifism and rebellion in *Mardi,* therefore, is not to be found in the sections concerned with Diranda, Porpheero and Vivenza, but in the closing chapters of the novel that deal with the island of Serenia, which, sharply contrasted to Maramma, symbolizes true Christianity.

The voyagers had not planned to stop at this island, but not far from its shore, they encounter a mild old man in a canoe, a foil to the blind Pani, who invites them to "turn aside to Serenia, a pleasant isle, where all are welcome; where many storm-worn rovers land at last to dwell".[48] Babbalanja expresses doubt about the nature of the island, but he is amazed at the kindly reception which he and his party receive in the name of Alma (Christ) from the inhabitants of Serenia. Turning to their guide, the philosopher says, " 'Old man! your lesson of brotherhood was learned elsewhere than from Alma; for in Maramma and in all of its tributary islands true brotherhood there is none'."[49] The old man replies that it is unfair to judge Alma by those who profess his faith. On Serenia, Alma's teachings are put into practice: the fatherless child is adopted as a son, the poor and naked man is clothed. Babbalanja asks what happens if the befriended one smites his benefactors. " 'Still we feed and clothe him' "[50] is the reply.

"Is this man divine?" mumured Babbalanja. "But thou speakest most earnestly of adoring Alma: – I see no temples in your groves."

"Because this isle is all one temple to his praise; every leaf is consecrated his. We fix not Alma here and there; and say – 'those groves for Him, and these broad fields for us.' It is all his own; and we ourselves; our every hour of life; and all we are, and have."

"Then, ye forever fast and pray; and stand and sing; as at long intervals the censer-bearers in Maramma supplicate their gods."

"Alma forbid! We never fast: our aspirations are our prayers; our

[48] *Ibid.,* p. 724.
[49] *Ibid.,* p. 725.
[50] *Ibid.,* p. 726.

lives our worship. And when we laugh, with human joy at human beings, – *then* do we most sound great Oro's praises, and prove the merit of sweet Alma's love! Our love in Alma makes us glad, not sad. Ye speak of temples; – behold! 'tis by not building *them*, that we widen the charity among us."[51]

By now Babbalanja is close to conversion. But one essential question remains – is faith in conflict with reason? " 'No brother! Right-reason, and Alma, are the same; else Alma, not reason we reject!' "[52]

"Oh, Alma, Alma! prince divine!" cried Babbalanja, sinking on his knees – "in *thee*, at last, I find repose. Hope perches in my heart like a dove; – a thousand rays illume; – all Heaven's a sun. Gone, gone! are all distracting doubts. Love and Alma now prevail. I see with other eyes: – Are these my hands? What wild, wild dreams were mine; – I have been mad. Some things there are, we must not think of. Beyond one obvious mark, all human lore is vain. Where have I lived till now? Had dark Maramma's zealot tribe but murmured to me as this old man, long since had I been wise! All I have said ere this, that wars with Alma's precepts, I here recant. Here I kneel, and own great Oro and his sovereign son."[53]

Babbalanja's conversion is reinforced by a vision he has shortly thereafter. In this dream, a guide appears and reveals many of the mysteries of earth and heaven. A small speck of doubt remains in the philosopher's mind, however – the question of evil.

"That," breathed my guide; "is the last mystery which underlieth all the rest. Archangel may not fathom it; that makes of Oro the everlasting mystery he is; that to divulge, were to make equal to himself in knowledge all the souls that are; that mystery Oro guards, and none but him may know."[54]

The next morning, before the other travellers leave Serenia, the philosopher makes a final speech.

"My voyage is ended. *Not because what we sought is found; but that I now possess all which may be had of what I sought in Mardi.* Here, I tarry to grow wiser still: – then I am Alma's and the world's. Taji!

[51] *Ibid.,* p. 727.
[52] *Ibid.,* p. 728.
[53] *Ibid.,* p. 729.
[54] *Ibid.,* p. 731.

for Yillah thou wilt hunt in vain; she is a phantom that but mocks thee; and for her thou madly huntest, the sin thou didst cries out, and its avengers still will follow. But here they may not come: nor those, who tempting, track thy path."[55] [Italics my own.]

During most of the novel, Babbalanja has been a great skeptic, a man whose intellectual rebellion against the world as it is reaches almost the same intensity as the philosophical defiance of Ahab in *Moby-Dick*. But as a result of his exposure to Serenia, the philosopher reverses himself, and his final position of Christian acceptance comes close to that of Starbuck's. Babbalanja's ultimate attitude hinges upon his new approach to the inter-related problems of evil and of faith. It is manifestly obvious to Babbalanja that evil is an essential part of the universe, and that there is nothing in our world or our experience to indicate that good is more prevalent. This, of course, is a key problem in determining the nature of God. The philosopher, echoing Epicurus, suggests that an all-knowing, all-good, all-powerful God would not permit the existence of evil; hence God cannot possess all three of these attributes in an absolute sense. Even after his conversion to Christianity, the problem of evil still plagues Babbalanja. The only answer that Christianity can give him is to say that if man knew how to explain the riddle of evil, he would be as wise as God, and this is no answer at all. Any concept of the goodness of God must be an act of faith. Now the willful boy, who looked for Oro on the isle of Maramma and whose search, to a great extent parallels the quest of both Taji and Babbalanja, specifically rejected faith ("I will climb Ofo with hope, not faith") as a means to salvation. The willful youth and the preconversion Babbalanja felt that for man to accept God or anything else on faith alone is an insult to human dignity, for to rely on faith is to admit man's own weakness and insignificance. But after his conversation, Babbalanja concludes that faith and right reason must be the same, and that it is only through an acceptance of the unknown that man can achieve understanding and wisdom, and make this life meaningful.

As Babbalanja indicates in his last speech, however, Serenia is not everything that man aspires for, but it is the best that he can

[55] *Ibid.*, p. 733.

hope for *in this world*. The philosopher's embracing of Serenia is a realistic compromise, but nevertheless a moral one. Man, Babbalanja would argue, must live within the bounds of the possible, recognize his own limitations, yet live as idealistic and ethical a life as he can. It should strongly be emphasized that Babbalanja is not weak but strong, and his acceptance of Christianity is not a surrender, it is the acceptance on the highest possible level of the inevitable.

If *Mardi* ended at this point, it would be a novel which expressed a strong message of the necessity for man's acceptance of the universe and which championed Christianity as the most common-sense and ethical form of salvation. But the book has not reached its conclusion, for Taji continues to pursue Yillah. After his unsuccessful search on the isle of Queen Hautia, Taji encounters Mohi and Yoomy, who have returned from Odo, the kingdom of Media. They inform Taji that there has been a revolution on Odo, and that Media has decided to remain behind to cope with it. The king's parting words to them are " 'In Serenia only, will ye find the peace ye seek; and thither must ye carry Taji, who else must soon be slain, or lost' "[56] But Taji scorns this advice.

An outlet in that outer barrier was nigh.

"Ah! Yillah! Yillah! – the currents sweep thee oceanward; nor will I tarry behind. – Mardi, farewell! – Give me the helm, old man!"

"Nay, madman! Serenia is our haven. Through yonder strait, for thee, perdition lies. And from the deep beyond, no voyager e'er puts back."

"And why put back? is a life of dying worth living o'er again? Let *me*, then, be the unreturning wanderer. The helm! By Oro, I will steer my own fate, old man. – Mardi, farewell!"

"Nay, Taji: commit not the last, last crime!" cried Yoomy.

"He's seized the helm! eternity is in his eye! Yoomy: for our lives we must now swim."

And plunging, they struck out for land: Yoomy buoying Mohi up, and the salt waves dashing the tears from his pallid face, as through the scud, he turned it on me mournfully.

"Now I am my own soul's emperor; and my first act is abdication! Hail! realm of shades!" – and turning my prow into the racing tide, which seized me like a hand omnipotent, I darted through.

[56] *Ibid.*, pp. 741-2.

Churned in foam, that outer ocean lashed the clouds; and straight in my white wake, headlong dashed a shallop, three fixed specters leaning o'er its prow: three arrows poising.

And thus, pursuers and pursued fled on, over an endless sea.[57]

Unlike Babbalanja, Taji is not a realist, nor will he compromise. Through his brief possession of Yillah, he has for a moment glimpsed the perfect and the absolute, and he will settle for nothing else. Serenia would be a false haven, and Taji is willing to continue his search even if it is hopeless, even if it is in one sense suicidal. Taji's rejection of Serenia, symbolizing pure Christianity, implies the rather interesting philosophy that there is an absolute good which transcends both the sphere of God and the sphere of man. Such a good may be unobtainable, but some strong and idealistic men will never abandon their quest for it. The boundary between the known world and the unknown sea, between the relative and the absolute, is symbolized by the "outer barrier". If Yillah can't be found in the world of man (Mardi) then Taji will press his search into as yet uncharted seas. (We find here the beginning of the association of pacifism with the land and rebellion with the sea, which is most fully developed in the imagery of *Moby-Dick*). When Yoomy says that Taji has committed the last crime, the poet means that the protagonist has turned his back on mankind in order to follow an impossible ideal. But this same act is also an act of salvation – "eternity is in his eye". Taji wishes to "steer his own fate", to be more than a passive object in the hands of the elements, even though this may lead to damnation, for he feels that man can achieve dignity only through self-assertation. This dualism of salvation-damnation reflects the initial ambiguity concerning Taji's slaying of Aleema to free Yillah, and the pursuer-pursued theme reiterated in the last line of the novel refers not only to the pursuit of Taji by the three avenging sons of Aleema, but also to Taji's helpless hunt for Yillah. That there can be no resolution to these ambiguities is indicated by the background of the "endless sea".

A somewhat similair treatment of the dilemma facing Taji and Babbalanja is to be found in Thomas Mann's *Bildungsroman*,

[57] *Ibid.*, p. 742.

Magic Mountain. In the climactic chapter "Snow", the hero, Hans Castorp, exhausted from skiing and lost in the mountains has a vision. In this vision, Hans imagines a sunny and lovely Arcadian landscape, inhabited by "Beautiful young human creatures, so blithe, so good and gay, so pleasing to see".[58] This is contrasted almost immediately with the apparition of a temple.

> Two grey old women, witchlike, with hanging breasts and dugs of finger-length, were busy there, between flaming braziers, most horribly. They were dismembering a child. In dreadful silence they tore it apart with their bare hands — Hans Castorp saw the bright hair bloodsmeared — and cracked the tender bones between their jaws, their dreadful lips dripped blood.[59]

The point that Mann wishes to develop here is that we can reach maturity only when we realize that both good and evil, both the beautiful landscape and the sinister temple, are an integral part of our lives, and though we can aspire to reach the sunny Arcadia, we must also recognize that the slaughtered babe too is an inescapable aspect of man's fate. This, roughly speaking, is the kind of recognition achieved by Babbalanja on the isle of Serenia. But Taji — and this is true of virtually all of Melville's rebels — refuses to accept evil as a part of human existence. Seeking to ignore the boundaries which limit him, he pursues an absolute and impossible good. In *Magic Mountain,* Hans' vision is a synthesis and a triumph. But *Mardi* presents us with no such triumph. Taji rejects Babbalanja's acceptance of Serenia as a form of weakness, and the novel ends on a note of tragic irony, for the more intensely Taji pursues Yillah, the more he becomes immersed in the evil which he seeks to avoid.

Though Melville does not fully develop a philosophy of either pacifism or rebellion in *Mardi,* he deals far more profoundly with these themes than he had previously done in *Typee* or *Omoo,* and at least the battle lines between the two viewpoints are drawn. Taji is an embryonic Ahab, a man of action, who lacks the introspective nature and articulate speech of the old whaling captain. But he,

---

[58] Translated by H. T. Lowe-Porter (New York, 1955), p. 491.
[59] *Ibid.,* p. 494.

like Ahab, comes to see human life primarily as a struggle against the universe, and his sailing out into the endless sea is a final act of defiance. Babbalanja cannot truly be called a pacifist, but when he surrenders his skepticism and remains in Serenia, he has made a giant step towards the philosophical position of Starbuck, Melville's pacifist-hero supreme. As seen in *Mardi,* pacifism would seem to include a belief in Christianity and faith in the essential order of the universe, a concern for the individual man, and an acceptance of man's weaknesses and limitations. Rebellion consists of a defiance of any or all powers stronger than man, an interest often with ideals rather than people, and a commitment to the cause of armed revolution as a means of social reform. The idealistic rebel is unable to compromise, but the pacifist is more of a realist, and though highly moral, is better able to adjust to life. To summarize briefly, we have in *Mardi,* for the first time in Melville's writings, a complex treatment of both pacifism and rebellion. But we do not find a comprehensive statement of pacifism in this novel as we do in *White-Jacket,* nor does rebellion emerge as a total philosophy until *Moby-Dick,* where the two outlooks collide for the first time in their fully developed form.

CHAPTER III

REDBURN: INNOCENCE AND EXPERIENCE

    "Father, father! where are you going?
    O do not walk so fast.
    Speak, father, speak to your little boy,
    Or else I shall be lost."

    The night was dark, no father was there;
    The child was wet with dew;
    The mire was deep, & the child did weep,
    And away the vapour fled.
            From *Songs of Innocence and Experience*
            by William Blake

In many ways, it seems unfortunate that *Redburn* (1849) is Melville's fourth book and not his first, for its hero, Wellingborough Redburn, is the youngest and most completely naive and unformed of Melville's protagonists. The novel, subtitled *His First Voyage,* concerns Redburn's round trip between New York City and Liverpool as a "boy" aboard the American ship, the *Highlander,* Redburn's journey is as much spiritual and psychological as it is physical, for as Newton Arvin comments, "The outward subject of the book is a young boy's first voyage as a sailor before the mast; its inward subject is the initiation of innocence to evil".[1]

This evil which Redburn encounters is of two types, social and metaphysical. The graphic and moving scenes describing the slums of Liverpool and the suffering of the Irish emigrants aboard the *Highlander* make of *Redburn* a strong work of social protest. In the person of Jackson, a figure who looks back to Queen Hautia and forward to Claggart and perhaps even to Moby-Dick, the

---

[1] *Herman Melville* (New York, 1957), p. 103.

young sailor glimpses a different kind of evil, an evil which is an inherent part of the universe and an evil which is beyond the control of man. With this awareness of the positive nature of evil in the universe is linked Redburn's realization that the traditional religious values can no longer give sufficient answers to the problems of the present age.

At the opening of the novel, Redburn lives in a world of daydream and delusion, and his ignorance of the actual world and the basic issues facing man is absolute. His interest in the sea, significantly enough, is a result, not so much of talking to real sailors or seeing a real ocean, but of looking at oil paintings, etc.

> But that which perhaps more than any thing else, converted my vague dreamings and longings into a definite purpose of seeking my fortune on the sea, was an old-fashioned glass ship, about eighteen inches long, and of French manufacture, which my father, some thirty years before, had brought home from Hamburg as a present to a great-uncle of mine...[2]

Redburn romantically envisions the reverence that people would show towards him if he were a world traveler, and how he would bring home "foreign clothes of a rich fabric and princely make, and wear them up and down the streets, and how grocers' boys would turn their heads to look at me, as I went by".[3] These youthful dreams are interwoven with images of his father, now deceased, who "had several times crossed the Atlantic on business affairs, for he had been an importer in Broadstreet".[4] Indeed, for half the novel, Redburn is dominated by a desire to imitate his dead parent, and this obsession is so strong that we find in the book not only an echo of Telemachus in pursuit of his father, but, as I hope to show later, the definite implication on another level of meaning, that the father Redburn pursues is God.

Thus Redburn sets out on his voyage with three clear — but not necessarily conscious — goals; the fulfillment of his romantic dreams, the desire to find his father or at least to identify himself

[2] *Redburn* (New York, 1957), p. 6.
[3] *Ibid.*, p. 3.
[4] *Ibid.*, p. 3.

with his father's values, and finally, the discovery of religious value. He fails in all three of these quests, but as a result of this failure and his concurrent realization that the world is a place more of evil than of good, Redburn becomes a man.

Redburn's romantic illusions are attacked by social reality immediately upon leaving his pleasant rural home near the Hudson River. On the steamboat to New York City, he is ostracized by the other passengers because of his poverty, and upon his arrival, he is cheated at a pawn shop. Soon after his ship, the *Highlander,* sets out to sea, a sailor suffering from delerium tremens throws himself overboard. Redburn is harried ceaselessly by the older members of the crew. And the first European he sees is not a creature of wonder, but a clever Irishman who succeeds in stealing part of the ship's ropes.

Such incidents, as might be expected, create in the youth a sense of moral indignation and isolation. Redburn feels himself to be "a sort of Ishmael in the ship, without a single friend or companion".[5] But, on the outbound voyage to Liverpool, Redburn's emotional reaction is perhaps based more on his own personal inadequacies than on any injustice he perceives or any cruelty of which he is the victim. For Redburn is a terrible snob, and his own exaggerated self-image is responsible for much of his unhappiness. After conversing with one of the other sailors, he remarks:

When I heard this poor sailor talk in this manner, showing so plainly his ignorance and absence of proper views of religion, I pitied him more and more, and contrasting my own situation with his, I was grateful that I was different from him; and I thought how pleasant it was, to feel wiser and better than he could feel . . .[6]

An ironic undercut immediately follows.

Thinking that my superiority to him in a moral way might sit uneasily upon this sailor, I thought it would soften the matter down by giving him a chance to show his own superiority to me, in a minor thing; *for I was far from being vain and conceited.*[7] [Italics my own.]

---

[5] *Ibid.*, p. 60.
[6] *Ibid.*, p. 46.
[7] *Ibid.*, pp. 46-7.

But Redburn comes to shun this perpetual egotism as a result of his experiences in Liverpool. His continual exposure in that city to pimps, beggars, cripples, prostitutes, and drunkards forces him into a realization that his own problems are comparatively petty and that all human existence is a form of suffering. Perhaps what is even more horrifying, many people, instead of trying to alleviate misery, exploit it for their own purposes. Noting the old men and women who search the docks for bodies hoping for a meagre reward, Redburn observes:

> There seems to be no calamity overtaking man, that can not be rendered merchantable. Undertakers, sextons, tomb-makers, and hearse-drivers, get their living from the dead; and in time of plague most thrive. And these miserable old men and women hunted after corpses to keep from going to the church-yard themselves; for they were the most wretched of starvelings.[8]

The incident which most moves Redburn, however, is the famous scene concerning what he saw in Launcelott's-Hey, a passage of such brilliancy and poignancy that an English critic is led to remark that "Melville does in five pages of quiet narrative what even Dickens could not have done in five hundred".[9] Walking through the narrow street one day, Redburn hears a "low, hopeless, endless wail of some one forever lost". Looking about him, he at last sees that

> some fifteen feet below the walk, crouching in nameless squalor, with her head bowed over, was the figure of what had been a woman. Her blue arms folded to her livid bosom two shrunken things like children, that leaned toward her, one on each side. At first, I knew not whether they were alive or dead. They made no sign: they did not move or stir; but from the vault came that soul-sickening wail.
>
> I made a noise with my foot, which, in the silence echoed far and near; but there was no response. Louder still; when one of the children lifted its head, and cast upward a faint glance; then closed its eyes, and lay motionless. The woman also, now gazed up, and perceived me; but let fall her eye again. They were dumb and next to dead with want. How they had crawled into that den, I could not tell; but there they crawled to die. At that moment I never thought of relieving

---

[8] *Ibid.*, p. 173.
[9] Ronald Mason, *The Spirit Above the Dust* (London, 1951), p. 71.

them; for death was so stamped in their glazed and unimploring eyes, that I almost regarded them as already no more. I stood looking down on them, while my whole soul swelled within me; and I asked myself, What right had any body in the wide world to smile and be glad, when sights like this were to be seen?[10]

The young sailor rushes to an open lot in the alley, hoping to find one of the old women who look for rags there. But these old hags either ignore his pleas entirely, or condemn the dying woman – " 'that Betsy Jennings desarves it – was she ever married? tell me that' ".[11] A policeman whom he finally encounters also refuses to help.

"It's none of my business, Jack," said he. "I don't belong to that street."
"Who does then?"
"I don't know. But what business is it of yours? Are you not a Yankee?"
"Yes," I said, "but come, I will help you remove that woman, if you say so."
"There, now, Jack, go on board your ship and stick to it; and leave these matters to the town."[12]

Others – porters, inn-keepers, etc. – will have nothing to do with the starving woman and her children. For several days Redburn brings them bread, but the inevitable occurs, and they die. Shocked not only by the horror of the poor woman's fate, but angered by the indifference of the rest of humanity, Redburn states, "Surrounded as we are by the wants and woes of our fellowmen, and yet given to follow our own pleasures, regardless of their pains, are we not like people sitting up with a corpse, and making merry in the house of the dead?"[13]

We find in Redburn's concern for the starving woman his first true act of kindness in the novel, and when he brings her food, he moves from a position of detachment to a position of commitment. For Redburn has reached the conclusion that no man is an island,

[10] *Redburn*, pp. 173-4.
[11] *Ibid.*, p. 175.
[12] *Ibid.*, p. 175.
[13] *Ibid.*, p. 178.

that to turn your back on one who is suffering is in reality to turn your back on yourself. To maintain any sort of self-respect, he feels that he must fight against all social evil and social injustice. Needless to say, after his initial act of kindness, most of Redburn's snobbishness and egotism disappears, and his major concern now is more with the misfortune of others than with his own discomforts and disappointments.

Thus far in the novel, human suffering has for the most part been related to poverty. But shortly after the scene in Launcelott's-Hey, Redburn meets Harry Bolton, a young nobleman. One day Harry mysteriously whisks the American to London, and they go to a gambling house, Aladdin's Palace, where Harry proceeds to lose all of his money. This scene in Aladdin's Palace, though not particularly well developed, is a balance to the numerous horrors of the slums of Liverpool, and the moral being illustrated is that there is almost as much tragedy and vice in the lives of the very rich as there is in the lives of the very poor.

No discussion of social protest in *Redburn* would be complete without mention of the plight of the Irish emigrants who return with Harry and Redburn on the homeward voyage of the *Highlander*. These five hundred Irishmen are packed into a foul hold, not given enough food, are forbidden from most parts of the ship, and are only permitted to have a fire for a few hours a day over which to cook their food. As a result of these horrendous conditions, a plague breaks out, and many of the Irish die. This tragedy leads to a general discussion of emigrant ships. Many Americans oppose further immigration, but Melville writes that people have the right to come to America if they can get here, "though they bring all Ireland and her miseries with them. For the whole world is the patrimony of the whole world; there is no telling who does not own a stone in the great Wall of China".[14] A specific list of recommendations to aid the plight of the emigrants then follows.

What ordinance makes it obligatory upon the captain of a ship, to supply the steerage-passengers with decent lodgings, and give them

---

[14] *Ibid.,* p. 282.

light and air in that foul den, where they are immured, during a long voyage across the Atlantic? What ordinance necessitates him to place the *galley,* or steerage-passengers' stove, in a dry place of shelter, where the emigrants can do their cooking during a storm, or wet weather? What ordinance obliges him to give them more room on deck, and let them have an occasional run fore and aft? — There is no law concerning these things.[15]

As we have seen, Redburn dreamed of making a spectacular return home, richly clothed and admired by all. But the actuality is far from the dream. He returns no financially richer than when he began the voyage. Moreover, his major concern upon reaching New York City again is not with his own impoverished condition, but with finding a job for his friend, Harry Bolton. Redburn's earlier romanticism and egotism have been purged. He has achieved maturity through his new awareness of man's inhumanity to man and through his own willingness to combat injustice. Such is not the case with Harry, who in many ways acts as a foil to Redburn. After the voyage, Harry complains about the tar-stains on his hands, crying: " 'They will not come out, and I'm ruined for life' ". Redburn replies " 'Never mind, Harry' ".[16] Redburn triumphs because he is willing to get his hands dirty and come to grips with life. Harry is destroyed because he tries to escape from reality. As Ronald Mason points out, "The sea that makes Redburn breaks Harry Bolton".[17]

In the course of *Redburn,* the young hero loses his innocence and becomes aware of the evil in the world. He is able to cope with the social injustice that he finds, actively rebelling against the evil produced by mortal man. But there is also portrayed in the novel a much more subtle and complex type of evil which Redburn lacks the maturity to deal with. This is the inherent or metaphysical evil represented by Jackson, the sickly sailor who dominates the crew of the *Highlander.* Jackson is often described in terms of the devil. He "was such a hideous looking mortal, that Satan himself would have run from him".[18] He tells horrible stories with a

[15] *Ibid.,* p. 282.
[16] *Ibid.,* p. 290.
[17] *Op. cit.,* p. 77.
[18] *Redburn,* p. 54.

64   "REDBURN": INNOCENCE AND EXPERIENCE

"*diabolical* relish",[19] expresses an "*infernal* opinion",[20] acts as if he had sold his soul "to Satan",[21] and presides over the dinner table "like a devil".[22] Even his death, where he plunges from the top of the rigging into the depths of the ocean, never to reappear at the surface, parallels the fall of Satan from heaven. Though he is physically the weakest man aboard the *Highlander* and is hated by the rest of the sailors, he is the acknowledged leader of the ship's crew. He is the final arbitrator in all disputes and rations out the food at dinner. The men rub his back, give him tobacco, and mend his clothes, but the more they cater to him, the more he abuses them. "He was a Cain afloat; branded on his yellow brow with some inscrutable curse; and going about corrupting and searing every heart that beat near him".[23]

Halfway across the Atlantic on the outbound voyage, the *Highlander* sights a wreck. Lashed to its taffrail are the grassy bodies of three dead sailors. Jackson immediately begins to ridicule these corpses.

"Don't laugh at dem poor fellows," said Max, looking grave; "do' you see dar bodies, dar souls are farder off dan de Cape of Dood Hope."

"Dood Hope, Dood Hope," shrieked Jackson, with a horrid grin, mimicking the Dutchman, "dare is no dood hope for dem, old boy; dey are drowned and d .... d, as you and I will be, Red Max, one of these dark nights."

"No, no," said Blunt, "all sailors are saved; they have plenty of squalls here below, but fair weather aloft."

"And did you get that out of your silly Dream Book, you Greek?" howled Jackson through a cough. "Don't talk of heaven to me – it's a lie – I know it – and they are all fools that believe it. Do you think, you Greek, that there's any heaven for *you*? Will they let *you* in there, with that tarry hand, and that oily head of hair? Avast! when some shark gulps you down his hatchway one of these days, you'll find, that by dying, you'll only go from one gale of wind to another; mind that, you Irish cockney! Yes, you'll be bolted down like one of your own pills: and I should like to see the whole ship swallowed down in

---

[19] *Ibid.*, p. 55.
[20] *Ibid.*, p. 257.
[21] *Ibid.*, p. 265.
[22] *Ibid.*, p. 271.
[23] *Ibid.*, p. 100.

the Norway maelstrom, like a box on 'em. That would be a dose of salts for ye!"[24]

Jackson's words may sound like Ahab's, but there are few other similarities between the two men. Ahab wishes to wage a wholehearted war against the evil which both he and Jackson describe. The latter, on the other hand, encourages and furthers this evil. Jackson, rather than being a rebel against the universe, is a concrete manifestation of what is wrong with it.

Redburn is horrified by Jackson and everything that he represents, and he searches for a philosophically satisfactory solution to the evil which the unholy sailor embodies. The answer initially suggested is some form of Christianity. Jackson is contrasted with Redburn's recurring image of his dead father.

> But then I remembered, how many times my own father had said he had crossed the ocean; *and I had never dreamed of such a thing as doubting him; for I always thought him a marvelous being, infinitely purer and greater than I was, who could not by any possibility do wrong, or say an untruth.*[25] [Italics my own.]

This description of a being who is "*infinitely* purer and greater" and who can never make a mistake certainly has connotations of the Almighty. Redburn's pursuit for his earthly father has become interwoven with a search for a heavenly father.

This religious symbolism is further developed in the chapters where Redburn tries to find his way around Liverpool, using his father's fifty year old guide book. Redburn regards the pages of this book, *The Picture of Liverpool,* as "sacred" and treats the book with "reverence".[26] Using it as a guide, Redburn proposes

> to visit Riddough's Hotel, where my father had stopped, more than thirty years before: and then, with the map in my hand, follow him through all the town, according to the dotted lines in the diagram. For thus would I be performing a filial *pilgrimage,* to spots which would be *hallowed* in my eyes.[27] [Italics my own.]

---

[24] *Ibid.,* pp. 99-100.
[25] *Ibid.,* p. 32.
[26] *Ibid.,* p. 151.
[27] *Ibid.,* p. 147.

66   "REDBURN": INNOCENCE AND EXPERIENCE

But Redburn only succeeds in getting lost, for the buildings mentioned in *The Picture of Liverpool* no longer are in existence.

But though I rose from the door-step a sadder and a wiser boy, and though my guide-book had been stripped of its reputation for infallibility, I did not treat with contumely or disdain, those sacred pages which had once been a beacon to my sire.[28]

I would agree with Lawrance Thompson, who suggests that Redburn's guidebook represents the Bible.[29] If Redburn's earthly father is linked with God, than the guide-book which he leaves his son should correspond to the Bible, if the analogy is to be consistent. Furthermore, not only is the guide-book presented in religious terms, but it is described as being "faded and dilapidated".[30] The only specific Bibles referred to in *Redburn* are in a similar condition. The Cook's copy is "very much soiled and covered with grease spots",[31] and the Bible belonging to Mrs. O'Brien is "black with age".[32]

The fact that all of the Bibles mentioned in the novel are in a rather battered condition suggests that the Scripture is outmoded for modern use. This is spelled out more clearly when Redburn generalizes on the nature of guide-books.

Guide-books, Wellingborough, are the least reliable books in all literature; and nearly all literature, in one sense, is made up of guide-books. Old ones tell us the ways our fathers went, through the thoroughfares and courts of old; but how few of those former places can their posterity trace, amid avenues of modern erections; to how few is the old guide-book now a clew! Every age makes its own guide-books, and the old ones are used for waste paper.[33]

As a result of his voyage to England and his experiences in Liverpool, Redburn sheds his innocence and learns a great deal about the nature of the universe. He discovers in the person of Jackson a form of evil of which he had previously been ignorant,

---

[28] *Ibid.*, p. 151.
[29] *Melville's Quarrel with God* (Princeton, 1952).
[30] *Redburn*, p. 142.
[31] *Ibid.*, p. 79.
[32] *Ibid.*, p. 258.
[33] *Ibid.*, p. 151.

a type of evil which seems structured into the very core of the universe. Concurrent with this recognition, Redburn comes to realize that he can never again find his father, either spiritual or physical. Odysseus is lost forever, and God no longer is considered to be infallible – the guide-book, symbolizing the Bible, is outdated, and those who follow it get lost. The religious values which have provided satisfactory answers for the problems raised in past ages are no longer sufficient, and modern man must find a new set of standards by which to guide his life. Redburn can't provide a solution to this riddle, but at least he arrives at an honest picture of the universe *as it really is,* not as it has been traditionally pictured. He is more successful in dealing with the social evil which he encounters, however. Redburn moves from his initial position of aloofness and self-centeredness to a position of involvement and identification with others. He feels that no man can be happy if his fellow humans are suffering, that to be a man is to fight against social injustice. Hence, *Redburn* is a novel of strong social protest, and though its hero does not defy the universe as does Taji in *Mardi,* he rebels actively against the injustices which are products of man's society.

CHAPTER IV

WHITE-JACKET: THE PHILOSOPHY OF PACIFISM

> But the New Testament produced a different impression, especially the Sermon on the Mount which went straight to my heart. I compared it with the *Gita*. The verses, "But I say unto you, that ye resist not evil: but whosoever smite thee on thy right cheek, turn to him the other also. And if any man take away thy coat let him have thy cloke too," delighted me beyond measure.... A Satyagrahi obeys the laws of society intelligently and of his own free will, because he considers it to be his sacred duty to do so. It is only when a person has thus obeyed the laws of society scrupulously that he is in a position to judge as to which particular rules are good and just and which are unjust and iniquitous.
>
> Mohandas Gandhi,
> *The Story of My Experiments with Truth*

White-Jack (1850), based on Melville's experiences as a sailor on the American frigate, the *United States,* is an even more direct and vigorous work of protest than is *Redburn*. The first-mentioned work suffers "more than the earlier books had done, from that humanitarian note that so dominates it as it dominates no other work of Melville's", observes one commentator.[1] But *White-Jacket* is also the only work of Melville's that led directly to some sort of reform, though the anonymous and over-enthusiastic critic who noted that "Placed on the desk of every member of Congress, possibly it had more influence in abolishing corporal punishment in the Navy than anything else", definitely overstates the impact of the novel.[2] Nevertheless, the book made enough of an impression

---

[1] Newton Arvin, *Herman Melville* (New York, 1957), p. 111.

[2] This comment is found on the back jacket of the Grove Press edition

for three admirals to comment upon it. Rear-Admiral Thomas O. Selfridge attacked Melville, saying that "he would have laws, democratic in all respects, for the rule of our Navy. What absurdity!" In 1930, another rear-admiral, Livingston Hunt, accused the book's author of being "a propagandist for world peace, a scoffer at gold braid and salutes and ceremonies, an anti-militarist, an apostle of leveling and democracy".[3]

Though *White-Jacket* makes use of symbols – the most conspicuous being the narrator's jacket – the critic who is interested in exploring Melville's attitude towards war and violence in this book has no problems with interpretation, for the major points which Melville wishes to make in this connection are stated clearly, often, and directly. *White-Jacket* takes issue not only with flogging, but also with a whole range of naval abuses, and furthermore develops a positive philosophy of pacifism, a philosophy based in part on religious values and in part on democratic principles, in part on the Bible and in part on the Declaration of Independence and the American Constitution, and a philosophy which is in dramatic conflict with the Articles of War, the Bible of the Navy, so to speak. The fact that Melville builds a philosophy based on the Bible, a work which he had previously rejected in *Redburn,* obviously precludes any sort of pat and simple chronological development of pacifism and rebellion in his writings. But a writer's craft or a thinker's philosophy never develop in a straight upward line: the growth of any man is marked by regression, reconsideration, and uncertainty. Between Beethoven's Eroica and Fifth symphonies is the modest little symphony in B-flat. Between the religious skepticism of *Mardi* and *Redburn* and the fiery denial of Christ and God in *Moby-Dick,* we find a work optimistic in attitude and orthodox in its attitude towards Christianity.

Floggings take place with frequency during the return voyage of the American warship, the *Neversink.* The first such incident

---

of *White Jacket,* New York, 1952. For the true story of the role played by White Jacket in abolishing flogging, see Charles Anderson, *Melville in the South Seas* (New York, 1937).

[3] Both of these quotations are cited by Charles Anderson, "A Reply to Herman Melville's *White-Jacket* by Rear Admiral Thomas O. Selfridge, Sr.", *AL,* VII, 123-44 (May, 1935).

discussed in any detail occurs one evening when White-Jacket – the narrator – and his fellow sailors are summoned to the mainmast to witness the punishment of four members of the crew, who had been fighting. Two of these sailors are sober, middle-aged men, who struck back only after repeated provocation. The other two include John, a bully and the real instigator of the trouble, and Peter, an innocent boy of nineteen years. John, the worst man, is flogged first, and later walks smiling among the crew, saying " 'D. . . .n me! It's nothing when you're used to it! Who wants to fight?' "[4] Next come one of the middle-aged men, who swears involuntarily when the blows hit him, and who, after he is cut down, vows to kill the captain. As a result of the whipping, the second middle-aged man "became silent and sullen for the rest of the cruise".[5] The youth is the last to be flogged. " 'I don't care what happens to me now!' wept Peter, going among the crew, with blood-shot eyes, as he put on his shirt. 'I have been flogged once, and now they may do it again if they will. Let them look out for me now' ".[6] As can readily be seen, Melville has gone to great lengths to show that while flogging in no way reforms a bad man, it either embitters or breaks the spirit of a good man.

This flogging scene is followed by three chapters of exposition entitled "Some of the Evil Effects of Flogging", "Flogging not Lawful", and "Flogging not Necessary". In the second of these chapters, it is noted that the Virginian, John Randolph, had declared in Congress that he had witnessed more floggings on one voyage aboard a man-of-war than he had seen on his own plantation in ten years. The narrator adds

But what torments must that seaman undergo, who, while his back bleeds at the gangway, bleeds agonised drops of shame from his soul! Are we not justified in immeasurably denouncing this thing? Join hands with me, then; and, in the name of that Being in whose image the flogged sailor is made, let us demand of legislators, by what right they dare profane what God Himself accounts sacred.[7]

---

[4] *White Jacket* (New York, Grove Press, 1952), p. 138.
[5] *Ibid.*, p. 138.
[6] *Ibid.*, p. 139.
[7] *Ibid.*, p. 142.

A more intellectual protest is made by White-Jacket in the last of these three chapters.

> If there are any three things opposed to the genius of the American Constitution, they are these: irresponsibility in a judge, unlimited discretionary authority in an executive, and the union of an irresponsible judge and an unlimited executive in one person.[8]

But, argues the protagonist, the Articles of War invest the captain of the ship with the powers of judge and executive, which is a clear violation of our Constitution. The sailor, therefore, "shares none of our civil immunities; the law of our soil in no respect accompanies the national floating timbers thereon, and to which he clings as his home. For him our Revolution was in vain; to him our Declaration of Independence is a lie."[9] Flogging violates not only the Constitution, but other laws as well.

> Now, in the language of Blackstone, again, there is a law, "coeval with mankind dictated by God Himself, superior in obligation to any other, and no human laws are of any validity if contrary to this." That law is the Law of Nature; among the three great principles of which Justinian includes "that to every man should be rendered his due." But we have seen that the laws involving flogging in the Navy do *not* render to every man his due, since in some cases they indirectly exclude the officers from any punishment whatever, and in all cases protect them from the scourge, which is inflicted upon the sailor.[10]

And finally, we are presented with the major argument,

> Irrespective of incidental considerations, we assert that flogging in the Navy is opposed to the essential dignity of man, which no legislator has a right to violate: that it is oppressive, and glaringly unequal in its operations; that it is utterly repugnant to the spirit of our democratic institutions; indeed, that it involves a lingering trait of the worst times of a barbarous feudal aristocracy; in a word, we denounce it as religiously, morally, and immutably *wrong*.[11]

There are several other chapters which deal with flogging, including one in which White-Jacket himself is brought before the

---

[8] *Ibid.*, p. 143.
[9] *Ibid.*, p. 144.
[10] *Ibid.*, pp. 145-6.
[11] *Ibid.*, p. 146.

mast, only to be saved by the intervention of Colbrook, the corporal of the marines, and by Jack Chase, but no new arguments against its abolition are advanced. The book continues to flay other naval abuses, however, and continually stresses that most of the injustice that takes place at sea is the result, not so much of the cruelty of the officers, but is the logical outcome of an adherence either to the Articles of War or to time-worn naval traditions.

Certainly one of the most striking aspects of *White-Jacket* is that no matter how apparently trivial the subject about which Melville is writing or how humorous this presentation initially is, sooner or later it becomes charged with protest against the cruelty of the Navy. For example, Melville begins to deal very amusingly with the times at which "the people" – the common sailors dine aboard a man-of-war. But it is quickly noted that on many warships, nobody is allowed to eat after the commodore has supped. "The people" eat breakfast at eight o'clock, and if the commodore dines at five in the afternoon, the crew must eat at four. Hence, the crew must go for sixteen hours without food. What seems at first to be a comic discussion of men's eating habits ends up with a serious appeal for reform.

Mr. Secretary of the Navy, in the name of *the people,* you should interpose in this matter. Many a time have I, a main-top man, found myself actually faint of a tempestuous morning-watch, when all my energies were demanded – owing to the miserable, unphilosophical mode of allotting the government meals at sea. We beg of you, Mr. Secretary, not to be swayed in the matter by the Honourable Board of Commodores, who will no doubt tell you that eight, twelve, and four are the proper hours for *the people* to take their meals; inasmuch, as at these hours the watches are relieved. For, though this arrangement makes a neater and cleaner thing of it for the officers, and looks very nice and superfine on paper, yet it is plainly detrimental to health . . . .[12]

And so it goes through the course of the book. Melville explores aspects of naval life which we take for granted, and finds them riddled with injustice. This type of protest is indicated even in the chapter headings. One such chapter, "Some of the Ceremonies in

[12] *Ibid.,* p. 42.

a Man-of-War Unnecessary and Injurious", closes with a demand for "discreet, but democratic legislation".[13] In another chapter, entitled "One Reason Why Man-of-War's Men Are Generally Short-Lived", Melville criticizes the fact that on a man-of-war, the hammocks are stored from sunrise until sunset, so the men are unable to catch a cat-nap below deck during the daytime. Even the continual washing and scrubbing of the ship's decks comes under scrutiny.

Now, against this invariably daily flooding of the three decks of a frigate, as a man-of-war's man, White Jacket most earnestly protests. In sunless weather it keeps the sailor's quarters perpetually damp; so much so, that you can scarcely sit down without running the risk of getting lumbago.[14]

Ship captains pride themselves on the speed with which their crews can furl and unfurl the sails. But on one occasion, an overzealous officer so harries and hurries a poor sailor called Baldy, that the latter, in his haste to fulfill orders, falls from one of the masts.

Why mince the matter? The death of most of these man-of-war's men lies at the door of the souls of those officers, who, while safely standing on deck themselves, scruple not to sacrifice an immortal man or two, in order to show off the excelling discipline of the ship. And thus do *the people* of the gun-deck suffer, that the commodore on the poop may be glorified.[15]

But a philosophy of pacifism must rest upon more than a protest against flogging and other naval injustices. If these were the only issues raised in *White-Jacket,* it would be a work expressing humanitarian — but not necessarily pacifistic — sentiments. Towards the close of the book, however, Melville makes fewer specific criticisms of life aboard a man-of-war, and begins to attack in general terms the basic concept of a battleship. As Richard Chase states, "Evil was organic with the kind of man-of-war society which had to exist as long as the Navy had to exist".[16] While dis-

---

[13] *Ibid.*, p. 164.
[14] *Ibid.*, p. 92.
[15] *Ibid.*, p. 193.
[16] *Herman Melville* (New York, 1949), p. 22.

cussing the differing attitudes of the crew of a man-of-war, who dread fighting, and the officers, who look forward to battle because it offers them a chance for glory and fame, White Jacket suddenly launches into an attack upon the very existence of a Navy.

When shall the time come, how much longer will God postpone it, when the clouds, which at times gather over the horizons of nations, shall not be hailed by any class of humanity, and invoked to burst as a bomb? *Standing navies, as well as standing armies, serve to keep alive the spirit of war even in the meek heart of peace.* In its very embers and smoulderings they nourish that fatal fire, and half-pay officers, as the priests of Mars, yet guard the temple, though no god be there.[17] [Italics my own.]

This theme is later expanded.

But the whole matter of war is a thing that smites common sense and Christianity in the face; so everything connected with it is utterly foolish, unchristian, barbarous, brutal and savouring of the Feejee Islands, cannibalism, saltpetre, and the devil.[18]

Not only is war wrong, but any sort of killing is in conflict with Christianity. In a chapter ironically entitled "Man-of-War Trophies", White-Jacket reminisces about a scene which he had once witnessed while visiting a small pioneer town on the western bank of the Mississippi. He had there encountered a gigantic Indian, parading proudly to and fro, wrapped in a blanket on the back of which were "a crowd of human hands, rudely delineated in red".[19]

Poor savage! thought I; and is this the cause of your lofty gait? Do you straighten yourself to think that you have committed a murder, when a chance falling stone has often done the same? *Is it a proud thing to topple down six feet perpendicular of immortal manhood, though that lofty living tower needed perhaps thirty good growing summers to bring it to maturity? Poor savage! And you account it so glorious, do you, to mutilate and destroy what God himself was more than a quarter of a century in building?*

And yet, fellow-Christians, what is the American frigate *Macedonian*, or the English frigate *President*, but as two bloody red hands

---

[17] *White Jacket*, p. 204.
[18] *Ibid.*, p. 299.
[19] *Ibid.*, p. 256.

painted on this poor savage's blanket?[20] [Italics in the first paragraph my own.]

The pacifistic position of the narrator has so strongly developed by the end of the book that even Jack Chase, White Jacket's hero and the man whom the work is dedicated, is reproached for his militarism. At the request of the sailors, Jack had been giving a vivid account of the battle of Navarino and of his own part in this naval encounter.

Now, this Jack Chase had a heart in him like a mastodon's. I have seen him weep when a man has been flogged at the gang-way; yet, in relating the story of the battle of Navarino, he plainly showed that he held the God of the Blessed Bible to have been the British Commodore in the Levant, on the bloody 20th of October, A.D. 1827. And thus it would seem that war almost makes blasphemers of the best of men, and brings them all down to the Feejee standard of humanity. Some man-of-war's men have confessed to me that, as a battle has raged more and more, their hearts have hardened in infernal harmony; and, like their own guns, they have fought without a thought.

Soldier or sailor, the fighting man is but a fiend; and the staff and bodyguard of the Devil musters many a baton. But war at times is inevitable. Must the national honour be trampled under foot by an insolent foe?

Say on, say on; but know you this, and lay it to heart, war-voting Bench of Bishops, that He on whom we believe himself *has enjoined us to turn the left cheek if the right be smitten. Never mind what follows. That passage you cannot expunge from the Bible; that passage is as binding upon us as any other; that passage embodies the soul and substance of the Christian faith; without it, Christianity were like any other faith. And that passage will yet, by the blessing of God, turn the world. But in some things we must turn Quakers first.*[21] [Italics my own.]

In light of the above quotation, it is not surprising that one of the things which Melville finds most abhorrent about the Navy is the role of the so-called Christian Church on a man-of-war. First, the sailors are forced to attend worship aboard ship, which Melvillle feels to be a violation of the Constitution. Moreover,

[20] *Ibid.*, pp. 256-7.
[21] *Ibid.*, p. 304.

How can it be expected that the religion of peace should flourish in an oaken castle of war? How can it be expected that the clergyman, whose pulpit is a forty-two pounder, should convert sinners to a faith that enjoins them to turn the right cheek when the left is smitten? How is it to be expected that when, according to the LXII. of the Articles of War, as they now stand unrepealed on the Statute Book, "a bounty shall be paid" (to the officers and crew) "by the United States government of twenty dollars for each person on board any ship of an enemy which shall be sunk or destroyed by any United States Ship"; and when by a subsequent section (vii.), it is provided, among other apportionings, *that the chaplain shall receive 'two-twentieths" of this price paid for sinking and destroying ships full of human beings? How is it to be expected that a clergyman, thus provided for, should prove efficacious in enlarging upon the criminality of Judas, who, for thirty pieces of silver, betrayed his Master?*[22] [Italics my own.]

Throughout all of the criticism of naval abuses and the championing of the cause of pacifism, Melville's attacks seem to be levelled primarily at the Articles of War, which reflect not only the worst aspects of naval life, but which also come to represent all that is brutal and arbitrary in the world of men. The Articles of War are continually contrasted with "that great non-combatant, the Bible".[23] Of the twenty offenses that a seaman can commit, as defined by the Articles, *thirteen* are punishable by death *"or such punishment as a court-martial shall adjudge"*.[24] The narrator suggests that perhaps some punishment worse than death is hereby implied.

Your honours of the Spanish Inquisition, Loyola and Torquemada! produce, reverend gentlemen, your most secret code, and match these Articles of War, if you can. Jack Ketch, *you* also are experienced in these things! Thou most benevolent of mortals, who standest by us, and hangest around our necks, when all the rest of the world are against us – tell us, hangman, what punishment is this, horribly hinted at as being worse than death? Is it, upon an empty stomach, to read the Articles of War every morning, for the term of one's natural life? Or is it to be imprisoned in a cell, with its walls papered from floor to ceiling with printed copies, in italics, of these Articles of War?

[22] *Ibid.*, pp. 156-7.
[23] *Ibid.*, p. 132.
[24] *Ibid.*, p. 279.

But it needs not to dilate upon the pure, bubbling milk of human kindness, and Christian charity, and forgiveness of injuries which pervade this charming document, so thoroughly imbued, as a Christian code, with the benignant spirit of the Sermon on the Mount. But as it is very nearly alike in the foremost states of Christendom, and as it is nationally set forth by those states, it indirectly becomes an index to the true condition of the present civilization of the world.[25]

As has been previously suggested, the Articles of War are in conflict not only with the Bible, but also with the democratic tradition of America, particularly as represented by the Constitution and the Declaration of Indepedence. White Jacket implies that the despotism of the Articles reflects their origin, for they came into existence in the reign of King Charles the Second of England. These Articles are condemned both for their cruelty and because they make an artificial distinction between men – the sailor and the officer. The arbitrary stripes which divide men into these two unequal and unbridgable groups are clearly a violation of our democratic principles. Once on board a man-of-war, an officer in his relationship with the crew or "the people" can never be wrong, simply because he is an officer. Even the most immature and vicious midshipman is always publicly backed by the captain, no matter how unjustly such a greenhorn maltreats a common sailor. The preposterous pomp and circumstances surrounding much of naval behaviour also is ridiculed. Even the president of the United States, Melville writes, enters the White House with "his umbrella under his arm, and no brass band or military guard at his heels".[26] Such should also be true aboard a man-of-war.

Is it not well to have our institutions of a piece? Any American landsman may hope to become President of the Union – commodore of our squadron of states. And every American sailor should be placed in such a position, that he might freely aspire to command a squadron of frigates.[27]

It should be remembered that Melville had also championed the cause of democracy in *Typee,* though his concept of democracy in

[25] *Ibid.,* pp. 279-80.
[26] *Ibid.,* p. 163.
[27] *Ibid.,* p. 119.

White Jacket is much more complex and profound. In *Typee*, Melville had pictured primitive man as being naturally good and dignified. He has no such illusions concerning the crew of a man-of-war, however. "The Navy is the asylum of the perverse, the home of the unfortunate. Here the sons of adversity meet the children of calamity, and here the children of calamity meet the off-spring of sin."[28] Again and again, White Jacket protests that he has no theoretical love of man.

Be it here, once and for all, understood, that no sentimental and theoretic love for the common sailor; no romantic belief in that peculiar noble-heartedness and exaggerated generosity of disposition fictitiously imputed to him in novels; and no prevailing desire to gain the reputation of being his friend, have actuated me in anything I have said, in any part of this work, touching the gross oppression under which I know that the sailor suffers. Indifferent as to who may be the parties concerned, I but desire to see wrong things righted, and equal justice administered to all.[29]

The narrator then goes on to add:

Nor, as has been elsewhere hinted, is the general ignorance or depravity of any race of men to be alleged as an apology for tyranny over them. On the contrary, it cannot admit of a reasonable doubt, in any unbiased mind conversant with the interior life of a man-of-war, that most of the sailor iniquities practised therein are indirectly to be ascribed to the morally debasing effects of the unjust, despotic, and degrading laws under which the man-of-war's man lives.[30]

Though *White Jacket* is set on a man-of-war, and though many of the specific protests against naval abuses would have meaning only in terms of life aboard a battleship, there can be no question that Melville is using the time-honored symbol of a ship to represent the whole world. The book is subtitled *The World in a Man-of-War*, and the phrase "our man-of-war world" appears at least twelve times in the course of the work. The relationship between the *Neversink* and the world as a whole is spelled out most clearly in the last chapter of the novel.

[28] *Ibid.*, p. 82.
[29] *Ibid.*, p. 289.
[30] *Ibid.*, p. 289.

As a man-of-war that sails through the sea, so this earth that sails through the air. We mortals are all on board a fast-sailing, never-sinking, world-frigate, of which God was the shipwright; and she is but one craft in a Milky-Way fleet, of which God is the Lord High Admiral. The port we sail from is ever astern. And though far out of sight of land, for ages and ages we continue to sail with sealed orders, and our last destination remains a secret to ourselves and our officers; yet our final haven was predestined ere we slipped from the stocks at Creation.[31]

The rest of this equation is simple to complete. "The people" or crew represent common man the world over. The officers stand for unjust authority, and the Articles of War symbolize those laws and rules which create artificial barriers – sailor and officer, king and serf – between men, and which are largely responsible for much of the brutality and tyranny in our world.

Only when it has been clearly established that *White Jacket* deals with considerably more than merely naval abuses, can we then proceed in evaluating the philosophy of pacifism which the book espouses. The most important aspect of this philosophy is that it is based on both religious *and* democratic values, on both the Bible *and* the Declaration of Independence. In the narrator's citation of Blackstone, which we have previously quoted, it is argued that no earthly law should violate the law of nature, which is "dictated by God Himself". This natural law, dictated by God, champions democracy; hence Melville argues, democracy is one of God's laws for man. Both democracy and Christianity have the same source, and both proclaim certain inalienable rights for man. To have Christianity without democracy, therefore, is impossible.

This democratic and Christian philosophy of pacifism contains three distinct and clear attitudes towards war and violence. First, war is "foolish, unchristian, barbarous, brutal", and savours of "cannibalism, saltpetre, and the devil", and standing armies and navies "keep alive the spirit of war even in the meek heart of peace". Second, *any sort* of killing or physical violence is wrong. Flogging sears the soul as well as the bodies of man, and the huge Indian who proudly exhibits his blanket on which the red hands

[31] *Ibid.*, p. 374.

are painted, has only succeeded in killing "a six foot perpendicular of immortal manhood". Finally, and most important of all, violence should be returned with kindness, good with evil. White Jacket refers us to Christ, who "has enjoined us to turn the left cheek if the right be smitten". Moreover, Christ's appeal "embodies the soul and substance of the Christian faith; without it, Christianity were like any other faith".

This philosophy based on Christianity and democracy is a tool of strength. As I have previously stated, *White Jacket* is the most powerful and effective work of social protest ever penned by Melville. Here is pacifism at its most effective – a philosophy based on love and tolerance, but a philosophy which declares war on every form of injustice.

It is interesting to compare the outlook of *White-Jacket* with Gandhi's concept of "Satyagraha". In his autobiography, *The Story of My Experiments with Truth,* Gandhi writes about the birth of Satyagraha.

> The principle called Satyagraha came into being before that name was invented. Indeed, when it was born, I myself could not say what it was. In Gujarati also we used the English phrase "passive resistance" to describe it. When in a meeting of Europeans I found that the term "passive resistance" was too narrowly construed, that it was supposed to be a weapon of the weak, that it could be characterized by hatred, and that it could finally manifest itself as violence, I had to demur to all these statements and explain the real nature of the Indian movement. It was clear that a new word must be coined by the Indians to designate their struggle.
>
> But I could not for the life of me find out a new name, and therefore offered a nominal prize through *Indian Opinion* to the reader who made the best suggestion on the subject. As a result Maganlal Gandhi coined the word "Sadagraha" (Sat – truth, Agraha – firmness) and won the prize. But in order to make it clearer I changed the word to "Satyagraha" which has since become current in Gujarati as a designation for the struggle.[32]

White Jacket represents the high-water mark of this philosophy of pacifism or "Christian Satyagraha" in Melville's writings. In a universe of which God is the Great Commodore, this vigorous type

---

[32] Translated by Mahadev Desai (Boston, 1957), pp. 318-9.

of pacifism is the most ethical and forceful approach to evil and injustice.

But Melville's ultimate philosophy in *White-Jacket* is possible only because he seems to have shifted radically from his intellectual position as seen in *Mardi* and *Redburn*. These two novels, particularly the former, had shown an increasing skepticism and a growing concern with the problem of evil. But *White Jacket* is probably the most orthodoxly Christian book that Melville ever wrote. It portrays a well-ordered universe, governed by an all-good God. The work is filled with appeals to Christ, natural law, and the Sermon on the Mount, and moreover, as William Braswell points out, Melville uses a great deal of New Testament phraseology in *White Jacket*.[33] The question of metaphysical evil is scarcely raised. True, there are a few pages on Bland, who is at best a watered-down Jackson, but his existence presents no real challenge to the traditional Christian viewpoint. But whether the Christian pacifism of *White Jacket* still is valid in a universe in which huge and malevolent white leviathans roam the seas is a question with which the rest of this study will concern itself.

[33] *Melville's Religious Thought* (Durham, 1943).

CHAPTER V

MOBY-DICK

> "I see a Whale in the South-sea drinking my soul away."
> William Blake, *America*

Introduction

Now that the fight for critical recognition has been won, it is no longer heresy to write that Moby-Dick is one of the great works of literature ever produced, that it is both an astute philosophical probing of the position of man in the universe and an organically whole, brilliantly conceived work of art. Melville's greatest novel is so vast and complex – a complexity, which unlike that of *Mardi*, is the conscious creation of a great artist fully in control of his genius – that it almost seems to defy analysis. Perhaps the best summary of the difficulties in coming to grips with *Moby-Dick* is to be found in Jean-Jacques Mayoux's study, *Melville*.

Melville's mixed and conflicting intensions are not easy to unravel: for example, the epic tone (a universally accepted convention) of the temptation to parody (a more dubious convention) and of the idea of the real greatness of modern man (proposition of a new truth). Affirmation of human valiance, a lament for nature, despoiled and destroyed by man? Or challenge flung at God and his nature by conquered and indomitable man, Promethean and Satanic? In some places the book is Homeric and traditional, in others Blakean and Miltonic, Christian and anti-Christian. Elsewhere it is modern in its very refusal of human enterprise, modern like Faulkner's *The Bear*: and its subject seems to be the mysterious opposition of man and a world of which he is never master.[1]

[1] New York, 1960, translated by John Ashbery, p. 81.

Even if one is intellectually successful in explicating some aspects of *Moby-Dick,* there is the overwhelming problem of how to organize this material on paper. Critics who try to deal with the whole book end up writing superficially about many things and profoundly about none, as is the case with M. O. Percival's *A Reading of Moby-Dick.*[2] On the other hand, a scholar who wishes to comment solely upon some particular facet of Ahab's nature, let us say, finds that in order to do so coherently he must also write about the White Whale, Starbuck, the symbolism of the ocean, etc.[3] All this is a prelude, obviously not to any sort of statement that I have resolved this dilemma, but rather it is an attempt to justify the rather odd structural organization of this chapter, which seems to me to be the best – though far from satisfactory – way possible to develop the material I wish to present.

In the introductory section, I will briefly discuss those aspects of *Moby-Dick* which seem most relevant to an exploration of pacifism and rebellion, and try to indicate those struggles and tensions in the novel with which this chapter will be concerned. This section will be followed by four longer sections: (1)"Loomings", which deals with Father Mapple's Sermon and with the character of Bulkington as foreshadowings of the main themes of the book; (2) "The Elemental Background", which concerns itself with the importance of land and sea, fire and sun, and the color white in the novel; (3) "Enter the Gladiators", an analysis of the characters of Ahab, Starbuck, and the White Whale himself, (4) and finally, "The Struggles", which attempts to evaluate the inter-relationship between the above-named gladiators.

Even on the simplest level of interpretation, *Moby-Dick* is concerned with three major struggles: the struggle between Ahab and Moby-Dick, the struggle between Ahab and Starbuck, and the struggle of Ishmael for survival and self-realization. The major emphasis in this chapter will be upon the first two of these strug-

[2] Chicago, 1950.
[3] It is probably because of the difficulty of successfully organizing material on *Moby-Dick* that such "poetic" readings as those of D. H. Lawrence and Charles Olson are far superior to most of the more conventional criticism.

gles. It should here be stressed that Ahab's conflict with Starbuck is at least as philosophically significant as is the old man's pursuit of the Whale who maimed him, and, of course, these two issues are hopelessly intertwined. Ishmael's struggle, for the most part, lies beyond the scope of this study, but one major point should be made. For the greater part of the *Pequod's* voyage, Ishmael is an oarsman in Starbuck's whaling boat. But the fact that Ishmael alone survives to tell the tale is largely a result of his replacing Fedallah in *Ahab's* boat on the last day of the chase. Moreover, Ishmael is slowly revolved "like another Ixion"[4] towards Queequeq's coffin, which serves as a life-raft, and eventually carries the narrator to safety. Ixion, it may be remembered, defied Zeus and was tortured by being chained to a wheel of fire in Hades. The fact that Ahab is a character clearly resembling Ixion, and that Ishmael is thrown free from Ahab's boat, at least suggests the possibility that Ishmael's survival is not based on a total rejection of Ahab and his philosophy.

Obviously, to all but the most naive critic,[5] the pursuit of Moby-Dick and the arguments between Starbuck and his captain have an importance far beyond the mere narrative level. Symbolically they represent the conflict between faith and atheism, between man and the elements, etc. In *White Jacket,* we have seen how Melville developed a philosophy of pacifism based on Christianity, opposition to physical force, democracy, and faith in nature law. This philosophy is carried over into *Moby-Dick* and is embodied in the character of Starbuck. Starbuck's position is challenged by Ahab, who, after he has been maimed by Moby-Dick, develops a philosophy of rebellion. The crux of the disagreement between the two men is initially seen in their differing attitudes and evaluations of the White Whale. This battle becomes more complicated, for various factions are lined up behind either the captain or his mate. On the side of Ahab, we find the members of the darker or primitive races, such as the harpooners Queequeq, Daggoo, and Tashtego,

---

[4] *Moby-Dick* (New York, 1930), p. 825.
[5] There are some critics like Montgomery Belgion, however, who insist that there is no symbolism in *Moby-Dick*. See his article, "Heterodoxy on *Moby-Dick*", *SR,* LV (January-March, 1947), 108-25.

the sinister Fedallah, and the supposedly mad Negro boy, Pip. Starbuck is backed by Stubb and Flask, the other two mates, and the people back home – the owners, wives, and children. In addition, the nine ships encountered by the *Pequod* espouse the "sane" voice-of-reason viewpoint as does Starbuck, though they are not consciously supporters of the Quaker mate. Therefore, some aspects of the struggle between Ahab and Starbuck become a conflict between primitivism and civilization, paganism and Christianity.

Now, in most cases in our culture, any time there is a choice between Christianity and paganism or civilization and primitivism, this choice is considered to be clear-cut. But this is certainly not true in Melville's writings, particularly *Moby-Dick*. Indeed, one of the great artistic and thematic complexities of the novel is, what for the lack of a better term, might be called the transvaluation of values. For example, we usually tend to associate whiteness with purity and innocence. But in *Moby-Dick,* whiteness is associated with terror and death. It should be pointed out, however, that Melville is far too subtle a thinker to deal with issues in absolute terms: hence, black does not come to symbolize absolute good nor white absolute evil. Yet Melville successfully breaks down our traditional associations with these colors. Instances such as this permeate the novel. The fact that Ahab is insane is stressed again and again, and he is also sometimes described in terms of the devil. But the critic who merely says that Ahab is obviously being condemned by Melville because he is pictured as being crazy and Satanic has really said nothing. For in *Moby-Dick,* Melville writes "So man's insanity is heaven's sense; and wandering from all mortal reason, man comes at last to that celestial thought, which, to reason, is absurd and frantic".[6] Also, Melville had underlined with double markings that section of Shelley's essay on *Paradise Lost* which suggests that Satan is morally superior to God.[7] This inversion of values helps to stress the differences between appearance and reality, which is another of the major themes of the novel. The state-

[6] *Moby-Dick*, p. 599.
[7] Cited by William Braswell, *Melville's Religious Thought* (Durham, 1945), p. 69.

ment most directly bearing upon this issue is made by Ishmael at the close of the chapter called "The Chapel".

Methinks we have hugely mistaken this matter of Life and Death. Methinks what they call my shadow here on earth is my true substance. Methinks that in looking at things spiritual, we are too much like oysters observing the sun through water, and thinking that thick water the thinnest of air. Methinks my body is but the lees of my better being.[8]

Loomings

Bulkington

Though Bulkington appears only briefly, Melville scholars feel that he is one of the most significant figures in the novel. Ishmael first spies him early in the book when a group of sailors, just returned from a three-year sea voyage, enter the Spouter Inn to drink up their savings. One of the crew, however, stands somewhat aloof from the others. This man is Bulkington, who "stood full six feet in height, with noble shoulders and a chest like a coffer-dam", though "in the deep shadows of his eyes floated some reminiscences that did not seem to give him much joy".[9] At the peak of the merriment, Bulkington slips away unnoticed, but his absence is discovered a few minutes afterwards, and his shipmates run out after him, calling his name.

Bulkington reappears twenty chapters later, and is the subject of a short but crucial section entitled "The Lee Shore". When the *Pequod* sets out to sea on Christmas Day, Ishmael is stunned to see that Bulkington is one of his fellow sailors. That a man could return from a long sea voyage, and then, several short days later, board another vessel which would be on the ocean for three years puzzles the narrator.

The land seemed scorching to his feet... The port would fain give succor; the port is pitiful; in the port is safety, comfort, hearthstone, supper, warm blankets, friends, all that's kind of our mortalities. But in that gale, the port, the land, is that ship's direst jeopardy; she must fly all hospitality; one touch of land, though it but graze the keel, would make her shudder through and through...

[8] *Moby-Dick*, p. 53.
[9] *Ibid.*, pp. 21-2.

Know ye, now, Bulkington? Glimpses do ye seem to see of that mortally intolerable truth; that all deep, earnest thinking is but the intrepid effort of the soul to keep the open independence of her sea; while the wildest winds of heaven and earth conspire to cast her on the treacherous, slavish shore?

But as in landlessness alone resides the highest truth, shoreless, indefinite as God – so, better is it to perish in that howling infinite, than be ingloriously dashed upon the lee, even if that were safety! ... Take heart, take heart, O Bulkington! Bear thee grimly, demigod! Up from the spray of thy ocean-perishing – straight up, leaps thy apotheosis![10]

The character of Bulkington is important for several reasons. In his attitude we find the first intense analysis of the difference between land and sea, a difference which provides perhaps the most dominant imagery of the novel. The shore offers comfort, a sort of static and fixed security, in one sense, a false but happy Absolute. The sea, on the other hand, represents hardship, isolation, and for Bulkington, who is destroyed while sailing on the ocean, death. Yet it is only at sea that we can find a sort of momentary truth, which is the only truth graspable by man, a truth which "is forced to fly like a scared white doe in the woodlands; and only by cunning glimpses will she reveal herself".[11] The shore may represent the world of happiness, but the ocean is the realm of actuality.

Bulkington's chief importance, however, is that he is at once a contrast, a foreshadowing, and a justification of Captain Ahab. There are numerous differences between the two men. Ahab is an old man, Bulkington, though his age is never divulged, gives the impression of youth. Bulkington's powerful and unmarked physique is in sharp contrast to the maimed and scarred body of the old captain. Ahab is often pictured in derogatory terms, but Bulkington is referred to as a "demigod". The moral aspect of Bulkington's pursuit is never questioned, which is far from the case with Ahab's. Perhaps most important, Bulkington is a common sailor and Ahab is captain of the *Pequod,* a man almost God-

---

[10] *Ibid.,* pp. 152-3.
[11] Herman Melville, "Hawthorne and His Mosses", in Jay Leyda, ed., *The Viking Portable Melville* (New York, 1952). p. 408.

like in his authority while at sea. Nevertheless, the actual quest of the two men is similar. Both men shun the lee shore, scorning the safety and comfort of land in order to go down to the sea in ships and come to grips with the basic elements of existence on the bare ocean. Part of the motivation for the search of both of these men lies in their tragic and unexplained pasts. Bulkington's "reminiscenses that did not give him much joy" can be roughly equated with many of the hidden mysteries of Ahab's former experiences that are hinted at by the crazy prophet Elijah. ("'Nothing about that deadly scrimmage with the Spaniard afore the altar in Santa? – heard nothing about that, eh? Nothing about the silver calabash he spat into?'")[12] Finally, it does not seem too extreme to suggest that, just as Fedallah symbolizes either Ahab's bad angel or all that is wrong with the old man, Bulkington represents the pure spirit of Ahab's search without any of its damning implications. For there is nothing wrong or demoniac about Ahab's pursuit of the While Whale *per se*. Ahab's sin is that he makes his will and his quest prevail upon his crew, and in so doing, leads them to destruction. Because Ahab is captain of the *Pequod* – not an ordinary sailor – and because he forces his own philosophy upon a for-the-most-part uninvolved crew, he becomes, in one sense, a ruthless dictator. But the fact that Ahab turns his back on the land in order to search out the true meaning of life at sea is a noble action, and his death in pursuit of Moby-Dick is a form of salvation, just as is Bulkington's death at sea. "Up from the spray of thy ocean-perishing – straight up, leaps thy apotheosis". If Bulkington, and not Ahab, had been the hero of *Moby-Dick,* we would have had a much less ambiguous novel, and a much less great one.

Father Mapple's Sermon

While in New Bedford shortly before the *Pequod* goes to sea, Ishmael visits the Whaleman's Chapel to hear the famous Father Mapple, who had himself been a harpooner in his youth. Father Mapple mounts the pulpit by means of a nautical perpendicular

---

[12] *Moby-Dick,* p. 134.

side ladder, and proceeds to deliver a sermon on Jonah and the Whale.

As with all sinners among men, the sin of this son of Amittai was in his wilful disobedience of the command of God — never mind now what that command was, or how conveyed — which he found a hard command. But all the things that God would have us do are hard for us to do — remember that — and hence, he oftener commands us than endeavors to persuade. *And if we obey God, we must disobey ourselves; and it is in this disobeying ourselves, wherein the hardness of obeying God consists.*[13] [Italics my own.]

Father Mapple then tells the story of how Jonah tried to flee from God by seeking passage on a ship bound for Tarshish. When the ship reaches the open sea, however, a dreadful storm arises, and the crew, in order to save the ship, casts the self-confessedly guilty Jonah overboard. He is swallowed by a waiting whale, and imprisoned in the leviathan's belly. Johan, realizing his crime, prays to the Lord repenting his sins but acknowledging the justice of God's punishment. God hears Jonah's prayers and speaks to the fish, "and from the shuddering cold and blackness of the sea, the whale came breaching up towards the warm and pleasant sun, and all the delights of air and earth; and 'vomited out Jonah upon dry land'."[14]

Moby-Dick most emphatically is not an allegory based on Jonah and the Whale. Nevertheless, Father Mapple's Sermon based on this text not only foreshadows the fate of the *Pequod*, but is applicable to three of the major characters in the novel — Ishmael, Starbuck, and Ahab. Ishmael, like Jonah, is emperiled by a whale, yet is almost miraculously cast out to safety. Starbuck is the only person aboard the *Pequod* who tries to introduce the word of God into an environment which is hostile to this word, paralleling the case of Jonah after he has been rescued from the whale. The character for whom Father Mapple's Sermon has most relevance, though, is Captain Ahab. Ahab's philosophical position is close to that of an unrepentant Jonah. The similarity between the two men is also brought out in the imagery. When the storm strikes the

[13] *Ibid.*, p. 60.
[14] *Ibid.*, p. 68.

ship aboard which Jonah is fleeing, he stumbles to the deck and "grasps a shroud, to look out upon the sea".[15] When Ishmael first views his captain, the latter is steadying his ivory leg in an auger hole, "one arm elevated, and holding a shroud; Captain Ahab stood erect, looking straight out beyond the ship's ever-pitching prow".[16] A great deal of attention is devoted to the lamp in Jonah's cabin.

Screwed at its axis against the side, a swinging lamp slightly oscillates in Jonah's room; and the ship, heeling over towards the wharf with the weight of the last bales received, the lamp, flame and all, though in slight motion, still maintains a permanent obliquity with reference to the room; though, in truth, infallibly straight itself, it but made obvious the false, lying levels among which it hung. The lamp alarms and frightens Jonah; as lying in his berth his tormented eyes roll round the place, and this thus far successful fugitive finds no refuge for his restless glance. But that contradiction in the lamp more and more appals him. The floor, the ceiling, and the side, are all awry. "Oh! so my conscience hangs in me!" he groans, "straight upward, so it burns; but the chambers of my soul are all in crookedness!"[17]

Very little of the novel's action takes place in Ahab's cabin, but there are three significant descriptions of the cabin's lamp or lanterns in the cabin. Late in the evening, Ahab is examining some yellowish sea charts, hoping to trace Moby-Dick's exact whereabouts.

While thus employed, the heavy pewter lamp suspended in chains over his head, continually rocked with the motion of the ship, and for ever threw shifting gleams and shadows of lines upon his wrinkled brow, till it almost seemed that while he himself was marking out lines and courses on the wrinkled charts, some invisible pencil was also tracing lines and courses upon the deeply marked chart of his forehead.[18]

Starbuck goes down to Ahab's cabin one night.

Never could Starbuck forget the old man's aspect, when one night going down into the cabin to mark how the barometer stood, he saw

[15] *Ibid.*, p. 65.
[16] *Ibid.*, p. 178.
[17] *Ibid.*, pp. 63-4.
[18] *Ibid.*, p. 286.

him with closed eyes sitting straight in his floor-screwed chair; the rain and half-melted sleet of the storm from which he had some time before emerged, still slowly dripping from the unremoved hat and coat. On the table beside him lay unrolled one of those charts of tides and currents which have been previously spoken of. His lantern swung from his tightly clenched hand. Though the body was erect, the head was thrown back so that the closed eyes were pointed towards the needle of the tell-tale that swung from a beam in the ceiling.[19]

Towards the end of the *Pequod's* voyage, on the night that Starbuck meditates killing the old man, the first mate again descends to the captain's cabin.

Ere knocking at his state-room, he involuntarily paused before it a moment. The cabin-lamp – taking long swings this way and that – was burning fitfully, and casting fitful shadows upon the old man's bolted door, – a thin one, with fixed blinds inserted, in place of upper panels. The isolated subterraneousness of the cabin made a certain humming silence to reign there, though it was hooped round by all the roar of the elements.[20]

These four descriptions are similar in major respects, suggesting the likeness of Ahab and Jonah. Each of these passages stresses the isolation of the protagonist. In each case, the swinging lamps are contrasted to the stillness of the human being in the cabin. But there are some differences. Whereas the lamp or lantern is in motion in each of these four scenes, it is pointed out that the light in Jonah's cabin, though moving, is really on an even keel, and that it is the ship which is aslant. Moreover, the light from the lantern disturbs Jonah, and is clearly the symbol of his guilty conscience. Ahab, on the other hand, makes use of the light or sleeps, ignoring it completely. And, in these three descriptions of Ahab's cabin, it is Ahab who seems to be fixed, and the lamp which is awry. The light for Jonah represents the light of God. Though he has rebelled against this light, Jonah still fears it, and acknowledges its moral superiority. Though it is difficult to determine Ahab's exact attitude towards the lamp in these short passages, it does seem clear that he neither worship nor fears

[19] *Ibid.*, pp. 341-2.
[20] *Ibid.*, p. 736.

the light; i.e. he does not admit his ethical inferiority to God.

If there are hints of both Starbuck and Ahab – two antithetical characters – in Father Mapple's rendition of the story of Jonah, his sermon most obviously contains some contradictions. These become apparent in the preacher's last comments.

Woe to him whom this world charms from Gospel duty! Woe to him who seeks to pour oil upon the waters when God has brewed them into a gale! Woe to him whose good name is more to him than goodness! Woe to him who, in this world, courts not dishonor! Woe to him who would not be true, even though to be false were salvation! ... But oh! shipmates! on the starboard hand of every woe, there is a sure delight; and higher the top of that delight, than the bottom of the woe is deep. ... Delight is to him – a far, far upward and inward delight – who against the proud gods and commodores of this earth, ever stands forth his own inexorable self. Delight is to him whose strong arms yet support him, when the ship of this base treacherous world has gone down beneath him. Delight is to him, who gives no quarter in the truth, and kills, burns, and destroys all sin though he pluck it out from under the robes of Senators and Judges. Delight, – top-gallant delight is to him, who acknowledges no law or lord, but the Lord his God, and is only a patriot to heaven.[21]

The two sentences stating that delight belongs to him who "ever stands forth his own inexorable self", who fights against "the proud gods and commodores of this earth", and who, in pursuit of truth, "kills, burns, and destroys", certainly suggest the rebellion of Captain Ahab. But the sentence following, which says that delight belongs to him "who acknowledges no law or lord, but the Lord his God, and is only a patriot to heaven", seems to refute the philosophy of Ahab, and point to the devout Starbuck. It could be argued that, as a result of Melville's clever manipulation of capitalization – "lord" and "gods" as contrasted to "Lord" and "Gods" – these sentences are not really in contradiction. But it will be recalled that early in his sermon, Father Mapple says "If we obey God, we must disobey ourselves". The man who is "his own inexorable self" obviously does not disobey himself. Ahab, in his "fatal pride"[22] acknowledges no master, and would never disobey himself. Starbuck, a man of humility, looks to God for guidance.

[21] *Ibid.*, pp. 68-9.
[22] *Ibid.*, p. 743.

A further complication in interpreting Father Mapple's closing comments is his frequent repetition of the word "delight". The last ship encountered by the *Pequod* is called the *Delight,* and it seems to me that this must bear some relationship to Father Mapple's Sermon. The *Delight* is indeed ill-named. It has engaged Moby-Dick and lost five of its men. The *Delight* reveals "shattered, white ribs, and some few splintered planks, of what had once been a whale-boat; but you now saw through this wreck, as plainly as you see through the peeled half-unhinged, and bleaching skeleton of a horse".[23] The type of delight mentioned by Father Mapple is a delusion and a mockery, for it is unattainable by man.

In this analysis of Father Mapple's Sermon, I have tried to show that though the story of Jonah and the Whale does not bear a fixed allegorical relationship to *Moby-Dick,* it foreshadows much of the action of the novel, and in Father Mapple's final words, he introduces, in a slightly variant form, the two major conflicting philosophies of the book, philosophies which are respectively represented by Starbuck and Ahab.

The Elemental Background

Land and Sea

In the chapter on Bulkington entitled "The Lee Shore", as we have seen, some of the differences between the land and the sea are brought out. But the tension between these two symbols is introduced in the first chapter of the novel. Ishmael writes "Whenever it is a damp, drizzly November in my soul; whenever I find myself involuntarily pausing before coffin warehouses, and bringing up the rear of every funeral I meet . . . then, I account it high time to get to sea as soon as I can".[24] The narrator ponders the enigma of why landsmen are continually drawn to the sea, even finding magic in the pool of a small brook. The sea has a magnetic power and inevitably leads men to reflection, for "meditation and water are wedded for ever".[25] Ishmael arrives at a conclusion which is both question and answer.

[23] *Ibid.*, p. 772.
[24] *Ibid.*, p. 1.
[25] *Ibid.*, p. 3.

> Why did the old Persians hold the sea holy? Why did the Greeks give it a separate deity, and own brother of Jove? Surely all this is not without meaning. And still deeper the meaning of that story of Narcissus, who because he could not grasp the tormenting, mild image he saw in the fountain, plunged into it and was drowned. But that same image, we ourselves see in all rivers and oceans. It is the image of the ungraspable phantom of life; and this is the key to all.[26]

This passage once again brings to mind the character of Ahab, whose "fatal pride" is a form of narcissism. Towards the close of the novel, Ahab too peers at his own image reflected in the water. "Slowly crossing the deck from the scuttle, Ahab leaned over the side, and watched how his shadow in the water sank and sank to his gaze, the more and the more that he strove to pierce the profundity".[27]

Not only does the land-sea antithesis recur throughout *Moby-Dick,* but two chapters – "Brit" and "The Gilder" – are entirely devoted to an analysis of this dichotomy. In an incisive article, J. A. Ward points out that the beginning of the chapter on brit, with its comparisons to meadows, etc., suggests the similarities between land and sea, but that the end of the chapter emphasizes the differences.[28] North-east of the Crozetts, the *Pequod* sights such "vast meadows of brit" that the ship seems to be sailing "through boundless fields of ripe and golden wheat". The Right Whales who feed upon the brit are described as "morning mowers who ... advance their scythes through the long wet grass of marshy meads".[29]

This charming and pastoral picture of the sea is quickly undercut.

> however baby man may brag of his science and skill, and however much, in a flattering future, that science and skill may augment; yet for ever and for ever, to the crack of doom, the sea will insult and murder him, and pulverize the stateliest, stiffest frigate he can make...[30]

---

[26] *Ibid.,* p. 4.
[27] *Ibid.,* p. 775.
[28] "The Function of the Cetological Chapters in *Moby-Dick*", *AL*, XXVII (May, 1956), 164-83.
[29] All of the quotations in this paragraph are from *Moby-Dick*, p. 396.
[30] *Ibid.,* p. 398.

Nor is that all – "not only is the sea such a foe to man who is alien to it, but it is also a fiend to its own offspring; worse than the Persian host who murdered his own guests; sparing not the creatures which itself hath spawned".[31] Perhaps most terrifying of all is that there is no force that masters the sea. "No mercy, no power but its own controls it. Panting and snorting like a mad battle steed that has lost its rider, the masterless ocean overruns the globe'".[32]

Consider, once more, the universal cannibalism of the sea; all whose creatures prey upon each other, carrying on eternal war since the world began.

Consider all this; and then turn to this green, gentle, and most docile earth; consider them both, the sea and the land; and do you not find a strange analogy to something in yourself? For as this appalling ocean surrounds the verdant land, so in the soul of man there lies one insular Tahiti, full of peace and joy, but encompassed by all the horrors of the half known life. God keep thee! Push not off from that isle, thou canst never return![33]

The chapter "The Gilder" adds little to this, except to again warn that when one beholds "the tranquil beauty and brilliancy of the ocean's skin, one forgets the tiger heart that pants beneath it".[34]

In my analysis of "The Lee Shore", I suggested that the land represents the Absolute, and that the sea stands for the relative. The chapter "Brit" leads us to further speculation. Land is associated with faith and the sea with skepticism. In the "soul" of man, there is a dot of land "full of peace and joy", and we find a final appeal to "God" to keep the individual from quitting the shore. Finally, it should be noted that throughout *Moby-Dick,* Ahab is linked with the sea, and Starbuck, though he too is a sailor, is identified with the shore, for his thoughts are constantly on his home, his wife, and his young child, and he continually appeals to Ahab to abandon the *Pequod's* ocean voyage and to return to Nantucket.

On one level of interpretation, it might seem as if this land-sea

[31] *Ibid.,* p. 398.
[32] *Ibid.,* p. 398.
[33] *Ibid.,* p. 399.
[34] *Ibid.,* p. 703.

antithesis presents the reader with two equal but mutually exclusive philosophies: a philosophy based on faith and acceptance, stressing the goodness of God and the joy and brightness of life, the other arguing that man exists in a world of chaos, that human life is darkness and misery, and that any philosophical position other than skepticism is sheer mental dishonesty. Critics who interpret the novel in this fashion suggest that Melville is saying that the wise man is he who views both the dark and the light aspects of life, and considering each, bases his actions accordingly. Such a man, they argue, is Ishmael, who survives a horrible ordeal, and having committed himself neither to the side of Ahab nor of Starbuck, achieves a kind of salvation through wisdom. I object strongly to any such interpretation. It seems to me that Melville clearly feels that the darker world – the ocean – is the dominant reality. "The sun hides not the ocean, which is the dark side of this earth and which is two thirds of this earth. So, therefore, that mortal man who hath more of joy than sorrow in him, that man cannot be true – not true, or undeveloped".[35] In the chapter "The Monkey Rope", Ishmael describes how Queequeg, while dangling from the ship by a rope, cuts away at a dead whale, whose corpse is surrounded by voracious sharks. To protect Queequeg from the mouths of these sharks, Tashtego and Daggoo flail with a pair of keen whale spades, which peril Queequeg's legs as much as they do the hungry fish. Commenting on this, Ishmael writes of Queequeg:

Are you not the precious image of each and all of us men in this whaling world? That unsounded ocean you gasp in, is Life; those sharks, your foes; those spades, your friends; and what between sharks and spades you are in a sad pickle and peril, poor lad.[36]

The ocean is much more than the setting of the *Pequod's* chase of Moby-Dick. The sea, which emerges as a far more powerful and sinister force than the land, becomes an active participant in the novel. Not only is the ocean the logical artistic choice to best portray man's struggle against the elements, but in terms of *Moby-*

---

[35] *Ibid.*, p. 612.
[36] *Ibid.*, pp. 464-5.

Dick itself, any solution found to the human situation on dry land would be, *ipso facto,* false.

Whiteness

The most striking thing about Moby-Dick is not his vast size, his malevolent intelligence, or his mythical power, but his whiteness. And conversely, the most striking example of whiteness in the novel is to be found in the whiteness of the whale. Even if Moby-Dick were not of this particular hue, however, the color white would still appear throughout the novel much like a leitmotif, and with a fairly fixed set of associations. The inn at which Ishmael stays in New Bedford has a white painting in front of it carrying the words "The Spouter-Inn: – Peter *Coffin*".[37] The fated *Pequod* is heavily inlaid with polished white ivory. After a sudden squall prevents a fight between the black Daggoo and the white Spanish Sailor, the still sane Pip whimpers, " 'Jimmini, what a squall! But those chaps are worse yet – they are your white squalls, they. White squalls? white whale, shirr! shirr! ... Oh, thou big white God aloft there somewhere in your darkness, have mercy on this small black boy down here' ".[38] But Pip's "white God" pays no attention to him, and shortly thereafter, the youth becomes a castaway and loses his sanity. The great squid which is momentarily mistaken for Moby-Dick and which cause Starbuck to exclaim " 'Almost rather had I seen Moby-Dick and fought him, than to have seen thee, thou white ghost!' "[39] is a cream-colored mass, resembling a "snow-slide".[40] In addition, the innumerable descriptions of the shattered hulls of ships, the huge skeletons of whales, etc., emphasize the whiteness of these objects. From the above examples, it can be seen that the color white is clearly associated with death.

But this is only a beginning. The most important section dealing with the color white is "The Whiteness of the Whale", in which Ishmael analyzes his own attitude towards whiteness. He begins by stating that "It was the whiteness of the whale that above all

[37] *Ibid.,* p. 13.
[38] *Ibid.,* pp. 256-7.
[39] *Ibid.,* p. 402.
[40] *Ibid.,* p. 401.

things appalled me".[41] It is true, argues Ishmael, that we traditionally associate white with royalty, with joy, with innocence, and even with religion. Nevertheless, there "lurks an elusive something in the innermost idea of this hue, which strikes more of panic to the soul than that redness which affrights in blood".[42] No matter how initially terrifying anything is, this terror is heightened if the object is coupled with whiteness. The white polar bear, the white shark, and the white squall are more terrible than their other-hued counterparts. Few people confess that whiteness is "the prime agent in exaggerating the terror of objects otherwise terrible".[43] But it is mistaken to think otherwise, says Ishmael. Man's reaction to whiteness is similar to a young Vermont colt's response when a fresh buffalo hide is shaken behind him. Though the colt has had no previous knowledge of buffalo, he stamps the ground with his fright. "Here thou beholdest even in a dumb brute, the instinct of the knowledge of the demonism in the world".[44]

What is the nature of this demonism? First, the analogy of the horse's reaction to the buffalo hide causes Ishmael to observe that "Though in many of its aspects this visible world seems formed in love, the invisible spheres were formed in fright".[45] Next, and somewhat related to the first explanation, is that whiteness is a means of deceiving man. Here again we are faced with the difference between appearance and reality. Whiteness implies joy but produces terror. Whiteness is compared to "deified Nature", which

absolutely paints like the harlot, whose allurements cover nothing but the charnel-house within; and when we proceed further, and consider that the mystical cosmetic which produces every one of her hues, the great principle of light, for ever remains white or colorless in itself, and if operating without medium upon matter, would touch all objects, even tulips and roses, with its own blank tinge – pondering all this, the palsied universe lies before us a leper...[46]

But the chief reason for the demonism inherent in whiteness can

[41] *Ibid.*, p. 272.
[42] *Ibid.*, p. 274.
[43] *Ibid.*, p. 279.
[44] *Ibid.*, p. 281.
[45] *Ibid.*, p. 282.
[46] *Ibid.*, p. 283.

perhaps not be directly stated, so Ishmael poses a question.

Or is it, that as in essence whiteness is not so much a color as the visible absence of color, and at the same time the concrete of all colors; is it for these reasons that there is such a dumb blankness, full of meaning, in a wide landscape of snow – a colorless, all-color of atheism from which we shrink?[47]

An exploration of the meaning of whiteness leads directly into the major philosophical issues of the novel – the difference between the visible and the invisible worlds and the question of value in the universe, for the whiteness which suggests the "visible absence" of color, "dumb blankness", and "a colorless all-color of atheism" also suggests that the world in which man finds himself is devoid of any real value. It should also be obvious by now that any intense analysis of the major imagery of *Moby-Dick* eventually points straight to Ahab. This is clearly the case in our exploration of the chapter "The Whiteness of the Whale". Ahab is the man who is not content with the world of appearance but is interested in looking at the lower layer, at striking through the mask. The old captain has no use for whiteness in any form, whether it is his white ivory leg or the White Whale, whether it be "the big white God" to whom Pip unsuccessfully appeals or the white members (with the possible exception of Starbuck) of the *Pequod's* crew. Significantly, when Ahab berates himself, he expresses his own guilt in terms of whiteness. " 'I leave a white and turbid wake; pale waters, paler cheeks, where'er I sail' ".[48]

Finally, it should be observed that Melville often brilliantly fuses together two major symbols or images. Perhaps the best example of this is to be found in the joining together of whiteness – representing death, lack of color and of value, and terror – with the sea, constantly changing but nevertheless immortal, in the final sentence of *Moby-Dick*. "Now small fowls flew screaming over the yet yawning gulf; a sullen white surf beat against its steep sides; all collapsed, and the great shroud of the sea rolled on as it rolled five thousand years ago".[49]

[47] *Ibid.*, p. 282.
[48] *Ibid.*, p. 241.
[49] *Ibid.*, p. 824.

Fire and Sun

Fire and sun, which produce heat and light and which scorch as well as illuminate, are re-inforcing symbols in *Moby-Dick*. No major distinction is made between them in the novel. They form perhaps the most difficult symbol of the book, for not only are they mutually dependent and inseparable, but also, they have little existence of their own and rather are hopelessly intertwined with the character of Ahab. This fire-sun symbolism is introduced when Ahab makes his initial appearance.

He looked like a man cut away from the stake, when the fire has overrunningly wasted all the limbs without consuming them, or taking away one particle of their compacted aged robustness. ... Threading its way out from among his grey hairs, and continuing right down one side of his tawny scorched face and neck, till it disappeared in his clothing, you saw a slender rod-like mark, lividly whitish. It resembled that perpendicular seam sometimes made in the straight, lofty trunk of a great tree, when the upper lightning tearingly darts down it, and without wrenching a single twig, peels and grooves out the bark from top to bottom, ere running off into the soil, leaving the tree still greenly alive, but branded.[50]

A further complication in interpreting this symbol is that Ahab's attitude toward fire and sun is ambivalent. Ahab's chief helper and adviser is the Parsee, Fedallah, a being who at times seems almost to dominate the captain. In his article "Sun and Fire in Melville's *Moby-Dick*" Paul Miller notes that a Parsee is a follower of Zoroaster, and that sun-worship is an integral part of this religion.[51] More important, it is clearly established in the context of the novel that Fedallah is a sun-fire worshipper. He not only kneels before the corposants, but also before *the image* of the sun on Ahab's doubloon, causing Stubb to comment, " 'Ah, only makes a sign to the sign and bows himself; there is a sun on the coin – fire worshipper, depend upon it' ".[52] Not only is Ahab's chief lieutenant a sun worshipper, not only, as we shall soon see, has Ahab been a fire worshipper himself, but there are times

---

[50] *Ibid.*, p. 177.
[51] *NCF*, XIII (Sept., 1958), 139-44.
[52] *Moby-Dick*, p. 625.

during the *Pequod*'s voyage when Ahab still seems to reverence the sun. One day, four whales are slain by the *Pequod's* men. Ahab, who himself has killed one of these monsters, watches their death throes.

For that strange spectacle observable in all Sperm Whales dying – the turning sunwards of the head, and so expiring – that strange spectacle, beheld of such a placid evening, somehow to Ahab conveyed a wondrousness unknown before.
"He turns and turns him to it, – how slowly, but how steadfastly, his homage-rendering and invoking brow, with his last dying motion. He too worships fire; most faithful, broad, baronial vassal of the sun!" [53]

Since Ahab's speech is a soliloquy, and hence not directed to anyone else, his statement that the whale "too" worships fire can only mean that the dying leviathan is being compared to the old man himself, and that therefore the *Pequod*'s captain is a sun-worshipper also.

If this is true, we are presented with a contradiction which I cannot solve, and which other critics ignore entirely, for the greater part of the fire-sun imagery is used to show that Ahab, though he may have once worshipped fire and sun, now rebels against them. Dying Sperm Whales face the sun. Moby-Dick and the whale who swallowed Jonah breach toward the sun. Even Pip, when he is cast away at sea, "turned his crisp, curling black head to the sun".[54] This form of religious devotion is antithetical to Ahab, who not only says that he himself would strike the sun, but whose last action is one of hostility towards that heavenly body – " 'I turn my body from the sun' ".[55]

Ahab demonstrates the same attitude to fire. It is true that Ishmael likens his captain to Prometheus. " 'God help thee, old man, thy thoughts have created a creature in thee; and he whose intense thinking thus makes him a Prometheus; a vulture feeds upon that heart for ever' ".[56] But Ahab is an odd sort of Promethe-

---

[53] *Ibid.*, p. 711.
[54] *Ibid.*, p. 598.
[55] *Ibid.*, p. 820.
[56] *Ibid.*, p. 292.

an figure, for he does not try to bring fire to man, as did the mythic figure to whom he is compared, but rather attempts to fling flame back to the gods from whence it came. He sees fire not as something which comforts man, but as something that scorches. This is most apparent in the chapter called "The Candles". While sailing on the usually mild waters off the coast of Japan, the *Pequod* is struck by a tremendous gale which bombards lightning upon the ship. Starbuck orders the lightning rods to be thrown overboard in order to protect the ship, but Ahab countermands these orders.

"Avast!" cried Ahab; "let's have fair play here, though we be the weaker side. Yet I'll contribute to raise rods on the Himmalehs and Andes, that all the world may be secured; but out on privileges! Let them be, Sir."[57]

No sooner has the old man uttered these words than each of the masts is touched with a pallid fire, making them appear like "three gigantic wax tapers before an altar".[58] The crew feels that "God's burning finger has been laid on the ship", and Stubb screams " 'The corposants have mercy on us all!' "[59] But Ahab, instead of being frightened, seizes the main-mast links in his hand, matching his blood against the fire. This is an odd re-enactment of the Prometheus legend. Prometheus, it may be remembered, smuggled fire to man in a hollow reed. Ahab attempts to hurl fire back to its source by grasping the slender lightning rods, which here correspond to a hollow reed. Holding the flaming links, he stands erect before the "lofty tri-pointed trinity of flames",[60] and delivers his credo of rebellion.

"Oh! thou clear spirit of clear fire, whom on these seas I as a Persian did worship, till in the sacramental act so burned by thee, that to this hour I bear the scar; I now know thee, thou clear spirit, and I now know that thy right worship is defiance. To neither love nor reverence wilt thou be kind; and e'en for hate thou canst but kill; and all are killed. No fearless fool now fronts thee. I own thy speechless, place-

[57] *Ibid.*, p. 722.
[58] *Ibid.*, p. 722.
[59] *Ibid.*, p. 723.
[60] *Ibid.*, p. 724.

less power; but to the last gasp of my earthquake life will dispute its unconditional, unintegral mastery in me. In the midst of the personified impersonal, a personality stands here. . . . . Oh, thou clear spirit, of thy fire thou madest me, and like a true child of fire, I breathe it back to thee." (*Sudden, repeated flashes of lightning; the nine flames leap lengthwise to thrice their previous height; Ahab, with the rest, closes his eyes, his right hand pressed hard upon them.*)

"I own thy speechless, placeless power; said I not so? Nor was it wrung from me; nor do I now drop these lines. Thou canst blind; but I can then grope. Thou canst consume; but I can then be ashes. Take the homage of these poor eyes, and shutter-hands. I would not take it. The lightning flashes through my skull; mine eye-balls ache and ache; my whole beaten brain seems as beheaded, and rolling on some stunning ground. Oh, oh! Yet blindfold, yet will I talk to thee. Light though thou be, thou leapest out of darkness; but I am darkness leaping out of light, leaping out of thee!"[61]

The development of the fire-sun symbolism reaches its culmination in "The Candles". In this chapter, we find a modern presentation of the Prometheus myth. Prometheus was a man who, because of his attitude towards both fire and mankind, defied the gods. Throughout Western literature, consequently, Prometheus has been used as a symbol of rebellion against unjust authority. Ahab also is much concerned with fire, and he too rebels against unjust authority. The authority in this case, however, is not *the gods,* but *God*. This is made quite clear through Melville's careful control of religious imagery in this chapter. The corposants make the masts to appear "like three gigantic wax tapers before an altar", the crew feels that "God's burning finger has been laid upon the ship", and Ahab refuses to kneel, but rather "stands erect before the lofty tri-pointed *trinity* of the flames". Much of the remainder of this chapter will deal with a more complete analysis of the nature of Ahab's rebellion.

Enter the Gladiators

Starbuck

Ahab issues his credo of rebellion while the storm-tossed decks of the *Pequod* are being illuminated by the terrifying corposants.

[61] *Ibid.,* pp. 724-5.

Starbuck's credo is uttered while he gazes into the sea on a calm day of incredible beauty. "'Loveliness unfathomable, as ever lover saw in his young bride's eye! — Tell me not of thy teeth-tiered sharks, and thy kidnapping cannibal ways. Let faith oust fact; let fancy oust memory; I look deep down and do believe'".[62] As can be seen from this speech, Starbuck is a man of faith, a man who when exposed to the reality of evil, can still believe that good forms the underlying foundation of the universe. The *Pequod*'s first mate is a Quaker, a member of a religion traditionally associated with pacifism, and he is also the only man of true Christian faith in the novel. When Starbuck speaks, the voice of Christianity is heard. After Ahab has delivered his long speech defying fire, Starbuck grasps his captain by the arm and says, " 'God, God is against thee, old man; forbear! tis an ill voyage!' "[63] When Moby-Dick batters into the *Pequod,* the first mate's dying words are " 'My God, stand by me now!' "[64]

The first of the two chapters entitled "Knights and Squires" gives a detailed description of the Quaker mate. Starbuck is a matter-of-fact and rugged man, whose "interior vitality was warranted to do well in all climates," but who has "domestic memories of his young Cape wife and child" which "tend to bend him still more from the original ruggedness of his nature". Unlike Ahab, he is not a crusader after perils. " 'For', thought Starbuck, 'I am here in this critical ocean to kill whales for my living, and not to be killed by them for theirs' ". Though his father and brother have died at sea, Starbuck fears not the terrors of the ocean, but has trouble withstanding "those more terrific, because more spiritual terrors, which sometimes menace you from the concentrating brow of an enraged and mighty man".[65]

Nevertheless, Starbuck does try to withstand Ahab, and this is of major significance in the novel. The Quaker mate is the only man aboard the *Pequod* who attempts to reason or argue with Ahab, the only man who dares to question his captain's orders.

---

[62] *Ibid.*, p. 705.
[63] *Ibid.*, p. 726.
[64] *Ibid.*, p. 819.
[65] All quotations in this paragraph are from *Ibid.*, pp. 163-4.

Starbuck's philosophy of pacifism, based on faith in God, love of one's fellow man, and a commitment, as we shall soon see, to the practice of non-violence, is the only way of life suggested in *Moby-Dick* as an alternative to Ahab's philosophy of rebellion. Indeed *Moby-Dick* is perhaps more concerned with the personal and philosophical struggle between Ahab and Starbuck than it is with Ahab's struggle with the White Whale.

The Great White Leviathan Himself

Does Moby-Dick really exist? If you were reading the novel for the first time and had almost finished it, you might suspect that the White Whale was nothing more than a mental projection of the crazy captain of the *Pequod*, and that the work was primarily a study in psychological deception. After all, *Moby-Dick* is a book of one hundred and thirty-five chapters, and through the first one hundred and thirty-two of these chapters, the White Whale has not yet made his appearance. It is true that Ahab and the captains of the *Delight,* the *Rachel,* and the *Samuel Enderby* claim to have encountered Moby-Dick, but the captains of the *Rose-Bud* and the *Bachelor* are equally emphatic in their doubts about such a whale. Even Stubb expresses skepticism about this particular leviathan's existence. But shortly after daybreak one morning, Moby-Dick is sighted, and this sighting partially answers some of the questions about Ahab's sanity.

At first glimpse, Moby-Dick seems to be an object of beauty, perhaps even a creature deserving D. H. Lawrence's description of "lovable".[66]

A gentle joyousness – a mighty mildness of repose in swiftness, invested the gliding whale. Not the white bull Jupiter swimming away with ravished Europa clinging to his graceful horns; his lovely, leering eyes sideways intent upon the maid; with smooth bewitching fleetness, rippling straight for the nuptial bower in Crete; not Jove, not that great majesty Supreme! did surpass the glorified White Whale as he so divinely swam.

On each soft side – coincident with the parted swell, that but once leaving him, then flowed so wide away – on each bright side, the whale shed off enticings.[67]

[66] *Studies in Classic American Literature* (New York, 1955), p. 157.
[67] *Moby-Dick*, p. 783.

But once again, the tiger heart that pants beneath the skin of the ocean shouldn't be forgotten, for so long as Moby-Dick swims in this position, he is "still withholding from sight the full terrors of his submerged trunk, entirely hiding the wrenched hideousness of his jaw".[68]

There can no longer be any question about the White Whale's existence. But what does he represent? He means different things for different people. For Ishmael, who is drawn to the sea by "one grand hooded phantom, like a snow hill in the air",[69] Moby-Dick is the foremost reason for undertaking a whaling voyage. For the crazy prophet Gabriel, the White Whale is the Shaker God incarnate. For the captain of the *Samuel Enderby,* who like Ahab has lost a limb to this leviathan, Moby-Dick stands for an unpleasant experience to be joked about, but which at all costs must be avoided in the future. For Steelkilt, the hero of the Town-Ho's story, Moby-Dick, as W. H. Auden points out, "is the justice and mercy of God, saving him from becoming a murderer and slaying the unjust Radney".[70] For the men of the *Pequod,* Moby-Dick represents death. And for Ahab, Moby-Dick symbolizes injustice and unmitigated evil.

The most important section dealing with the White Whale is called "Moby-Dick". In this chapter, Ishmael records what is known of the history of the Whale. The first point that Ishmael makes is that much of what is said about Moby-Dick is true about Sperm Whales in general, creatures who are "so incredibly ferocious as continually to be athirst, for human blood".[71] Moby-Dick, much in the tradition of the American tall story, is the biggest, strongest, most intelligent and most malignant of Sperm Whales — in short, he is sort of the quintessence of the Sperm-Whaleness. Moby-Dick is said to be ubiquitous and immortal, but "even stripped of these supernatural surmisings, there was enough in the earthly make and incontestable character of the monster to strike the imagination with unwonted power".[72] More terrifying than his

---

[68] *Ibid.,* p. 784.
[69] *Ibid.,* p. 8.
[70] *The Enchaféd Flood,* New York, 1950, p. 76.
[71] *Moby-Dick,* p. 261.
[72] *Ibid.,* p. 264.

great strength and bulk is "that unexampled, intelligent malignity which, according to specific accounts, he had over and over again evinced in his assaults".[73] Moby-Dick had reaped the leg from one whaling captain who had dared to fight him. "No turbaned Turk, no hired Venetian or Malay, could have smote him with more seeming malice".[74] That captain was Ahab, who as a result of this experience, came to look upon the Whale as the cause not only of his physical woes, but his intellectual and spiritual torments as well.

That intangible malignity which has been from the beginning; to whose dominion even the modern Christians ascribe one-half of the worlds; which the ancient Ophites of the east reverenced in their statue devil; – Ahab did not fall down and worship it like them; but deliriously transferring its idea to the abhorred White Whale, he pitted himself, all mutilated, against it. All that most maddens and torments; all that stirs up the lees of things; all truth with malice in it; all that cracks the sinews and cakes the brain; all the subtle demonisms of life and thought; all evil, to crazy Ahab, were visibly personified, and made practically assailable in Moby-Dick. He piled upon the whale's white hump the sum of all the general rage and hate felt by his whole race from Adam down.[75]

The symbol of the White Whale, as is the case with all of the major symbols of the novel, cannot be pinned down to one fixed meaning. As we have seen, Moby-Dick symbolizes different things for different characters in the novel. Nevertheless, some evaluation of these various views can be made. No one has yet been able to solve the riddle of how to make human existence meaningful for all men. Yet it is certainly more worthwhile to listen to what Mahatma Gandhi has to say on this subject than Governor Wallace. Such also is the case with interpreting the symbol of the White Whale. Ahab has the most profound vision of life of any character in the novel, and his vision of the whale, while oversimplified, is the best single evaluation of Moby-Dick.

Finally, be the White Whale an agent of the great powers of the universe or that power itself, he has two of the attributes which we

[73] *Ibid.*, pp. 264-6.
[74] *Ibid.*, p. 266.
[75] *Ibid.*, p. 267.

normally associate with God – ubiquity and immortality. He is also an intelligent and thinking creature, capable of making decisions by himself. Despite this, on one level, Moby-Dick stands for fate or blind chance. There is no reason why Ahab, in the normal course of his whaling duties, should have his leg shorn off, and why the captain of the *Bachelor*, the most successful of whale ships, should, in the normal course of his whaling duties, not even have heard of the White Whale. On a cosmic level, this is the height of injustice. On a cosmic level, the White Whale not only is a concrete embodiment of evil, but also represents the chaos which pervades the universe.

Ahab

We have learned a great deal about Ahab already. We have seen how he is identified with Prometheus, how he too rebels against what he considers to be the unjust authority of the gods. We have seen also how Ahab has come to attribute all of his spiritual and intellectual woes to the White Whale that took off his leg. In Ahab, Melville has created one of the great figures of Western literature, a man who possesses the tragic vision of life, and a figure who completely dominates the novel. Virtually any passage of *Moby-Dick,* if fully explored, eventually leads to Ahab. As the Catskill eagle, which "even in his lowest swoop ... is still higher than other birds upon the plain, even though they soar",[76] so Ahab, despite the dark depths of his despair, towers intellectually and spiritually above the other characters in the novel. Yet there is no question that he is mad. In his monomaniacal obsession with the Whale, the old man loses his contact with everyday reality. Certainly he is mad, but his madness is the madness of Don Quixote and King Lear, men who because of their greater awareness, more fully realize the horror underlying all human life, and therefore are considered to be insane by their less sensitive brethren. As Ahab himself comments, "'Gifted with the high perception I lack the low, enjoying power; damned, most subtly and most malignantly damned in the midst of Paradise'".[77] But despite his

[76] *Ibid.*, p. 612.
[77] *Ibid.*, p. 242.

madness and his suffering and his obsession with the Whale, "stricken, blasted, if he be, Ahab has his humanities!" to borrow the words of Captain Peleg.[78] One of the purposes of this section will be to discuss the nature of these humanities.

Ahab's minor humanities can be almost negatively stated. There is no cruelty or brutality about the *Pequod*. At times, indeed, Ahab shows a consideration for others almost unbecoming a ship's captain. On warm summer nights, for instance, Ahab abstains from walking on the quarter-deck, for he does not wish to disturb the sailors sleeping there. On another occasion, Stubb pokes fun at a passing wreck. "'What soulless thing is this that laughs before a wreck? Man, man! did I not know thee brave as fearless fire (and as mechanical) I could swear thou wert a poltroon'."[79] The above examples are trivial when compared to Ahab's major humanities. These can best be seen, Gordon Mills suggests, in the captain's relationship with Pip and Starbuck.[80]

Shortly after Pip has been temporarily abandoned at sea, and as a result has lost his sanity, Ahab orders that the log be thrown overboard. Pip rushes up to see what is happening and is accosted by Ahab. "'And who art thou, boy? I see not my reflection in the vacant pupils of thy eyes. Oh God! that man should be a thing for immortal souls to sieve through! Who art thou, boy?'"[81] Pip responds with gibberish.

"Oh, ye frozen heavens! look down here. Ye did beget this luckless child, and have abandoned him, ye creative libertines. Here, boy; Ahab's cabin shall be Pip's home henceforth, while Ahab lives. Thou touchest my inmost centre, boy; thou art tied to me by cords woven of my heart-strings. Come, let's down."

"What's this? here's velvet shark-skin," intently gazing at Ahab's hand, and feeling it. "Ah, now, had poor Pip but felt so kind a thing as this, perhaps he had ne'er been lost! This seems to me, Sir, as a man-rope; something that weak souls may hold by. Oh, Sir, let old Perth now come and rivet these two hands together; the black one with the white, for I will not let this go."

[78] *Ibid.*, p. 116.
[79] *Ibid.*, p. 791.
[80] A fine article on Captain Ahab's humanities is Gordon E. Mills, "The Cast-away in *Moby-Dick*", UTSE, XXIX (1950), pp. 231-48.
[81] *Moby-Dick*, p. 747.

"Oh, boy, nor will I thee, unless I should thereby drag thee to worse horrors than are here. Come, then, to my cabin. Lo! ye believers in gods all goodness, and in man all ill, lo you! see the omniscient gods oblivious of suffering man; and man, though idiotic, and knowing not what he does, yet full of the sweet things of love and gratitude. Come! I feel prouder leading thee by thy black hand, than though I grasped an Emperor's!"[82]

The last section of this chapter will deal in detail with the relationship between Ahab and Starbuck. It will suffice for now to say that though the first mate is the only man to openly oppose the captain, Ahab places great trust in him. When the old man wishes to look for Moby-Dick himself, he has to be hauled up into the riggings in a basket. The handling of the rope by which Ahab is raised and lowered is a tricky business, for one false move and the old man would be pitched into the sea. Surprisingly, Ahab unhesitatingly hands the rope to Starbuck, thus "freely giving his whole life"[83] to the first mate. When Moby-Dick is first sighted, Ahab demonstrates his solicitude for Starbuck by ordering him to remain aboard the *Pequod,* presumably a far safer place than aboard one of the tiny whale boats pursuing the leviathan. On the final day of the chase, when Ahab is quitting the ship for the last time, he makes a point of shaking Starbuck's hand, an action which brings tears to the latter's eyes.

Ahab's humanities can be seen not only in his actions but also in the imagery. When Ahab first appears, "he looked like a man cut away from the stake".[84] He stood before the crew "with a crucifixion in his face".[85] There is something unquestionably Christ-like about old Ahab and his humanities.

But Ahab's humanities make up only part of his personality. It may be remembered that Ahab is divided in two by a lightning-like scar which runs from his crown to his sole. The ship's carpenter also remarks of Ahab, "'Seems to me some sort of Equator cuts yon old man, too, right in his middle'."[86] If Ahab's humanities rep-

[82] *Ibid.,* pp. 747-8.
[83] *Ibid.,* p. 770.
[84] *Ibid.,* p. 177.
[85] *Ibid.,* p. 178.
[86] *Ibid.,* p. 756.

resent one side of this Equator, his "fatal" pride, first suggested by the reference to the legend of Narcissus in the opening chapter, represents the other side, and these two halves are continually at war within him.

Ahab has lost his leg to Moby-Dick, but instead of accepting the inevitable, he is egotistical enough to think that he can destroy those immortal forces, symbolized by the Whale, which govern the universe.

"Aye! I lost this leg. I now prophesy that I will dismember my dismemberer. Now, then, be the prophet and the fulfiller one. That's more then ye, ye great gods, ever were. I laugh and hoot at ye, ye cricket-players, ye pugilists, ye deaf Burkes, and blinded Bendigoes! I will not say as schoolboys do to bullies, – Take some one of your own size; don't pommel *me*! No, ye've knocked me down, and I am up again; but *ye* have run and hidden. Come forth from behind your cotton bags! I have no long gun to reach ye. Come, Ahab's compliments to ye; come and see if ye can swerve me. Swerve me? ye cannot swerve me, else ye swerve yourselves! man has ye there. Swerve me? The path of my fixed purpose is laid with iron rails, whereon my soul is grooved to run. Over unsounded gorges, through the rifled hearts of mountains, under torrents' beds, unerringly I rush! Naught's an obstacle, naught's an angle to the iron way." [87]

Ahab's pride causes him to lose sight of everything except himself and his vengeful pursuit of the Whale. Looking at the doubloon, made in Ecuador and now nailed to the masthead, Ahab says,

"There's something ever egotistical in mountain-tops and towers, and all other grand and lofty things; look here, – three peaks as proud as Lucifer. The firm tower, that is Ahab; the volcano, that is Ahab; the courageous, the undaunted and victorious fowl, that, too, is Ahab: all are Ahab." [88]

While the Carpenter is making him a new leg, the old man exclaims, " 'Here I am, proud as a Greek god, and yet standing debtor to this blockhead for a bone to stand on! Cursed be that mortal inter-indebtedness which will not do away with ledgers' ". [89] Ahab

---

[87] *Ibid.*, pp. 242-3.
[88] *Ibid.*, p. 620.
[89] *Ibid.*, p. 678.

comes more and more to rely solely on his own judgment as the voyage progresses. First, he smashes the *Pequod*'s quadrant. After a severe storm has reversed the ship's compass, Ahab magnetizes the needle back to its proper position. "'Look ye, for yourselves, if Ahab be not lord of the level load-stone! The sun is East, and that compass swears it!' ... In his fiery eyes of scorn and triumph, you then saw Ahab in all his fatal pride".[90] When the log-line parts, Ahab's pride reaches its zenith. "'I crush the quadrant, the thunder turns the needles, and now the mad sea parts the log-line. But Ahab can mend all'".[91]

Ahab's pride and his humanities are incompatible and he himself realizes this, as is implied in his previously quoted speech about human inter-indebtedness. The more that Ahab becomes drawn into the world of human kindness, the more he is removed from the pursuit of Moby-Dick, and the more intensely that he pursues the Whale, the more he is removed from the world of human kindness. There are numerous examples of the conflict between Ahab's pride, identified with his desire for vengeance upon Moby-Dick, and his humanities, but two will suffice. Towards the close of the novel, the *Pequod* meets the *Rachel,* which has just encountered Moby-Dick, with the usual consequences: one of the ship's boats is missing. On board that boat is the youngest son of the *Rachel*'s captain. The father appeals to Ahab to join in the search for the missing boy, reminding Ahab that he too has a young son, and offering to hire the *Pequod* if necessary. Even the usually callous Stubb feels that his captain must agree to help look for the boy. But Ahab refuses, saying, "'May I forgive myself'", and rushes away with "averted face".[92] Discussing Ahab's refusal of the *Rachel*'s request, Merlin Bowen writes, "The ties that hold us to the breathing human beings whom we love are the same ties, the head realizes, that fetter us to the compromises and half-truths of our past; there can be no freeing ourselves of the one and clinging to the other".[93] Another example of this conflict centers upon

[90] *Ibid.*, p. 743.
[91] *Ibid.*, p. 746.
[92] *Ibid.*, p. 762.
[93] *The Long Encounter. Self and Experience in the Writings of Herman Melville* (Chicago, 1960), p. 26.

Pip. Shortly after Pip has been taken in by Ahab, the old man is about to leave his cabin and go out on deck.

"Lad, lad, I tell thee thou must not follow Ahab now. The hour is coming when Ahab would not scare thee from him, yet would not have thee by him. There is that in thee, poor lad, which I feel too curing to my malady."

. . . .

"They tell me, Sir, that Stubb did once desert poor little Pip, whose drowned bones now show white, for all the blackness of his living skin. But I will never desert ye, Sir, as Stubb did him. Sir, I must go with ye."

"If thou speakest thus to me much more, Ahab's purpose keels up in him. I tell thee no; it cannot be."

"Oh good master, master, master!"

"Weep so, and I will murder thee! have a care, for Ahab too is mad." [94]

Ahab, because of his fatal pride, forces the *Pequod*'s crew to make his own personal chase *their* chase, his own personal vengeance *their* vengeance. What the White Whale is to Ahab, Ahab in one sense becomes to his crew. The old man, who hates injustice, leads his men to an unjust end, for the crew follow Ahab not because of any real conviction on their part, but because his will is stronger than theirs. As Starbuck remarks of Ahab, " 'Aye, he would be a democrat to all above; look, how he lords it over all below!' " [95]

The Struggles

Ahab Versus the Whale

Thus far, I have stressed only the negative aspects, the selfish aspects of Ahab's pride. But this fatal pride is the old man's triumph as well as tragedy. Ahab's pursuit of Moby-Dick is not only one isolated individual's attempt for personal revenge, but on the highest level, it is Everyman's effort to assert the dignity of mankind in the face of the hostile elements. As Charles Cook notes, Ahab "inflates his own private hurt into the hurt of all mankind,

[94] *Moby-Dick*, pp. 763-4.
[95] *Ibid.*, p. 244.

and allegorizes the infliction of this hurt into the dwelling place of all human evil".[96] Towards the end of the novel, Ahab makes a speech on the wind.

"And yet, 'tis a noble and heroic thing, the wind! who ever conquered it? In every fight it has the last and bitterest blow. Run tilting at it, and you but run through it. Ha! a coward wind that strikes stark naked men, but will not stand to receive a single blow. Even Ahab is a braver – a nobler thing than *that*. Would now the wind but had a body; but all the things that most outrage mortal man, all these things are bodiless, but only bodiless as objects, not as agents."[97]

For Ahab, Moby-Dick is the embodiment of "the things that most exasperate and outrage mortal man", and the *Pequod*'s captain thinks that if he can sink a harpoon into the White Whale, he will be able to liberate mankind from these exasperations. Since Ahab is identified not only with Prometheus, the traditional champion of mankind, but also, as we shall later see, with Adam, there can be no question as to the universality of his quest.

To sink a harpoon into the life spot of the White Whale and thus to free mankind from the forces which plague him – this is a noble thought, but it is impossible. Man can fight against the elements, but he can't destroy them. Lances may be plunged into Moby-Dick, but he is, nonetheless, immortal. Ahab does not realize this initially. When he first addresses his crew, Ahab cries, " 'And this is what ye have shipped for, men! to chase that white whale on both sides of land, and over all sides of earth, till he spouts black blood and rolls fin out'."[98] Even in his sleep he screams " 'Stern all! the White Whale spouts thick blood!' "[99]

To insure his being able to slay the Whale, Ahab has a special harpoon made, forged from the gathered nail-stubs of the shoes of race horses, the best and strongest steel in the world. Ahab scorns water to temper the newly forged harpoon, using instead the volunteered blood of his three heathen harpooners. " 'Ego non

---

[96] "Ahab's Intolerable Allegory", *BUSE*. I (Spring-Summer, 1955), p. 45.
[97] *Moby-Dick*, p. 807.
[98] *Ibid.*, p. 234.
[99] *Ibid.*, p. 693.

baptizo te in nomine patris, sed in nomine diaboli!' deliriously howled Ahab, as the malignant iron scorchingly devoured the baptismal blood".[100] This exclamation – "I baptize you not in the name of the Father, but in the name of the devil!" – reintroduces a clearly religious element into the novel. Ahab is similar to Milton's Satan or to an unrepentant Job, who instead of bowing before God, decides to fight Him. As W. H. Auden suggests in *The Enchafèd Flood,* Ahab's mental processes are as follows: Ahab "neither says 'I am justly punished' if he has been quilty, nor 'though He slay me yet will I trust in Him' but 'Thou art guilty and shall be punished'".[101] He baptizes the harpoon with which he hopes to slay the Whale in the name of the devil, and not the name of God, because Ahab sees Moby-Dick as either being God himself or His agent. In his fight against the White Whale, he employs the forces traditionally at war with God, the forces of darkness represented by the three dusky harpooners and by Fedallah, who in many ways is a reincarnation of the devil. With their help, and with his specially forged harpoon, Ahab believes that the death of Moby-Dick is inevitable. When the *Pequod* crosses the path of the battered *Delight,* recently staved by the White Whale, Ahab shouts to the latter ship's captain, asking him whether he has killed Moby-Dick.

"The harpoon is not yet forged that will ever do that," answered the other, sadly glancing upon a rounded hammock on the deck, whose gathered sides some noiseless sailors were busy in sewing together.

"Not forged!" and snatching Perth's levelled iron from the crotch, Ahab held it out, exclaiming – "Look ye, Nantucketer; here in this hand I hold his death! Tempered in blood, and tempered by lightning are these barbs; and I swear to temper them triply in that hot place behind the fin, where the White Whale most feels his accursed life!"[102]

If there is a major epiphany in the novel, it is at the very end of the book when Ahab at last realizes that Moby-Dick is immortal, that he will never be able to slay the White Whale. At the close of the second day of the chase of Moby-Dick, after the Parsee has been lost at sea, Starbuck once again warns the old man that his pursuit is hopeless and can only lead to destruction. Though Ahab

[100] *Ibid.,* p. 701.
[101] Auden, pp. 139-40.
[102] *Moby-Dick,* pp. 772-3.

answers that on the next day Moby-Dick will rise once more " 'but only to spout his last!' " he remarks to himself " 'Oh! how valiantly I seek to drive out of others' hearts what's so fast clinched in mine!' "[103] This hint of doubt in Ahab's mind becomes a certainty after Moby-Dick has smashed into the *Pequod*. Ahab now knows beyond question that the Whale cannot be destroyed. Ahab himself, however, can still escape, for the White Whale does not threaten his boat, but lies "quiescent"[104] a little way off. Knowing that the Whale cannot be destroyed, knowing that the Whale is not at the moment threatening him, knowing that any sort of attack on the leviathan will prove fatal, Ahab nevertheless darts his harpoon into the monster. His last words are:

"Towards thee I roll, thou all-destroying but unconquering whale; to the last I grapple with thee; from hell's heart I stab at thee; for hate's sake I spit my last breath at thee. Sink all coffins and all hearses to one common pool! and since neither can be mine, let me then tow to pieces, while still chasing thee, though tied to thee, thou damned whale! *Thus*, I give up the spear!"[105]

For Ahab, rebellion has become a philosophy. Man finds himself thrust into a world in which he is continually buffeted and battered by the elements. At times he seems to be the victim of blind chance, at times the victim of a ubiquitous malevolent intelligence. Thus, the world in which man finds himself is either chaotic or is governed, not by a good God, but by an evil God. Positive value as such does not exist in the universe. Man's life is necessarily unhappy – two thirds of this earth is water – but his pride, his desire to get back up after he has been knocked down, is a saving virtue. Ahab, by pursuing Moby-Dick, is also attempting to pursue positive value and truth. The essence of Ahab's philosophy is reached, however, when he realizes that the Whale can't be destroyed, that chaos and evil can never be eliminated. For despite this realization, Ahab continues his struggle. Value and truth cannot be achieved in any absolute sense, but in his pursuit of them, man finds salvation. Or so it seems to Ahab.

[103] *Ibid.*, pp. 804-5.
[104] *Ibid.*, p. 820.
[105] *Ibid.*, p. 820.

Ahab Versus Starbuck

Starbuck, however, is not concerned with rebelling against the gods. He sees human life as being made meaningful through faith, and for him, the comforts of home – both physical and spiritual – are reason enough to rejoice in living. "I look deep down and do believe". Needless to say, such a man as Starbuck would find Ahab's view of life antithetical to his own. Hence, every time Starbuck and Ahab clash, it is a battle not only between individuals, but between mutually exclusive philosophies. This section will attempt to analyze some of the encounters between these two men.

Ahab and Starbuck first come into conflict in the chapter entitled "The Quarter-Deck". The captain addresses his crew for the first time, and reveals that the true purpose of the *Pequod*'s voyage is to hunt for Moby-Dick. The men in the heat of emotion, passionately pledge to aid their captain in his pursuit, but Ahab notices that Starbuck has a long face, and asks his mate whether he is willing to chase the White Whale, whether he is game for Moby-Dick.

"I am game for his crooked jaw, and the jaws of Death too, Captain Ahab, if it fairly comes in the way of the business we follow; but I came here to hunt whales, not my commander's vengeance. How many barrels will thy vengeance yield thee even if thou gettest it, Captain Ahab? it will not fetch thee much in our Nantucket market."

"Nantucket market! Hoot! But come closer, Starbuck; thou requirest a little lower layer." . . .

"Vengeance on a dumb brute!" cried Starbuck, "that simply smote thee from blindest instinct! Madness! To be enraged with a dumb thing, Captain Ahab, seems blasphemous."

"Hark ye again, – the little lower layer. All visible objects, man, are but as pasteboard masks. But in each event – in the living act, the undoubted deed – there, some unknown but still reasoning thing puts forth the mouldings of its features from behind the unreasoning mask. If man will strike, strike through the mask! How can the prisoner reach outside except by thrusting through the wall? To me, the white whale is that wall, shoved near to me. Sometimes I think there's naught beyond. But 'tis enough. He tasks me; he heaps me, I see in him outrageous strength, with an inscrutable malice sinewing it. That inscrutable thing is chiefly what I hate; and be the white whale agent, or be the white whale principal, I will wreck that hate upon him. Talk not to me of blasphemy, man; I'd strike the sun if it insulted me." [106]

Several things are immediately apparent in this crucial passage. First, Ahab singles out Starbuck as the one man aboard the *Pequod* who needs a more profound reason than he has previously given for hunting Moby-Dick. Ahab can sway the crew by his control of their emotions, but Starbuck is a far more dangerous and complicated opponent, and consequently requires "the little lower layer". Secondly, we have in this passage the clash between the tragic vision of life and, what for a better term, might be called the commonplace view of reality. If a man bases his life on believing things are as they appear, and through this viewpoint finds meaning and happiness, he would naturally maintain that a flower is a flower, or that a whale is nothing but a dumb brute. This is Starbuck's position. But if a man has been deeply scarred physically, spiritually, and psychologically, as Ahab has been, he comes to reject the beliefs that he has previously held and begins to ask the fatal question "Why?" Perhaps a flower isn't a flower, perhaps a whale isn't merely a dumb brute. Let us say a man, while walking down a mountain path, has his leg crushed by a falling boulder. Is this merely an unexplainable accident? Perhaps. But perhaps also, the boulder is a physical manifestation of some higher reasoning force. Ahab comes to this latter conclusion – "All visible objects, man, are but as pasteboard masks". To come to grips with the real forces of the universe, to be free from the prison of concrete physical objects which surround one, man must strike through this mask.

In the first encounter between Ahab and Starbuck, the battle lines between the two men are drawn. Shortly after this scene, Starbuck, in a long soliloquy, vows that he will try to fight against Ahab.

"My soul is more than matched; she's overmanned; and by a madman! Insufferable sting, that sanity should ground arms on such a field! ... Oh, life! 'tis now that I do feel the latent horror in thee! but 'tis not

---

[106] *Ibid.*, pp. 235-6.

me! that horror's out of me! and with the soft feeling of the human in me, yet will I try to fight ye, ye grim, phantom futures! Stand by me, hold me, bind me, O ye blessed influences!" [107]

Ahab too is cognizant that he faces a never-ending struggle with Starbuck.

He knew, for example, that however magnetic his ascendency in some respects was over Starbuck, yet that ascendency did not cover the complete spiritual man any more than mere corporeal superiority involves intellectual mastership; for to the purely spiritual, the intellectual but stand in a sort of corporeal relation. Starbuck's body and Starbuck's coerced will were Ahab's, so long as Ahab kept his magnet at Starbuck's brain; still he knew that for all this the chief mate, in his soul, abhorred his captain's quest, and could he, would joyfully disintegrate himself from it, or even frustrate it.[108]

One day, Starbuck enters Ahab's cabin to tell him that the oil is leaking and that the Burtons should be hoisted. Ahab replies in no uncertain terms. " 'Begone! Let it leak! I'm all aleak myself. Aye! leaks in leaks! not only full of leaky casks, but those leaky casks are in a leaky ship!' "[109] Starbuck persists in his argument, however, and Ahab once again orders him from the cabin.

"Nay, Sir, not yet; I do entreat. And I do dare, Sir – to be forbearing! Shall we not understand each other better than hitherto, Captain Ahab?"
Ahab seized a loaded musket from the rack ... and pointing it towards Starbuck, exclaimed: "There is one God that is Lord over the earth, and one Captain that is lord over the Pequod. – On deck!"
For an instant in the flashing eyes of the mate, and his fiery cheeks, you would have almost thought that he had really received the blaze of the levelled tube. But, mastering his emotion, he half calmly rose, and as he quitted the cabin, paused for an instant and said: "Thou hast outraged, not insulted me, Sir; but for that I ask thee not to beware of Starbuck; thou wouldst but laugh; but let Ahab beware of Ahab; beware of thyself, old man."[110]

[107] *Ibid.*, pp. 244-5.
[108] *Ibid.*, p. 306.
[109] *Ibid.*, p. 681.
[110] *Ibid.*, p. 682.

After Starbuck's leaves, however, Ahab observes that the mate is but too good a fellow, and orders the Burtons to be raised, either because of a "flash of honesty in him; or mere prudential policy which, under the circumstance, imperiously forbade the slightest symptom of open disaffection, however transient, in the important chief officer of his ship".[111]

Shortly thereafter, a far more important scene takes place in the captain's cabin. Starbuck descends to tell the sleeping Ahab that the weather is no longer stormy and that a fair wind is rising. Pausing before the old man's door, Starbuck's eyes alight upon the musket with which Ahab had previously threatened to shoot him.

"I come to report a fair wind to him. But how fair? Fair for death and doom, – *that's* fair for Moby-Dick. It's a fair wind that's only fair for that accursed fish. – The very tube he pointed at me! – the very one; *this* one – I hold it here; he would have killed me with the very thing I handle now. . . . But shall this crazed old man be tamely suffered to drag a whole ship's company down to doom with him? – Yes, it would make him a wilful murderer of thirty men and more, if this ship come to any deadly harm; and come to deadly harm, my soul swears this ship will, if Ahab have his way. If, then, he were this instant – put aside, that crime would not be his. . . . Great God forbid! – But is there no other way? no lawful way? – Make him a prisoner to be taken home? What! hope to wrest this old man's living power from his own living hands? Only a fool would try it. . . . What, then, remains? The land is hundreds of leagues away, and locked Japan the nearest. I stand alone here upon an open sea, with two oceans and a whole continent between me and law. – Aye, aye, 'tis so. – Is heaven a murderer when its lightning strikes a would-be murderer in his bed, tindering sheets and skin together? – And would I be a murderer, then, if" – and slowly, stealthily, and half sideways looking, he placed the loaded musket's end against the door.

"On this level, Ahab's hammock swings within; his head this way. A touch, and Starbuck may survive to hug his wife and child again. – Oh, Mary! Mary! – boy! boy! boy! – But if I wake thee not to death, old man, who can tell to what unsounded deeps Starbuck's body this day week may sink, with all the crew! Great God, where art thou? Shall I? shall I?"[112]

[111] *Ibid.*, p. 683.
[112] *Ibid.*, pp. 736-7.

It has been previously noted that F. O. Matthiessen says that in this scene, Starbuck finds himself in the same position as is Tommo, who, in order to escape from the Typees, is forced to brain with an oar the savage who is pursuing him. Gerhard Friedrich suggests that Starbruck's inner conflict during this passage makes of him a Quaker Hamlet.[113] Most important of all, we here find Starbuck faced with the choice of continuing his philosophy of pacifism, or rejecting it, and turning to rebellion as a way of life. The problem is very simple. If Starbuck were to kill Ahab, he would save not only himself, but all the rest of the *Pequod*'s crew. If he doesn't slay Ahab, the destruction of the *Pequod* and all the men aboard seems inevitable. If Starbuck kills Ahab, however, he must do so at the cost of rejecting everything he believes in – nonviolence, the idea that a just God would somehow prevent the horror that is being perpetrated upon the *Pequod* by its captain, and the belief in the sanctity of all human beings, including Ahab. If Starbuck murders Ahab, he might save the ship, but only, ironically, at the expense of being converted to the old man's philosophy. For Starbuck to attempt to murder the captain would be identical with Ahab's trying to harpoon the White Whale. In each case, both men would be trying to destroy the unjust fate or force which attempts to overpower them. But Starbuck decides not to shoot Ahab. He puts the rifle down and asks Stubb to tell the captain that the wind has changed. Like Ahab, Starbuck would rather be destroyed than to abandon his principles.

Since Starbuck doesn't kill Ahab, it seems as if nothing can now deter the old man from his chase. Yet one bright and gorgeous day, he weakens. While looking at the supreme beauty of nature, Ahab drops a tear into the Pacific. Starbuck sees this and approaches his captain.

"Oh, Starbuck! it is a mild, mild, wind, and a mild looking sky. On such a day – very much such a sweetness as this – I struck my first whale – a boy harpooner of eighteen! Forty – forty – forty years ago! – ago! Forty years of continual whaling! forty years of privation, and peril, and storm time! forty years on the pitiless sea! for forty years has Ahab forsaken the peaceful land, for forty years to make

[113] *In Pursuit of Moby-Dick* (Pendle Hill, 1958), p. 25.

war on the horrors of the deep! ... Why this strife of chase? why weary, and palsy the arm at the oar, and the iron, and the lance? how the richer or better is Ahab now? ... I feel deadly faint, bowed, and humped, as though I were Adam, staggering beneath the piled centuries since Paradise. ... Close! stand close to me, Starbuck; let me look into a human eye; it is better than to gaze into sea or sky; better than to gaze upon God. By the green land; by the bright hearth-stone! this is the magic glass, man; I see my wife and my child in thine eye."

"Oh, my Captain! my Captain! noble soul! grand old heart, after all! why should any one give chase to that hated fish! Away with me! let us fly these deadly waters let us home! Wife and child, too, are Starbuck's ... I think, Sir, they have some such mild blue days, even as this, in Nantucket."

"They have, they have. I have seen them — some summer days in the morning. About this time — yes, it is his noon nap now — the boy vivaciously wakes; sits up in bed; and his mother tells him of me, of cannibal old me; how I am abroad upon the deep, but will yet come back to dance him again."

"'Tis my Mary, my Mary herself! She promised that my boy, every morning, should be carried to the hill to catch the first glimpse of his father's sail! Yes, yes! no more! it is done! we head for Nantucket! Come, my Captain, study out the course, and let us away! See, see! the boy's face from the window! the boy's hand on the hill!"

But Ahab's glance was averted; like a blighted fruit tree he shook, and cast his last, cindered apple into the soil.

"What is it, what nameless inscrutable, unearthly thing is it; what cozzening, hidden lord and master, and cruel remorseless emperor commands me; that against all natural lovings and longings, I so keep pushing, and crowding, and jamming myself on all the time; recklessly making me ready to do what in my own proper, natural heart, I durst not so much as dare?" [114]

This mild Pacific day has again brought to the forefront the conflict between sea and land, pride and humanities. Ahab himself realizes that he has nothing to show for forty years of truth-searching at sea. Indeed, this very search has carried him away from the ones he loves, has isolated him from every comfort. Starbuck has previously tried to sway the old man from his course by implying that the Whale is a phantom of his own creation, that pursuit of Moby-Dick can only lead to sure doom, and he has even

[114] *Moby-Dick*, pp. 776-8.

considered killing Ahab in order to save the ship. But sensing his captain's changed mood, Starbuck tries a different tack. He now suggests that Ahab can find a meaningful existence on shore beside his wife and young son. He does not argue that his captain has not been unjustly and malevolently maimed by Moby-Dick. He says that it is even now not too late for Ahab to find a type of salvation in the world of man through human love. " 'See, see! the boy's face from the window! the boy's hand on the hill!' " But Ahab turns his glance away. The inscrutable thing which drives him on is his fatal pride.

Starbuck makes one final appeal. At the close of the second day of the chase, after the Parsee has disappeared, he turns to the captain.

"Great God! but for one single instant show thyself," cried Starbuck: "never, never wilt thou capture him, old man – In Jesus' name no more of this, that's worse than devil's madness. Two days chased; twice stove to splinters; thy very leg once more snatched from under thee; thy evil shadow gone – all good angels mobbing thee with warnings; ... Impiety and blasphemy to hunt him more!"

"Starbuck, of late I've felt strangely moved to thee; ever since that hour we both saw – thou know'st what, in one another's eyes. But in this matter of the whale, be the front of thy face to me as the palm of this hand – a lipless, unfeatured blank. Ahab is for ever Ahab, man."[115]

Starbuck's appeal to Jesus is the only time in the novel that a character utters the name of Christ. In *White Jacket*, as we have seen, the concept of Christ dominates the novel. Jesus is pictured as being not only just and loving, but perhaps most of all, strong. It is through the force of Christ that the inequities of human life can be corrected. This philosophy seems to be rejected in *Moby-Dick*, however. The only other reference to Christ in the novel condemns him and his way of life as a form of weakness. After suggesting that real power never impairs beauty, the narrator goes into a brief discussion of painting.

And whatever they may reveal of the divine love in the Son, the soft, curled hermaphroditical Italian pictures, in which his idea has been

---

[115] *Ibid.*, pp. 803-4.

most successfully embodied; these pictures, so destitute as they are of all brawniness, hint nothing of any power, but the mere negative, feminine one of submission and endurance, which on all hands it is conceded, form the peculiar virtues of his teachings.[116]

This is certainly one of the most damning statements ever made about Christianity. Neither Jesus nor his teachings are strong enough to save either Starbuck from Ahab or Ahab from the White Whale.

Ahab's reply to Starbuck that he is "forever Ahab" harks back to Father Mapple's Sermon. "And if we obey God, we must disobey ourselves; and it is in this disobeying ourselves, wherein the hardness of obeying God consists". So long as Ahab remains true to his own inexorable self, his actions are as inevitable and fixed as fate. Though on that mild blue Pacific day Ahab momentarily weakens, he is too strong a man ever to willfully disobey himself. His own inexorable self commands that he hunt Moby-Dick. "Delight is to him, who . . . in his own inexorable self . . . gives no quarter in the truth, and kills, burns, and destroys all sin though he pluck it out from under the robes of Senators and Judges". Ahab does not find delight in his chase, but he finds greatness.

Ahab and Starbuck present us with two different ways of life. The Quaker mate advocates a philosophy based on faith in the goodness of God and love of fellow men. Through this philosophy, at least a limited amount of joy is possible for every man in his relationship with his fellow humans, particularly his family. But, as developed in *Moby-Dick,* this philosophy is not only weak, but it is essentially dishonest, for it is based on a false premise. All evidence indicates that the universe is not governed by forces sympathetic to man. Nevertheless, Starbuck's philosophy is a satisfactory compromise, for it permits man some happiness and allows him to maintain his sanity. The alternative to this way of life is offered by Ahab. Man can refuse to compromise and rebel against the universe. To do so, he must cut himself off from his friends and his family, for any tie to the world of man weakens him in his defiance of the elements. Ahab's way is the way of madness and destruction, but it is also the way of strength and honesty. Though

[116] *Ibid.,* p. 544.

Ahab's philosophy is inevitably suicidal, there is no question that Melville's sympathies lie with the *Pequod*'s captain.

In *Moby-Dick,* we find the first full-fledged clash of pacifism and rebellion in Melville's writings. Though Melville could never reconcile these two attitudes, he does redefine and alter them, as we shall see.

CHAPTER VI

PIERRE: THE FOOL OF VIRTUE

> The laws of God, the laws of man,
> He may keep that will and can;
> Not I: let God and man decree
> Laws for themselves and not for me;
> And if my ways are not as theirs
> Let them mind their own affairs.
> Their deed I judge and much condemn,
> Yet when did I make laws for them?
> Please yourselves, say I, and they
> Need only look the other way,
> But no, they will not; they must still
> Wrest their neighbour to their will,
> And make me dance as they desire
> With jail and gallows and hell-fire.
> And how am I to face the odds
> Of man's bedevilment and God's?
> I, a stranger and afraid
> In a world I never made.
> They will be master, right or wrong;
> Though both are foolish, both are strong
> And since, my soul, we cannot fly
> To Saturn nor to Mercury,
> Keep we must, if keep we can,
> These foreign laws of God and man.
>
> A. E. Housman, "The Laws of God, The Laws of Man"

Intellectually and philosophically, *Pierre* covers much the same ground as *Moby-Dick,* posing the same questions and arriving at the same conclusions as does the earlier book. Both novels are concerned with how an idealistic and uncompromising man reacts when confronted with the problem of evil, and in each instance, the unyielding idealism of the protagonist leads to inevitable destruction. Yet *Pierre* and *Moby-Dick* are so unalike that it is often difficult to believe that they were written by the same man. The reason for this is the complete artistic collapse of the latter novel. In *Moby-Dick,* the threads of the narrative, the transcendental, the humorous, etc., are woven into a tight organic pattern. But the elements of the adventurous, the satiric, and the philosophical don't blend together in *Pierre.* As Ronald Mason observes of this novel, "Melodrama and metaphysics are dangerous companions".[1] Moreover, the characters in *Moby-Dick,* no matter what their symbolic significance, are vital and believable beings. In the later novel, the characters are poorly developed and seem merely to be figures in an intellectual jig-saw puzzle. Also, as a more-or-less general rule in Melville's prose, his works dealing with transcendental evil are more successful if this evil is given concrete form, as is the case with the figures such as Jackson, Claggart, and the White Whale. Though evil is an active force in *Pierre,* this evil exists as an abstract – not as an embodied – force. Finally, again broadly speaking, Melville's best fiction is set either against the sea or in some exotic locale such as Nukahiva, or the Galapagos. With the possible exception of "Bartleby the Scrivener", Melville never seemed to be able to write well about man in a civilized, Western, urban society. And *Pierre* is a novel which attempts to deal both with man in this type of society and with social morality.

The plot of *Pierre* is relatively complex. Pierre Glendinning is the scion of a wealthy and aristocratic American family, a descendent from a long line of heroes and patriots. He is a handsome and likeable young man of nineteen, proud of his heritage and happy with his life. In a superficial way, too, he is a kind and intelligent youth. Though his "dear perfect father is dead",[2] Pierre finds consolation in the sacred and immaculate memory left by his deceased parent. Pierre's mother, Mary, is a still-beautiful woman, and she and her son act as if they were contemporaries. Pierre shows a "lover-like adoration"[3] towards Mrs. Glendinning, and the two call each other not "mother" and "son", but "brother" and "sister". Pierre is shortly to marry a beautiful and charming girl,

---

[1] *The Spirit Above the Dust* (London, 1951), p. 158.
[2] *Pierre* (New York, 1957), p. 25.
[3] *Ibid.,* p. 20.

Lucy Tartan, whom he worships. This proposed union has the blessings of Mrs. Glendinning, not only because she recognizes Lucy's inherent qualities and because she is delighted that Pierre will be married to someone of an equal social background, but also because she thinks that Lucy is a weak person, and hence, the forthcoming marriage will not in any real way alter her present relationship with her son.

Life, to borrow a phrase from Cary McWilliams, lay before Pierre like an unopened bottle of wine. Only one thing mars his otherwise perfect existence. He had no real sister.

"Oh, had my father but had a daughter!" cried Pierre; "someone whom I might love, and protect, and fight for; if need be. It must be a glorious thing to engage in a mortal quarrel on a sweet sister's behalf! Now, of all things, would to heaven, I had a sister!" [4]

Pierre's plea, made in the opening pages, foreshadows all of the action of the novel. For Pierre's father did have a daughter sometime in the distant past, though her mother was not Mary Glendinning, but probably a mysterious and tragic French beauty with whom he had been in love during his youth. As a result of numerous complex adventures, this daughter, who has been an outcast since birth, is now working as a menial near Saddle Meadows, the Glendinning family estate. She eventually comes to believe that Pierre is her brother, and consequently reveals her identity to him. Pierre, convinced that Isabel is really his sister, is horrified by the cruelty she has been subjected to. The existence of Isabel not only shatters Pierre's almost God-like concept of his father, but plunges him into a psychological and philosophical crisis. Until now, Pierre had believed in the goodness and simplicity of life, and he himself was a devout and unquestioning Christian. But the discovery of Isabel's existence destroys all of Pierre's former beliefs. Shocked though he is, Pierre vows to devote his life to righting the wrong that has been done to her. But this is not an easy task. Pierre knows that his mother would never be willing to acknowledge Isabel as his sister. Moreover, if he tells the truth concerning

[4] *Ibid.*, p. 7.

Isabel's parentage, he will ruin his father's reputation, which is the last thing that Pierre wishes to do. Thinking that "sometimes a lie is heavenly, and truth infernal",[5] Pierre decides that he will tell the world that he is married to Isabel, though in actuality they will live as brother and sister. "Then, for the time, all minor things were whelmed; his mother, Isabel, the whole wide world; and one thing only remained to him; – this all-including query – Lucy or God?"[6]

Pierre chooses the way of God. After this initial decision, all of Pierre's conscious motivations are directed to the pursuit of virtue, and what follows as a result of this choice seems inevitable. He tells Lucy that he is already married, causing her to fall into an almost death-like illness. Mrs. Glendinning banishes Pierre from Saddle Meadows and disinherits him, so he decides to go to the city with Isabel and her "fallen" friend Delly. His boyhood chum and cousin, Glendinning Stanly, had offered Pierre the use of a house in the metropolis. But when Pierre arrives with Isabel, no house is available, and Glen pointedly insults him. Pierre, by now almost penniless, moves into a converted church, known as the Apostles, with Isabel and Delly, and attempts to make his living as a writer. This happy threesome is, surprisingly enough, now joined by the recuperated Lucy, who realizes that Pierre's actions must be virtuous, though she herself cannot comprehend them. She pretends to be nothing more than a platonic cousin of Pierre's, and she herself believes that Isabel and Pierre are man and wife. Lucy is followed by her angry brother Frederic, an equally angry Glen Stanly, who is now Lucy's suitor, and the especially angry mother of Lucy. All three try to pursuade or force Lucy to move away from Pierre, but she refuses.

Pierre, Delly, and the two women who love him live on in poverty, despair, and deception until one day Pierre, who has virtually no communication with the outside world, unexpectedly receives two letters. The first, from Pierre's publisher, accuses him of being a swindler, for Pierre, instead of writing the usual romantic claptrap which had in his Saddle Meadow days made him a minor literary sensation, has attempted to write a serious and

---

[5] *Ibid.*, p. 128.
[6] *Ibid.*, p. 253.

mature novel. His publisher finds this attempt "A blasphemous rhapsody, filched from the vile Atheists, Lucian and Voltaire".[7] The other letter is from his cousin Glen and Lucy's brother Frederic, denouncing Pierre as a liar. This is the final straw. Turning to the outer two doors of the rooms of Isabel and Lucy, he screams " 'For ye two, my most undiluted prayer is now, that from your here unseen and frozen chairs, ye may never stir alive: – the fool of Truth, the fool of Virtue, the fool of Fate, now quits ye forever!' "[8] Seizing a brace of pistols from a friend's chambers, he rushes out into the street, where, as luck would have it, he encounters Glen and Fred. The former strikes Pierre in the face, and he responds by emptying both pistols into his cousin. Pierre is taken to prison where he is visited by Isabel and Lucy. In the strain of the moment, Isabel shrieks " 'Oh, ye stony roofs, and seven-fold stony skies! – not thou art the murderer, but thy sister hath murdered thee, my brother, oh my brother!' "[9] When Lucy hears these words, she at last understands the true relationship between Pierre and Isabel, and promptly drops dead. This is quickly followed by the double suicide of Pierre and Isabel, and on this melodramatic note, the novel closes.

Pierre is sub-titled *The Ambiguities*. The most obvious of these ambiguities, obvious even in terms of mere plot alone, is that the more intensely Pierre pursues truth and virtue, the greater the catastrophes and the more the horror that result from his actions. As a direct consequence of Pierre's unflagging and uncompromising quest for goodness and right, he murders his cousin, causes the death of Lucy and his mother as well as the suicide of Isabel, and brings to a close the long and honorable line of Glendinnings. This is the central ambiguity of the novel, and I will deal with it in much greater detail in my discussion of "Chronometricals and Horologicals". There are, however, many other major ambiguities in the book. I intend to discuss three of these at some length: the exact nature of the attraction and relationship between Pierre and Isabel, the contrast between Isabel and Lucy, and the conflicting

[7] *Ibid.*, p. 497.
[8] *Ibid.*, p. 499.
[9] *Ibid.*, p. 503.

evidence offered by the various portraits which appear in crucial sections throughout the novel.

When Pierre first decides to aid Isabel, he feels himself to be "divinely dedicated ... with divine commands upon him to befriend and champion Isabel, through all conceivable contingencies of Time and Chance".[10] But another subtle and less noble, though unconscious, explanation for Pierre's behavior is at least implied. This explanation is sexual. Pierre had seen Isabel long before he has talked to her, though he did not then know her identity. Consequently, when he receives Isabel's letter in which she identifies herself as his sister, "already, and ere the proposed encounter, he was assured that, in a transcendent degree, womanly beauty, and not womanly ugliness, invited him to champion the right".[11] In describing the attraction which Pierre and Isabel feel for each other, Melville uses the word "magnetic" again and again. When Pierre first informs Isabel of his plan to tell the world that she is his wife, "He imprinted repeated burning kisses upon her".[12] The love between Pierre and Lucy, on the other hand, seems to be almost completely spiritual. Though Pierre kisses Lucy, these kisses are never described as being even remotely "burning."

Despite the fact that Melville writes that when Pierre first meets Isabel, the thought of anything other than a brotherly embrace never entered his uncontaminated mind, it is clearly indicated – or at least as clearly as the mores of the times would permit – that on one occasion, the love between Pierre and Isabel is consumated.

"My brother! this is some incomprehensible raving," pealed Isabel, throwing both arms around him: – "my brother, my brother!"

"Hark thee to thy furthest inland soul," thrilled Pierre in a steeled and quivering voice. "Call me brother no more! How knowest thou I am your brother? Did thy mother tell thee? Did my father say so to me? – I am Pierre, and thou Isabel, wide brother and sister in the common humanity, – no more. For the rest, let the gods look after their own combustibles. If they have put powder kegs in me – let them look to it! let them look to it! Ah! now I catch glimpses, and

[10] *Ibid.*, p. 148.
[11] *Ibid.*, p. 151.
[12] *Ibid.*, p. 268.

seem to half see, somehow, that the uttermost ideal of moral perfection in man is wide of the mark. The demigods trample on trash, and Virtue and Vice are trash!"

. . . .

"Pierre, when thou just hovered on the verge, thou wert a riddle to me; but now, that thou art deep down in the gulf of the soul, – now, when thou wouldst be lunatic to wise men, perhaps – now doth poor ignorant Isabel begin to comprehend thee. Thy feeling hath long been mine, Pierre. Long loneliness and anguish have opened miracles to me. Yes, it is all a dream!"

Swiftly he caught her in his arms: – "From nothing proceeds nothing, Isabel! How can one sin in a dream?"

"First, what is sin, Pierre?"

"Another name for the other name, Isabel."

"For Virtue, Pierre?"

"No, for Vice."

"Let us sit down again, my brother."

"I am Pierre."

"Let us sit down again, Pierre; sit close; sit close; thy arm!"

And so, on the third night, when the twilight was gone, and no lamp was lit, within the lofty windows of that beggarly room, sat Pierre and Isabel hushed.[13]

The possible incestuous relationship between Pierre and Isabel has significance not only on the philosophical level, but also on the psychological level, for *Pierre* is perhaps more the study of the human mind than it is an analysis of the meaning of virtue and truth. Melville uses incest as a means by which to explore the hidden recesses of the human psyche, and *Pierre*, no matter what its artistic flaws, is an important and amazingly modern psychological document. If Pierre is to be anything more than a symbol of pure good, there must at least be the suggestion that *all* of his actions are not solely dedicated by the pursuit of virtue. Though Pierre's conscious motivations in helping Isabel are certainly noble, there is at least the possibility that his subconscious motivations are not so self-sacrificing. Moreover, *Pierre* illustrates that while in pursuit of virtue, it is possible to commit the most horrible crimes, since nineteenth century America would regard incest as one of the cardinal sins. Finally, the incestuous tie be-

---

[13] *Ibid.*, pp. 381-2.

tween Isabel and Pierre is merely one aspect of the theme of incest which recurs again and again throughout the novel. As we have seen, the relationship between Pierre and Mrs. Glendinning is closer to that of lovers than it is to mother and son. Lucy, though not a close relative, is Pierre's cousin. Glen Stanly, with whom Pierre had one of those childish friendships "which sometimes transcends the bounds of mere boyishness, and revels for a short while in the empyrean of a love which only comes short, by one degree, of the sweetest sentiment entertained between the sexes",[14] is Pierre's cousin. This motif is continued in Pierre's dream of Enceladus, in which the hero comes to identify himself with the rebellious giant.

Old Titan's self was the son of incestuous Coelus and Terra, the son of incestuous Heaven and Earth. And Titan married his mother Terra, another and accumulative incestuous match. And thereof Enceladus was one issue. So Enceladus was both the son and grandson of an incest..."[15]

At the close of the novel, when Pierre and Isabel are looking at a picture called "The Stranger", Isabel finds herself fascinated by a painting of the Cenci by Guido. Beatrice Cenci, a blonde who physically resembles Lucy, is involved in two of the "most horrible crimes possible to civilized humanity – incest and parricide".[16] In addition to the psychological insights and complexities it develops, the recurrent theme of incest is used by Melville to attack the concept of an American aristocracy, a social class which suffers from too much in-breeding and whose values are too self-contained and removed from the rest of mankind.

Another source of ambiguity is the contrast between Lucy Tartan and Isabel. Pierre is torn between the two polarities represented by Isabel and Lucy, but it is never quite definite what these two women symbolize. The only certainty is that Pierre can't possess both of them wholly, nor can he be happy with only one of them. Though Isabel herself says that Lucy is Pierre's good angel and that she is his bad angel, this statement is not true.

[14] *Ibid.*, p. 301.
[15] *Ibid.*, p. 483.
[16] *Ibid.*, p. 489.

Isabel and Lucy represent antitheses, but these antitheses are not good and evil. Isabel is just as kind and self-sacrificing as is Lucy. Though Pierre first becomes aware of evil as a result of his discovery of Isabel, she herself is not evil, rather the forces which produced her misery are evil. Pierre is physically destroyed as a result of his attempt to aid his sister, but he at least gains knowledge of the world as it really is through his contact with her. Although Pierre's destruction is inevitable after he has been banished from Saddle Meadows, his end is hastened with the arrival of Lucy, for Glen and Frederic's note, which provokes Pierre to murder, would never have been written if she hadn't decided to live in a ménage-à-trois at the Apostles. The major differences between Isabel and Lucy, therefore, are not moral or philosophical, and are expressed primarily in terms of imagery.[17] Lucy is a blonde, and as her name indicates, is associated with light and the day. The raven-tressed Isabel is dark, wears black dresses, and at first, Pierre sees her only during the night. Furthermore, Lucy is wealthy, from an aristocratic family, and is readily accepted by society. Isabel is a penniless outcast, ignored by everyone except Pierre, and is often described as "supernatural".[18] Henry Murray, in his lengthy introduction to the Hendricks House edition of *Pierre*,[19] suggests that Isabel represents the unconscious. Though one cannot with any confidence attach a fixed meaning to either Isabel or Lucy, it is safe to say that in a comparison of the two, we find the contrast between the conscious and the unconscious, the known and the unknown, the world of man and the supernatural, the explainable and the unexplainable.

A third ambiguity is to be found in the various portraits in the novel. There are two pictures of Pierre's father. One, painted at the request of his wife, shows "a middle-aged, married man, and

---

[17] For a fuller discussion of the differences between Lucy and Isabel, see Richard Chase, *Herman Melville* (New York, 1949), and F. I. Carpenter, "Puritans Preferred Blondes: The Heroines of Melville and Hawthorne", *NEQ*, IX (June, 1936), 257-64.

[18] *Pierre, op. cit.*, p. 157.

[19] Murray's introduction to this edition of *Pierre* (New York, 1949), though more psychiatric than critical in approach, is extremely useful and provocative.

seemed to possess all the nameless and slightly portly tranquilities incident to that condition when a felicitous one".[20] The other, a smaller portrait, is of "a brisk, unentangled, young bachelor, gaily ranging up and down in the world",[21] who has on his lips an "ambiguous, unchanging smile".[22] This latter portrait was painted by an amateur friend of Pierre's father when the elder Glendinning was rumored to be in love with a beautiful and mysterious French girl. Isabel bears a striking resemblance to the portrait of Pierre's father as a young man, and, in all probability, the mysterious French girl is her mother. The larger portrait, a favorite of Pierre's mother, hangs in the drawing room. But Mrs. Glendinning always disliked the smaller portrait, which was given to Pierre by his aunt, so Pierre keeps it hanging in a small closet in his chambers. He cannot understand why his mother hates this portrait, but even to him, "these two paintings had always seemed dissimilar".[23] Pierre often puzzles over this and wonders if the same man can be the subject of both pictures.

Obviously, these two portraits indicate not only the ambiguity of human life and the dual nature of every man, but perhaps more important, suggest a split in the universe itself. Just as Wellingborough Redburn worshipped the idea of his father, so too does Pierre. There was

> in the inmost soul of Pierre, the impression of a bodily form of rare manly beauty and benignity, only rivalled by the supposed perfect mould in which his virtuous heart had been cast. ... and again, and again, still deeper and deeper. was stamped in Pierre's soul the cherished conceit, that his virtuous father, so beautiful on earth, was now uncorruptibly sainted in heaven.[24]

There is at least the suggestion that his sainted memory of his father is coupled with Pierre's belief in the inherent goodness of God. After Pierre has discovered how Isabel has been wronged and neglected as a result of his father's callousness, he loses faith in both his earthly and his heavenly father. Shortly after meeting

---

[20] *Pierre* (New York, 1957), p. 100.
[21] *Ibid.*, p. 100.
[22] *Ibid.*, p. 273.
[23] *Ibid.*, p. 100.
[24] *Ibid.*, p. 94.

Isabel, Pierre burns the smaller portrait of his father, indicating that he is unwilling to accept the existence of evil in the world, and asserts his own moral equality with the powers of the universe. As the flames devour the painting, Pierre screams, " 'Henceforth, cast out Pierre hath no paternity, and no past; and since the Future is one blank to all; therefore, twice-disinherited Pierre stands untrammelledly his ever-present self! – free to do his own self-will and present fancy to whatever end.' "[25]

To some extent, Isabel's true identity is established by her striking similarity to the smaller portrait of Pierre's father. But at the close of the novel, another painting casts some doubt on the veracity of this previous means of identification. Pierre, Isabel, and Lucy go to an art gallery one day. While Lucy[26] is examining the aforementioned painting of the Cenci by Guido, the other two step in front of a painting called "The Stranger" by an unknown artist.

"My God! see! see!" cried Isabel, under strong excitement, "only my mirror has ever shown me that look before! See! see!" ... "The Stranger" was a dark comely, youthful man's head, portentously looking out of a dark shaded ground, and ambiguously smiling. There was no discoverable drapery; the dark head, with its crisp, curly, jetty hair, seemed just disentangling itself from out of curtains and clouds. But to Isabel, in the eye and on the brow, were certain shadowy traces of her own unmistakable likeness; while to Pierre, this face was in part as the resurrection of the one he had burnt at the inn. Not that the separate features were the same; but the pervading look of it, the subtler interior keeping of the entirety, was almost identical; still, for all this, there was an unequivocal aspect of foreignness, of Europeanism, about both the face itself and the general painting.[27]

Here we find ambiguity piled on ambiguity. The existence of the

[25] *Ibid.*, p. 277.

[26] Lucy herself is a painter and thinks that she can make a living by sketching portraits of various tenants who live in the Apostles.

[27] *Pierre* (New York, 1957), pp. 488-90. Note that the use of the word "resurrection" in this paragraph, the fact that Pierre's mother's name is Mary, and the fact that Pierre lives in a building called the Apostles suggests that some sort of fairly orthodox religious interpretation of the novel might be possible.

"PIERRE": THE FOOL OF VIRTUE

painting "The Stranger" makes impossible any remotely certain solution to the mystery of Isabel's past, the exact relationship between Isabel and Pierre, or to the riddle posed by the two seemingly conflicting portraits of Pierre's father.

After our discussion of the narrative line of *Pierre* and of some of the supplementary ambiguities, we can now deal in more detail with the central ambiguity of the novel, the ambiguity of how the more intensely Pierre pursues truth and virtue, the more evil and unhappiness he brings about. In the middle of the book, Pierre, accompanied by Isabel and Delly, is riding on a carriage to the city, leaving forever the rural life which he has previously known. While the two women sleep, Pierre meditates. Suddenly he sees a sleazy mass of paper, which turns out to be a pamphlet by one Plotinus Plinlimmon, entitled "Chronometricals and Horologicals". This pamphlet is the philosophical center of the novel, being a commentary on Pierre's actions and the resulting ambiguities. The pamphlet to some extent reflects the same struggle that exists between Ahab and Starbuck in *Moby-Dick*, and hence "Chronometricals and Horologicals" is the most important section in *Pierre* in terms of our topic of pacifism and rebellion.

Plinlimmon's pamphlet begins with a discussion of types of earthly time. If a sailor in England sets his watch by Greenwich time and sails to China without adjusting his watch to Chinese time, he would do all sorts of foolish things, such as going to bed at noon, etc. This doesn't indicate that Chinese time is better than English time. It merely shows that Chinese time is appropriate for China and English time is apppropriate for England.

> Now in an artificial world like ours, the soul of man is further removed from its God and the Heavenly Truth, than the chronometer carried to China, is from Greenwich....
>
> Bacon's brains were mere watchmaker's brains; but Christ was a chronometer; and the most exquisitely adjusted and exact one, and the least affected by all terrestrial jarrings, of any that have ever come to us. And the reason why his teachings seemed folly to the Jews, was because he carried that Heaven's time in Jerusalem, while the Jews carried Jerusalem time there. Did he not expressly say – My wisdom (time) is not of this world?[28]

[28] *Ibid.*, pp. 294-5.

138 "PIERRE": THE FOOL OF VIRTUE

Thus it follows that "though the earthly wisdom of man be heavenly folly to God; so also, conversely, is the heavenly wisdom of God an earthly folly to man".[29] If we carry this to its logical extreme, we must conclude that

> he who finding in himself a chronometrical soul, seeks practically to force that heavenly time upon the earth; in such an attempt he can never succeed, with an absolute and essential success. And as for himself, if he seek to regulate his own daily conduct by it, he will but array all men's earthly time-keepers against him, and thereby work himself woe and death. Both these things are evinced in the character and fate of Christ, ... almost invariably, with inferior beings, the absolute effort to live in this world according to the strict letter of the chronometricals is, somehow, apt to involve those inferior beings eventually in strange, *unique* follies and sins, unimagined before.[30]

This chronometrical conceit in no ways justifies the actions of wicked men.

> For in their wickedness downright wicked men sin is as much against their own horologes, as against the heavenly chronometer. ... No, this conceit merely goes to show, that for the mass of men; the highest abstract heavenly righteousness is not only impossible, but would be entirely out of place, and positively wrong in a world like this.[31]

Consequently, "A virtuous expediency... seems the highest desirable or attainable earthly excellence for the mass of men, and is the only earthly excellence that their Creator intended for them."[32] The pamphlet is unfinished, breaking off with the words "Moreover: if..."[33] indicating that it is "more the excellently illustrated restatement of a problem, than the solution of the problem itself".[34]

It is important to realize that the pamphlet discusses three – not merely two – attitudes of life. There is not only the way of man and the way of God, but a median way, the way of "virtuous

[29] *Ibid.*, p. 295.
[30] *Ibid.*, p. 296.
[31] *Ibid.*, pp. 297-8.
[32] *Ibid.*, p. 299.
[33] *Ibid.*, p. 300.
[34] *Ibid.*, p. 293.

expediency". Horological time is the time represented by the mores of society, by people such as Mary Glendinning. Virtuous expediency, a compromise time, is equated with Christianity and is embodied in the Reverend Falsgrave. Chronometrical time is not only the time of God, but also the time of strong and virtuous individuals. This latter type of time is Absolute and leaves no possible chance for compromise. Pierre attempts to adjust his life by chronometrical time, and hence is involved in "strange, *unique* follies and sins, unimagined before". Needless to say, the man who follows chronometrical time, such as Pierre, is continually at war not only with society, but with Christianity as well.

Melville finds little to justify man's being governed by horological time or the mores of society. Society has no real concern with virtue, only with expediency. The representatives of society in this novel – Mrs. Glendinning, Glen Stanly, Mrs. Tartan – have no interest in truth or goodness. They are selfish and shallow people, interested at best in improving their own station and well-being in any way that does not conflict with the letter of the law. Mrs. Glendinning, for example, "loves" her son only because he is an adornment for her and makes her life pleasant and companionable. When Pierre for the first time goes against his mother's wishes, she banishes him from Saddle Meadows and disinherits him. Such too is the case with Mrs. Tartan. She comes, at the request of Glen and Frederic, to urge Lucy to leave Pierre. "Had Mrs. Tartan been a different woman than she was; had she indeed any disinterested agonies of a generous heart, and no mere match-making mortifications, however poignant; then the hope of Frederic and Glen might have had more likelihood in it".[35]

A stronger attempt is made to justify "virtuous expediency" or Christianity as a philosophy. If man is governed solely by the codes of society, he would destroy himself through his own selfishness. If, on the other hand, all men were like Pierre, man would destroy himself because of his uncompromising search for goodness and truth. Only Christianity offers both morality and the type of compromise necessary for getting along in the world of man. ("A vituous expediency... seems the highest desirable or attain-

[35] *Ibid.*, p. 454.

able excellence for the mass of men, and is the only earthly excellence that their Creator intended for them".) As has been suggested earlier, this position is represented by Reverend Falsgrave, whose very name indicates that this attitude leaves something to be desired. His spiritual softness is reflected in his body. When the minister dines at the Glendinnings, he tucks a napkin into his "snowy bosom", and Pierre notices "the gentle humane radiations which come from the clergyman's manly and rounded beautifulness".[36] After Pierre has committed himself to the cause of Isabel, Reverend Falsgrave comes to visit Mrs. Glendinning, but when he can offer her no comfort, she screams, " 'Begone! and let me not hear thy soft, mincing voice, which is an infamy to man! Begone, thou helpless and unhelping one!' "[37] These descriptions of the minister immediately bring to mind "the soft hermaphroditical Italian pictures" of Christ mentioned in *Moby-Dick*.

When Pierre is confused as to what his exact course should be in regards to Isabel, he goes to Falsgrave for advice. Pierre asks the minister about Delly Ulver, who has had an illegitimate child, hoping to eventually bring the subject around to Isabel and her plight. The clergyman hems and haws, refusing to giving anything resembling a concrete answer.

"I perfectly comprehend the whole, sir. Delly Ulver, then, is to be driven out to starve or rot; and this, too, by the acquiescence of a man of God. Mr. Falsgrave, the subject of Delly, deeply interesting as it is to me, is only the preface to another, still more interesting to me, and concerning which I once cherished some slight hope that thou wouldst have been able, in thy Christian character, to sincerely and honestly counsel me. But a hint from heaven assures me now, *that thou hast no earnest and world-disdaining counsel for me. I must seek it direct from God Himself, whom, I now know never delegates His holiest admonishings. But I do not blame thee; I think I begin to see how thy profession is unavoidably entangled by all fleshly alliances, and cannot move with godly freedom in a world of benefices.*[38] [Italics my own.]

[36] *Ibid.*, pp. 138-9.
[37] *Ibid.*, p. 270.
[38] *Ibid.*, p. 230.

Reverend Falsgrave represents another step downward from the philosophy developed in *White-Jacket*. In that work, Melville presented pacifism as a philosophy of strength and an instrument with which to combat evil and injustice. Starbuck, who carries this philosophy over into *Moby-Dick,* is not only a good man, but a strong and courageous man as well, though he is overpowered by Ahab and the latter's philosophy of rebellion. Reverend Falsgrave may be a good man, but he is weak and cowardly. In *Pierre,* pacifism has become nothing but a watered down version of Christianity, a way of life which may be a modus vivendi, but which lacks real moral force and depth.

As might be excepted, the most complex of these three times to adjust to is chronometric, or the time of God. Before he met Isabel, Pierre lived by horological time, or was governed by virtuous expediency. When, through the plight of Isabel, he becomes aware of evil, he vows to live in the future only by chronometric time. " 'Henceforth I will know nothing but Truth; . . . I will know what *is,* and do what my deepest angel dictates' ".[39] Pierre's commitment to Truth causes him to break from the world of man. "Thus, in the Enthusiast to Duty, the heaven-begotten Christ is born; and will not own a mortal parent, and spurns and rends all mortal bonds".[40] Pierre fully realizes that he is spurning and rending all mortal bonds in the cause of righteousness, and because of this understanding, he delivers an ultimatum to the powers that be.

"On my strong faith in ye Invisibles, I stake three whole felicities, and three whole lives this day. If ye forsake me now, – farewell to Faith, farewell to Truth, farewell to God; exiled for aye from God and man, I shall declare myself an equal power with both; free to make war on Night and Day, and all thoughts and things of mind and matter, which the upper and nether firmaments do clasp!" [41]

Pierre has two great moments of revelation in the novel. The first comes when he meets Isabel and becomes aware of man's inhumanity to man. The second is when he realizes that, though he

[39] *Ibid.,* p. 90.
[40] *Ibid.,* p. 149.
[41] *Ibid.,* p. 150.

has dedicated himself body and soul to the cause of virtue and truth, God does not necessarily side with him.

That hour of the life of a man when first the help of humanity fails him, and he learns that in his obscurity and indigence humanity holds him a dog and no man; that hour is a hard one, but not the hardest. There is still another hour which follows, when he learns that in his infinite comparative minuteness and abjectness, the gods do likewise despise him, and own him not of their own clan. Divinity and humanity then are equally willing that he should starve in the street for all that either will do for him.[42]

After this realization, Pierre – though he continues in his pursuit of virtue and truth – acknowledges no power as being morally superior. When Glen accuses him of being a fiend, Pierre responds "'I am what I am'".[43] He now realizes that he is not only in conflict with horological time, but with God as well.

Pierre never thinks of surrendering, however. He persists in his futile yet noble quest for virtue. Even "the very blood in his body had rebelled in vain against his Titanic soul".[44] The linking of his iron will with Titanism is further developed in a dream which Pierre has towards the end of the book. In this dream, Pierre sees once again the Mount of Titans, a mountain not far from his home in Saddle Meadows. At the bottom of this mountain is a huge, scarred, and armless rock.

You paused; fixed by a form defiant, a form of awfulness. You saw Enceladus the Titan, the most potent of all the giants, writhing from out the imprisoning earth; – turbaned with upborne moss he writhed; still, though armless, resisting with his whole striving trunk, the Pelion and the Ossa hurled back at him; – turbaned with upborne moss he writhed; still turning his unconquerable front toward that majestic mount eternally in vain assailed by him, and which, when it had stormed him off, had heaved his undoffable incubus upon him, and deridingly left him there to bay out his ineffectual howl.[45]

As the dream continues, the rocks at the bottom of the mountain rally and attack the unconquerable slope.

[42] *Ibid.*, pp. 412-3.
[43] *Ibid.*, p. 452.
[44] *Ibid.*, p. 475.
[45] *Ibid.*, p. 480.

But no longer petrified in all their ignominious attitudes, the herded Titans now sprung to their feet; flung themselves up the slope; and anew battered at the precipice's unresounding wall. Foremost among them all, he saw a moss-turbaned, armless giant, who despairing of any other mode of wrecking his immitigable hate, turned his vast trunk into a battering ram, and hurled his own arched-out ribs again and yet again against the invulnerable steep.

"Enceladus! it is Enceladus!" Pierre cried out in his sleep. That moment the phantom faced him; and Pierre saw Enceladus no more; but on the Titan's armless trunk, his own duplicate face and features magnifiedly gleamed upon him with prophetic discomfiture and woe.[46]

In the dream, Pierre not only identifies himself with the Titan, but the vision of Enceladus, the son of Earth who warred against the heavens, both explains and justifies the actions of Pierre.

the present mood of Pierre — that reckless sky-assaulting mood of his, was nevertheless on one side the grandson of the sky. For it is according to eternal fitness, that the precipated Titan should still seek to regain his paternal birthright ever by fierce escallade. Wherefore whoso storms the sky gives best proof he came from thither! But whatso crawls contented in the moat before that crystal fort, shows it was born within that slime, and there forever will abide.[47]

Pierre's fight is hopeless. He can never defeat the forces which humiliate man, but so long as he rebels, he is saved from completely sinking into the slime from which he is trying to escape.

In discussing the central ambiguity of why a man completely dedicated to the cause of good can produce nothing but evil, we have also uncovered another related and perplexing problem: Pierre devotes his life to following God, and as a result, is led inevitably into direct conflict with Him. Pierre had early puzzled over the following lines from *Hamlet,* which so aptly reflect the young American's dilemma.

The time is out of joint; — Oh cursed spite
That ever I was born to set it right!

[46] *Ibid.,* p. 482.
[47] *Ibid.,* p. 483.

Plinlimmon's pamphlet seizes upon this time analogy, and warns that any man who tries to follow God's time or a path of complete virtue will be an outcast in the world of man. But "Horologicals and Chronometricals" does not go far enough, for its author fails to realize that the completely virtuous man is not only in conflict with his fellows, but with God as well. Pierre's rebellion, which initially seems to be antithetical to that of the Captain of the *Pequod* in that Pierre attempts to follow God and to right social injustice, eventually — as seen in his dream of Enceladus — leads him to Ahab's position, to a war against heaven itself. Unfortunately for Pierre, there is no Moby-Dick, a symbol of all that is wrong with the cosmos, for him to harpoon. The best available substitute is his cousin Glen, whom Pierre shoots.

One inescapable conclusion amidst all this confusion is, that at some point, the way of God and the way of absolute virtue part company. Furthermore, God indiscriminately destroys those who follow his teachings and those who don't. As Melville writes early in the novel, "we shall see whether this wee little scrap of latinity be very far out of the way — *Nemo contra Deum nisi Deus ipse* [No one against God if not God himself]".[48] A good man must eventually war against God, because God is not all good, or to re-phrase this, the more God-like a man, the more inevitable is his rebellion against God.

In *Pierre,* we probably find the most unsympathetic presentation of pacifism and the most fanatic representation of rebellion in all of Melville's works. The philosophy of pacifism which dominates *White-Jacket* and is sympathetically and strongly represented in *Moby-Dick* by Quaker Starbuck, has so dwindled in strength by *Pierre,* that its sole representative is the hapless and effeminate Reverend Falsgrave. Though he often makes Captain Ahab appear to be the epitome of moderation in contrast and though his actions include murder, suicide, and incest, Pierre and his philosophy emerge as infinitely superior to the other characters in the novel and their way of life — the selfish but strong figures such as Mrs. Glendinning and Glen Stanley, and the good but weak figure of Reverend Falsgrave. Nevertheless, there is something radically

[48] *Ibid.,* p. 17.

wrong with Pierre. If an artist wishes to dramatize a rather unusual philosophy, the character who embodies this approach to life must be a magnetic and powerful figure, capable of holding the reader's interest and respect, if nothing else. Now the ultimate philosophical position reached by Pierre is not too far from that of Ahab. Yet no matter how much we may disagree with Ahab, he always commands our respect, and no matter how much we may agree with Pierre, he usually seems puerile and foolish. The season that Pierre's rebellion so often appears ridiculous is not so much a result of philosophical weakness as it is the result of Melville's inability to create a protagonist of stature in this novel. *Moby-Dick* is a work of great tragic scope because of Ahab's nobility. *Pierre* seldom rises above mediocre melodrama because we find its hero not so much tragic or misguided, but ludicrous.

CHAPTER VII

ISRAEL POTTER AND THE CONFIDENCE MAN

> "Shall we their fond pageant see?
> Lord, what fools these mortals be."
> Shakespeare, *A Midsummer Night's Dream*

Israel Potter (1854) and *The Confidence Man* (1857) have little in common except their chronological position, for they are Melville's last two full-length novels, and the yoking of these works together in one chapter is highly artificial. Since this study attempts to deal with all of Melville's fiction and poetry, however, something must be said about the earlier of these two novels, yet it is obvious that devoting an entire chapter to *Israel Potter* is impossible. Commenting briefly on this work in a section devoted primarily to *The Confidence Man*, therefore, seems the best solution.

Israel Potter portrays the adventures of an obscure and unfortunate American soldier who is captured by the British during America's struggle for independence. From its subject matter, no book would seem to initially be more appropriate for a discussion of pacifism and rebellion, for *Israel Potter* concerns itself with not only war but with revolution as well. This promise is not fulfilled, though, for the novel contains little beyond the level of simplest narration. There are no philosophical digressions, and Israel, though by no means unintelligent, is one of the least contemplative heroes imaginable, never for a moment considering any of the broader implications of the Revolutionary War. Melville tries halfheartedly to broaden the scope of the work by introducing some symbolism into the closing sections. This is indicated by chapter headings such as "Israel in Egypt" and "In the City of Dis". In addition, Potter works for a short time in a great brickyard whose kiln becomes a symbol of hell. But such symbolism appears infrequently, only at the end of the novel, and most important of all, has no organic connection with anything that happens in the rest of the book.

Only once during the novel does Melville comment on the nature of war. At the close of the titanic battle between the *Bon Homme Richard* and the *Serapis*, he writes:

The loss of life in the two ships was about equal; one-half of the total number of those engaged either killed or wounded.

In view of this battle, one may ask – What separates the enlightened man from the savage? Is civilization a thing distinct, or is it an advanced stage of barbarism?[1]

If this passage were further developed, it could possibly have been an indication of the beginning of a return to the philosophy of *White-Jacket*, but Melville seems content to let the matter rest.

Israel Potter's autobiography, upon which the novel is based, would seem to have offered the author of *Moby-Dick* ideal material for a profound and moving work. But Melville ignored any of the deeper suggestion of the story, and merely produced an enjoyable but trivial historical novel.

In *Pierre*, Melville reached an artistic and philosophical dead end. The novel was failure as a piece of literature, and the philosophy expounded by its hero was so extreme as to make the general reading public think that its author was insane, though it seems to me that any direct identification of Pierre with Melville himself is extremely dubious. *Israel Potter*, which followed two years later, is too slight a work to indicate that Melville had developed further as a thinker or had regained his artistic touch. With the writing of *The Piazza Tales* and *The Confidence Man*, his last full-length novel,[2] however, we once again find Melville in full artistic

---

[1] *Israel Potter*, in *The Romances of Herman Melville* (New York, 1931), p. 1438.

[2] Though this thesis supposedly deals with Melville's works in chronological order, I have discussed *The Confidence Man*, which was published in 1857, before I have talked about *The Piazza Tales*, which were collected and published a year earlier. All evidence indicates that the novel and most

control. *The Confidence Man* is not another *Moby-Dick*, to be sure, but it is, nonetheless, a well-written and important work. This book differs in many ways from any of the preceeding novels. To begin with, it is the only lengthy work of Melville's which is a sustained satire. In addition, though the heroes of the earlier novels may have a great many shortcomings, they are always presented sympathetically. This is not true of the title figure of *The Confidence Man*, who is at best portrayed in a neutral light. Finally, it is the only novel by Melville which contains neither any physical action nor has any pretense of plot, being merely a string of episodes tied together by a tight control of imagery, a dominating central theme, and the continued presence – in various guises – of the Confidence Man himself.

Specifically in terms of our topic, *The Confidence Man*, like *White-Jacket*, might be regarded as throwing a monkey wrench into the otherwise more-or-less smooth chronological development of pacifism and rebellion, or, more constructively, as a healthy philosophical muddying of the waters. Pacifism and rebellion do not entirely disappear in *The Confidence Man*. The deaf-mute, who returns the blows of the crowd with a message of love would be a pacifist in the best tradition of *White-Jacket*, were he not, in all probability, a fraud. In the person of Colonel John Moredock, a man who because he thinks all red men are evil, dedicates his life with an almost religious-like zeal to the hating and killing of Indians, we recognize a character not dissimilar to Captain Ahab in his remorseless pursuit of the White Whale. For the most part, though, pacifism and rebellion do not play an integral role in the novel, nor do they appear as polarities. In fact, some of the previously antithetical aspects of these two philosophies are mixed

---

of the tales were written at approximately the same period, however. For a fuller discussion of the time of writing, see Leon Howard, *Herman Melville*, Berkeley and Los Angeles, 1958, and Elizabeth Foster's introduction to the Hendricks House *The Confidence Man*, New York, 1954. Therefore, since there is no real time difference between the two works, and since I have linked *The Confidence Man* with *Israel Potter* (1854), I decided to deal with Melville's short stories after these two works, simply because it enables me to analyze all of Melville's novels in one block before moving on to a discussion of his writings in a different genre.

together in this work. Generally speaking, Christianity has been associated with pacifism, the use of physical violence – as seen in the actions of Taji and Pierre – has been linked with rebellion. But in *The Confidence Man*, not only does the stooped Titan, who is a misanthrope and opposed to the granting of confidence, strike the herb-doctor, but a Methodist minister, a champion of confidence and Christianity, assaults the man with the wooden leg because the latter insists that only a fool would have confidence in mankind. What *The Confidence Man* does do is to explore some of the foundations upon which the philosophies of pacifism and rebellion are based: the nature of God and the nature of man, the conflict between truth and faith, etc. As regards our topic, *The Confidence Man* represents re-examination and suspended judgment rather than restatement and further development.

The action of the novel takes place on April Fool's Day aboard the ironically named steamer, the *Fidèle*, which travels between Saint Louis and New Orleans. The Mississippi River, on which the *Fidèle* sails, not only divides American in two, but there is at least the hint that this implies a similar division in the nature of man. This river reflects the spirit of the West, and "uniting the streams of the most distant and opposite zones, pours them along, helter-skelter, in one *cosmopolitan* and *confident* tide."[3] [Italics my own.] The passengers aboard the *Fidèle* constitute every conceivable type of human being, "a piebald parliament, an Anacharsis Cloots congress of all kinds of that multiform pilgrim species, man."[4] Not only is Melville once again using a ship to symbolize the entire world, but we find here also that the trip from Saint Louis to New Orleans represents the journey of man's life.

The first scene sets the tone for the entire novel. On the lower deck of the *Fidèle*, a milling throng has gathered around a poster which offers a reward for a mysterious imposter from the East. Through this crowd edges a strange-looking man without luggage, "in the extremest sense of the word, a stranger".[5] Finally arriving near the reward-offering poster, he holds up a small slate on

[3] *The Confidence Man* (New York, 1955), p. 18.
[4] *Ibid.*, p. 18.
[5] *Ibid.*, p. 11.

which appear the words *"Charity thinketh no evil."* The crowd responds to this message by jostling the stranger, who turns out to be deaf as well as mute. Apparently undiscouraged however, he erases his tablet and holds up a different saying: *"Charity suffereth long, and is kind."* With this, the crowd's jostles turn to blows. But the mute, "apparently a non-resistant",[6] changes his writing to *"Charity endureth all things."* followed by *"Charity believeth all things."* and finally, *"Charity never faileth."* As the crowd still continues to shove the unfortunate man, however, he retires to a secluded part of the deck where he falls asleep, and soon quietly disappears.

While the mute is writing this message of charity from *Corinthians* on his slate, the ship's barber rudely pushes aside the crowd and elevates a pasteboard sign on which appears the image of an upraised razor with the words "NO TRUST" underneath it. Oddly enough, the crowd, which had responded with hostility to the mute, seems not at all to object either to the barber's shoving or to his sign. This juxtaposition of charity or confidence against no trust or lack of confidence and the reaction of people to these two beliefs appear throughout the novel in an infinite variety of situations and forms. But it must be emphasized that the exact nature of confidence and lack of trust are not static, but always are changing in one way or another. This constant shifting of positions gives the novel a certain enigmatic quality, for as John Cawelti notes, Melville "presents something for the reader to hold unto and then snatches it away by presenting its contrary".[7]

After the disappearance of the deaf-mute, the center of the stage is taken by Black Guinea, a crippled Negro who shuffles around like a Newfoundland dog, expertly catching in his mouth pennies that are thrown by the crowd. At the height of this game of charity, "a limping gimlet-eyed, sour-faced person"[8] with a wooden leg accuses Black Guinea of being a sham, a white man assuming the guise of a deformed Negro for financial purposes.

---

[6] *Ibid.*, p. 13.
[7] "Some Notes on the Structure of *The Confidence Man*", *AL*, XXIX (Nov., 1957), p. 281.
[8] *The Confidence Man* (New York, 1955), p. 20.

The hitherto sympathetic crowd turns on the Negro and demands that he show them documentary proof that he is what he appears. When the Negro moans that he has none, a friendly Episcopal clergyman asks him if there is no one who will vouch for him.

"Oh yes, oh yes, ge'mmen," he eagerly answered, as if his memory, before suddenly frozen up by cold charity, as suddenly thawed back into fluidity at the first kindly word. "Oh yes, oh yes, dar is aboard here a werry nice, good ge'mman wid a weed, and a ge'mman in a gray coat and white tie, what knows all about me; and a ge'mman wid a big book, too; and a yarb-doctor; and a ge'mman in a yaller west; and a ge'mman wid a brass plate; and a ge'mman in a wiolet robe; and a ge'mman as is a sodjer; and eber so many good, kind, honest ge'mman more aboard what knows me and will speak for me, God bress 'em; yes, and what knows me as well as dis poor old darkie knows hisself, God bress him! Oh, find 'em, find 'em," he earnestly added, "and let 'em come quick, and show you all, ge'mmen, dat dis old darky is werry well wordy of all you kind ge'mmen's kind confidence."[9]

This list of men suggested by Black Guinea is, generally speaking, the list of disguises assumed by the Confidence Man. Black Guinea is followed by the man with the weed, who is in turn followed by the man in the gray coat and white tie, then the man with the big book, then the herb doctor, and then the man with the plate. There is no man in a yellow vest, the soldier who appears briefly is himself gulled by the herb-doctor – ergo it is impossible for him to be the Confidence Man – and the gentleman in the "wiolet robe", though he does appear, presents a special problem, with which we will concern ourselves shortly.

Critics who argue that *The Confidence Man* is an unfinished work – and a poorly organized one at that – should take a careful look at the divisions of the book and at the careful progression from one type of confidence man to another. *The Confidence Man* contains forty-five chapters. Chapters 1-22 concern the Confidence Man – excluding for a moment the problem presented by the deaf-mute – in six disguises. Chapter 23, with the exception of the last sentence, has as its subject the meditations of the dyspeptic Missourian after he realizes that the has been fleeced. The final twenty-

[9] *Ibid.*, pp. 22-3.

two chapters deal with Frank Goodman, the confidence man supreme. Thus we can see that the book is divided exactly in the middle. Furthermore, the nature of the Confidence Man changes as the book progresses. Discounting the deaf-mute, the first three guises the Confidence Man assumes (Black Guinea, the man with the weed who tells a hard luck story, and the man in the gray coat who claims to be an agent of the Seminole Widow and Orphan Asylum) appeal to the charity and kind-heartedness of his victims. In his next three guises (John Truman who is the man with the book and the agent for the Black Rapids Coal Company, the herb doctor, and the man with the brass plate who represents the Philosophical Intelligence Office) the Confidence Man is not a charity case, but is a man who offers some sort of service to his victim. In each of these three cases, he appeals not to man's kindness and charity but to his greed or self-interest. Frank Goodman, though he retains many of the characteristics of the preceeding confidence men, has a subtlety and complexity lacking in the others, and is interested in somewhat higher and different stakes.

With the appearance of Frank Goodman, Melville begins to play a guessing game with the reader. One critic has noted that much of the suspense of the novel is generated by sudden reversals, reversals of roles and characters, etc.[10] Melville combines this technique of reversal with the inexact description by Black Guinea of one of his friends to successfully camouflage the identity of the Confidence Man, and in this way, to further confuse and amuse the reader. According to the list of friends advanced by old Guinea, the man with the brass plate should be followed by a man in a "wiolet robe". Shortly after the Missourian has been swindled by the man with the brass plate, he is approached by someone sporting "a vesture barred with various hues, that of the cochineal predominating, in style participating of a Highland plaid, Emir's robe, and French blouse",[11] who identifies himself as "A cosmopolitan, a catholic man".[12] Despite his protestations of being a philan-

---

[10] John Cawelti, *op. cit.*
[11] *The Confidence Man* (New York, 1955), p. 158.
[12] *Ibid.*, p. 159.

thropist, the man in the Emir's robe is accused by the Missourian of being Diogenes masquerading in the guise of a cosmopolitan, so the former quickly retreats. The cosmopolitan is in turn approached by a stranger wearing a "violet vest sending up sunset hues".[13] Both men, therefore, are not only dressed similarly, but both are clothed somewhat like the man in a "wiolet robe" in which garb we expect the Confidence Man to appear. At this stage it is impossible for us to decide which man is the novel's protagonist.

Both the stranger and the cosmopolitan spout forth the same line of brotherly love, profess everlasting friendship, and attempt to get each other drunk over a comradely bottle of port. Suddenly the cosmopolitan, taking advantage of the stranger's continual protestations of esteem and trust, asks to borrow some money. The stranger, one Charles Arnold Noble, leaps to his feet, crying "'Go to the devil, sir! Beggar! imposter! – never so deceived in a man in my life.'"[14] "At last," we think, "It is the cosmopolitan who is the Confidence Man." But we have reached our decision too soon, for the cosmopolitan draws ten half-eagles out of his pocket and "with the air of a necromancer"[15] lays them in a circle around his erstwhile friend, claiming that his request for money was just a joke. The stranger, pretending to relish this exposure as a good prank also, claims that his reactions of anger was also part of the fun. After a few minutes, however, Noble staggers off to bed.

The problem of identification becomes more complicated immediately thereafter, for the cosmopolitan is promptly approached by one Mark Winsome, a mystic, who warns him that his supposed friend Charles is nothing but a "Mississippi operator",[16] at the same time protesting that he, Mark Winsome, is confident that the cosmopolitan "must be a beautiful soul – one full of all love and truth; for where beauty is, there those must be".[17] If we accept Mark Winsome's evaluations, it would appear that the stranger is

[13] *Ibid.*, p. 167.
[14] *Ibid.*, p. 213.
[15] *Ibid.*, p. 213.
[16] *Ibid.*, p. 229.
[17] *Ibid.*, p. 221.

the Confidence Man and that the cosmopolitan isn't. But since Egbert Olivar[18] has pretty clearly established that Mark Winsome is a caricature of Ralph Waldo Emerson, it seems quite possible that Melville could here be satirizing Emerson's inability to recognize evil when confronted with it, to be unable to tell who is a fraud and who isn't. If we accept this interpretation, the fact that Winsome thinks that the cosmopolitan has such a beautiful soul would be just so much added irony.

Eventually we conclude that the cosmopolitan, whose name is Frank Goodman, is the Confidence Man, primarily because he succeeds in conning the barber, the one who had posted a "NO TRUST" sign outside of his shop in the first chapter, for a free shave, and also because he stays on the scene for the rest of the novel.

Before any interpretation of the book can be developed, it must first be determined whether the deaf-mute is in reality the Confidence Man or not. A majority of the critics think that the mute and Frank Goodman are one and the same man, but they give no reasons for their conclusions. It seems to me that two arguments might be advanced which would at least suggest that both are the identical person. The first is structural. After the first two chapters, there is never a time in the novel in which either the Confidence Man or someone he has swindled or both are not the center of attention. Therefore, it seems as if the structure of the novel would demand that the Confidence Man should appear at the beginning of the book as well, and if this is true, the only person who he could be is the deaf-mute, a man who champions the cause of charity in the face of a hostile crowd. There is a much better argument, though, and this is to be found in the imagery. Though the mute is not described in great detail, it is stated that he had a hat with "a long *fleecy* nap",[19] and shortly thereafter, a member of the crowd with an unobserved stroke" dextrously flattened down his *fleecy* hat upon his head".[20] When Black

---

[18] "Melville's Picture of Emerson and Thoreau in *The Confidence Man*", CE, VIII (Nov., 1946), 61-72.
[19] *The Confidence Man* (New York, 1955), p. 11.
[20] *Ibid.*, p. 12.

Guinea appears immediately after the mute's exit, his hair is pictured as being "knotted black *fleece*".[21] Not only are variations of the same word used in describing both men, but since one of the meanings of the verb "to fleece" means "to swindle", there seems to be a good chance that the words "fleecy" and "fleece" are consciously being used by the author as a means of linking together the mute and the Negro.

If the deaf-mute is one of the guises of the Confidence Man, another complication arises, for there is no question that he is described in Christ-like terms. After he brings a message of charity and meekly endures the blows of the unruly crowd, he lies down next to a ladder "leading to a deck above",[22] where "gradually overtaken by slumber, his flaxen head drooped, his whole *lamb-like* figure relaxed . . ."[23] [Italics my own.] Critics such as James Miller seize upon this imagery and go so far as to say that the Confidence Man appears as Jesus in the opening chapter, and thus conclude that the theme of the novel is "that Christ's heavenly doctrine of charity (love) is unworkable, at least in any absolute sense, among human beings on earth".[24] If this approach is accepted, *The Confidence Man* would be a continuation of the conflict between chronometrical and horological time that we have found in *Pierre*, and thus the work would fit snugly into our study of pacifism and rebellion.

Unfortunately, this interpretation is challenged in a brilliant article by J. W. Schroeder, who argues that the Confidence Man should be equated with Satan because of the satanic and snake imagery which is constantly associated with him.[25] There are innumerable examples of this throughout the novel. The herb-doctor is called a snake by the stooped Titan who boards at the houseless landing. Later, Frank Goodman talks of the "latent

---

[21] *Ibid.*, p. 18.
[22] *Ibid.*, p. 14.
[23] *Ibid.*, p. 15.
[24] "*The Confidence Man:* His Guises", *PMLA*, LXXIV (March, 1959), p. 106.
[25] "Sources and Symbols for Melville's *The Confidence Man*", *PMLA*, LXVI (June, 1951), 363-80.

benignity of that beautiful creature, the rattle-snake",[26] and "as he breathed these words, he seemed to enter into their spirit – as some earnest and descriptive speakers will – as unconsciously to wreathe his form and sidelong crest his head, till he all but seemed the creature described". After the Confidence Man finally succeeds in taking in the misanthropic Missourian, he immediately leaves the ship at a place known as the Devil's Joke.

Could the Confidence Man represent both Christ and the Devil? This possibility is at least humorously implied by the man with the big book who is at once an agent for the Black Rapids Coal Company (hell) and who also sells shares in a concern known as New Jerusalem (heaven). Though there is no one-to-one relationship between the Confidence Man and either Christ or Satan, he contains elements of both. These contradictory qualities within *The Confidence Man* serve many purposes. Not only do they make a more interesting and complex figure of the Confidence Man and prepare the reader for the partial metamorphosis of the central figure when he assumes the guise of Frank Goodman, but they suggest the duality inherent in human life. An awareness of the Christ and Satan imagery associated with the Confidence Man prevents the reader from falling into the same trap that many of the characters in the novel fall into; assuming that the Confidence Man represents either unmitigated evil and must be rejected no matter what the means, or that he stands for pure good, and that to question his motives in some way reflects badly upon the questioner himself. Finally, both the Christ and Satan imagery help to emphasize the almost supernatural quality of the protagonist. Melville's Confidence Man is no mere mortal, nor is the novel a realistic account of the actions of a swindler. No person could exchange a disguise as rapidly, or for that matter, be such a master of disguise as our Confidence Man. Not only does the Missourian refer to the herb doctor and the man from the Philosophical Intelligence Agency as "extraordinary metaphysical scamps",[27] but he is continually being described in terms which stress his more-than-human aspect. In the scenes with Charles

---

[26] *The Confidence Man* (New York, 1955), p. 222.
[27] *Ibid.*, p. 163.

"ISRAEL POTTER" AND "THE CONFIDENCE MAN" 157

Noble, for instance, he is called a "necromancer" and creates a "magic ring".[28]

If the Confidence Man is a metaphysical scamp, exactly what is the nature and purpose of his game? Obviously, his major interest is not cash but confidence, for he will accept money only if his victim also puts faith in him as well. His real motivations are pegged by the wooden-legged man who accuses Black Guinea of being a fraud. "'Money, you think, is the sole motive to pains and hazard, deception and deviltry, in this world. How much money did the devil make by gulling Eve?'"[29]

Not only is his object the transfer of confidence, but, in her exhaustive introduction to the Hendricks House edition of the novel, Elizabeth Foster suggests that the type of confidence being peddled varies with the guise of the protagonist. Thus, Miss Foster argues, "the message of the man with the big book is "Trust God"; that of the herb-doctor, "Trust Nature"; and that of the man with the brass plate and the cosmopolitan, "Trust Man'".[30]

The premise which the Confidence Man offers to his prospective victims is that the universe, the world, nature, man, etc., are, in all but the most minor ways, perfect. As James Miller notes, "The constant argument of all these individuals is that suspicion and pessimism are evil, and an optimistic confidence, particularly in the speaker as an individual, is the greatest of virtues."[31] The Confidence Man uses this proposition with endless variations. When the crippled Thomas Fry, who had unjustly been imprisoned for murder, makes sarcastic comments about "free Ameriky", the Confidence Man replies.

"You, my worthy friend, to my concern, have reflected upon the government under which you live and suffer. Where is your patriotism? Where your gratitude? True, the charitable may find something

---

[28] *Ibid.*, p. 213.
[29] *Ibid.*, p. 45.
[30] *Op. cit.*, pp. lvi-lvii. Miss Foster's lengthy introduction to the Hendricks House edition is one of the most thorough and useful pieces of Melville criticism in existence.
[31] *Op. cit.*, p. 103.

in your case, as you put it, partly to account for such reflections coming from you. Still, be the facts how they may, your reflections are none the less unwarrantable. Grant, for the moment, that your experiences are as you give them; in which case I would admit that government might be thought to have more or less to do with what seems undesirable in them. *But it is never to be forgotten that human government, being subordinate to the divine, must needs, therefore, in its degree, partake of the characteristics of the divine. That is, while in the general efficacious to happiness, the world's law may yet, in some case, have, to the eye of reason, an unequal operation, just as, in the same imperfect view, some inequalities may appear in the operations of heaven's law; nevertheless, to one who has a right confidence, final benignity, is, in every instance, as sure with the one law as the other.* I expound this point at some length, because these are the considerations, my poor fellow, which, weighed as they merit, will enable you to sustain with unimpaired trust the apparent calamities which are yours.[32] [Italics my own.]

Shortly after this statement, the herb-doctor succeeds in selling some herbs to the sickly old miser, convincing the latter that if anything is a pure product of nature, it must be *ipso facto* good. This phony type of optimism peddled by the Confidence Man is effectively countered by the Missourian, who overhearing the transaction between the herb-doctor and the miser, ridicules the latter for his trust in nature.

"Because a thing is nat'ral, as you call it, you think it must be good. But who gave you that cough? Was it, or was it not, nature?"
"Sure, you don't think that natur, Dame Natur, will hurt a body do you?"
"Natur is good Queen Bess; but who's responsible for the cholera?"
"But yarbs, yarbs, yarbs are good?"
"What's deadly-nightshade? Yarb, ain't it?"
"Oh, that a Christian man should speak agin natur and yarbs – ugh, ugh, ugh! – ain't sick men sent out into the country; sent out to natur and grass?"
"Ay, and poets send out the sick spirit to green pastures, like lame horses turned out unshod to the turf to renew their hoofs. A sort of yarb-doctors in their way, poets have it that for sore hearts, as for sore lungs, nature is the grand cure. But who froze to death my

---

[32] *The Confidence Man* (New York, 1955), pp. 119-20.

teamster on the prairie? And who made an idiot of Peter the Wild Boy?"[33]

In keeping with the ironic reversals upon which the novel revolves, the Missourian is soon gulled by the man with the brass plate, who persuades the former that he should have trust in man.

I have mentioned earlier that the appearance of Frank Goodman adds a quality of dramatic tension to the novel. More important, the character of Goodman introduces much of the thematic complexity of *The Confidence Man*. Frank Goodman differs radically from all of his predecessors. They are without exception swindlers, even though their primary interest is confidence and not cash, and their voices are the voices of falsehood. In this respect, Goodman is almost antithetical to the Confidence Man in his other disguises. He takes money from no one, rather he gives it away with compassion to the haggard peddlar of philosophical tracts, with scorn to Egbert, the ice-hearted disciple of Mark Winsome. His goal no longer seems to be the deception of the greedy and naive, but rather exposure of false do-gooders such as Charles Noble and Mark Winsome. The voice of the Confidence Man, which throughout the novel has been the voice of falsehood, becomes, for the greater part, in the person of Frank Goodman the voice of truth. When Frank Goodman turns in anger to Egbert, Mark Winsome's disciple, and denounces the latter's philosophy for its coldness and lack of humanity, we find in his words real feeling and real condemnation, not merely the pat phrases that he has previously used to gull his victims.

"Enough, I have had my fill of the philosophy of Mark Winsome as put into action. And moonshiny as it in theory may be, yet a very practical philosophy it turns out in effect, as he himself engaged I should find. But, miserable for my race should I be, if I thought he spoke truth when he claimed, for proof of the soundness of his system, that the study of it tended to much the same formation of character with the experiences of the world. – Apt disciple! Why wrinkle the brow and waste the oil both of life and the lamp, only to turn out a head kept cool by the under ice of the heart? What your illustrious magian has taught you, any poor, old, broken-down,

[33] *Ibid.*, pp. 128-9.

heart-shrunken dandy might have lisped. Pray, leave me, and with you take the last dregs of your inhuman philosophy. And here, take this shilling, and at the first wood-landing buy yourself a few chips to warm the frozen natures of you and your philosopher by." [34]

The association of both Christ and Satan imagery with the protagonist and the apparent differences between Frank Goodman and the earlier guises assumed by the Confidence Man make the meaning of the last chapter of the novel, entitled "The Cosmopolitan Increases in Seriousness," somewhat ambiguous. While the others sleep, Goodman and a kindly old man sit beneath the last remaining lighted lamp in the gentlemen's cabin, discussing the Bible. While the aged gentleman is protesting his confidence in his fellow man, a strange young boy enters the cabin and sells the old man a lock for his state-room door and a money belt to prevent him from being robbed, and also gives him, free of charge, a little pamphlet called the *Counterfeit Detector*. After checking two recent bills with the *Counterfeit Detector* to determine their genuineness and being unable to decide whether they are real or not, torn between confidence and distrust, the old man decides to go to bed.

"Ah, my way now," cried the old man, peering before him, "where lies my way to my state-room?"
"I have indifferent eyes, and will show you; but, first, for the good of all lungs, let me extinguish this lamp."
The next moment, the waning light expired, and with it the waning flame of the horned altar, and the waning halo, round the robed man's brow; while in the darkness which ensued, the cosmopolitan kindly led the old man away. Something further may follow of this Masquerade.[35]

This final scene, I believe, is somewhat allegorical of the human situation in general. Man lives in a world of darkness in which nothing is certain, and neither the cabin lamp nor the *Counterfeit Detector* are sufficiently certain or illuminating to act as a cicerone for the human race. All men must grope their way in the dark, sure of nothing, torn, as is the old man, between skepticism and

[34] *Ibid.*, p. 261.
[35] *Ibid.*, p. 294

faith. Re-enforcing this interpretation is Elizabeth Foster's argument that the cabin lamp "variegated, in transparency, with the image of a horned altar, from which flames rose, alternate with the figure of a robed man, his head encircled by a halo",[36] symbolizes Christianity,[37] and hence the waning light indicates that religion no longer offers hope or meaning to modern man.

On a more specific level, the old gentleman surrenders his fate into the hands of Frank Goodman, whom we know to be the Confidence Man. The chances are great that he will be led out into the dark and fleeced, as has been the case with the miser and the good merchant. Yet, because Frank Goodman seems different than the other swindlers, there is a faint possibility that the old gentleman's confidence will not be betrayed, and that he will be guided safely and "kindly" to his destination. There is a faint chance, perhaps, that confidence in one's fellow man many result in salvation.

The philosophy of rebellion as advocated by Ahab and Pierre is sharply challenged in *The Confidence Man*, while at the same time, the previous skepticism concerning pacifism as a way of life is still apparent in the novel. The rebel-hero had felt that the universe is essentially amoral or evil and that to have faith in the powers of the cosmos is basically a dishonest position. In Melville's earlier novels, there seems to be the tacit assumption that truth must be pursued at all costs. Ahab, Pierre, and probably Taji pursue truth so intensely and uncompromisingly that it leads to their own destruction. The opposite of the man of truth is the man of faith such as Starbuck, who believes in the essential order and morality of nature and God. The man of truth and the man of faith are constantly at odds with one another, and generally speaking, Melville sides with the former. Though *The Confidence Man* still pictures the universe as being hostile to man, the choice between faith and trust is no longer as clear cut as it has been in the previous novels.

The conflict between truth and faith or confidence is quite apparent in the novel and is readily recognized by both those who

[36] *Ibid.*, p. 279.
[37] *Op. cit.*, p. lxxxiv.

place their trust in the Confidence Man and those who withhold their confidence. The man with the wooden leg, who is the first to challenge the veracity of Black Guinea's lameness, hits the nail on the head when he is asked by the Methodist minister why he has no charity. "'Charity is one thing, and truth another',"[38] he rejoins. Even Mr. Roberts, the good-natured merchant who is duped three times by the Confidence Man, realized the dichotomy between truth and confidence. Over a bottle of wine, he confides the following to the man who represents the Black Rapids Coal Company:

"Ah, wine is good, and confidence is good; but can wine or confidence percolate down through all the stony strata of hard considerations, and drop warmly and ruddily into the cold cave of truth? Truth will *not* be comforted. Led by dear charity, lured by sweet hope, fond fancy essays this feat; but in vain; mere dreams and ideals, they explode in your hand, leaving naught but the scorching behind!"[39]

So bitterly satirical is *The Confidence Man*, however, that the conflict between truth and faith is usually presented in much simpler and less euphemistic terms. The Missourian suggests that all mankind can be divided into two classes, fools and knaves, and this is the point made over and over again by the Confidence Man. Perhaps the best gauge as to the pessimism of the novel is that Melville apparently feels that there is no middle ground between truth and faith, knaves and fools. The novel is conspicuous for its lack of just one character who can in all honesty and sincerity say to the Confidence Man, "I would gladly give to any worthy charity or to any person in real need of assistance, but I will give nothing to you because you are a fraud." If someone has pity on Black Guinea or believes the hokum about nature being essentially kind, he is a fool, no matter how good-hearted and noble his motivations might be. Indeed, the more kindly and generous the individual – as is the case with Mr. Roberts and the Episcopal minister – the more often is he gulled, and hence the bigger fool is he. On the other hand, men such as the stooped Titan and the

[38] *The Confidence Man* (New York, 1955), p. 23.
[39] Ibid., p. 84.

man with the wooden leg – men who immediately recognize the Confidence Man for what he is – are out and out misanthropes. Melville underlines the misanthropy of those who reject the Confidence Man by continually describing them as not only being personally disagreeable, but as also being in some ways deformed or dressed in the skins of animals, etc. The choice between truth and faith is here presented as a Hobson's choice between malevolence and stupidity, no longer dramatized in terms of Ahab and Starbuck, but in terms of the old miser and the woodenlegged misanthrope.

Related to the above point, *The Confidence Man* further challenges another of the tenets of rebellion. In his other novels, Melville's rebel-heroes had concluded that mankind, at least in the abstract, was far nobler than the elements which surrounded him or the powers which had created him. Even in *Pierre*, which is certainly a strong indictment of human society, there is no condemnation of mankind in the abstract. In *The Confidence Man*, however, Melville not only continues to ridicule the concept that nature or God are basically good, but he also attacks the idea that man is any better than the powers which govern the cosmos. As we have seen, the novel implies that *all* men are either knaves or fools. Every character in the book falls into one of these two categories except for the Confidence Man himself, and as I have suggested earlier, he is no mere mortal but perhaps symbolizes the inscrutable and treacherous forces at work both in the world of man and the world of nature. The foundations of Melville's philosophy of pacifism as developed in *White-Jacket* had been shaken when the concept of the goodness or even the existence of God had been attacked. On the other hand, when the basic integrity and intelligence of the whole of mankind is questioned, the type of rebellion practiced by Ahab, who is a Promethean-like champion of the human race and who says that a man is a far nobler thing than the wind, must be re-examined.

The Confidence Man does not fit neatly into our thesis that the conflict between pacifism and rebellion is to be found at the center of most of Melville's works. Rather it is a novel which examines some of the assumptions basic to the philosophies of pacifism and rebellion. As a result of this re-evaluation, when pacifism and rebellion appear as polarities once again in Melville's later writings, they are in a somewhat different and more complex form.

CHAPTER VIII

THE SHORT STORIES:
A PARTIAL RECONCILIATION
OF DIFFERENCES

> To suffer woes which Hope thinks infinite
> To forgive wrongs darker than death or night;
> To defy Power, which seems omnipotent;
> To love, and bear; to hope till Hope creates
> From its own wreck the thing it contemplates
> Neither to change, nor falter, nor repent; –
> This, like thy glory, Titan, is to be
> Good, great and joyous, beautiful and free;
> This is alone Life, Joy, Empire, and Victory!
> Shelley, *Prometheus Unbound*

Melville's short stories, which along with *Moby-Dick* and *Billy Budd* represent his best prose writing, were all composed between 1853 and 1856. The most impressive of these tales – "Benito Cereno", "Bartleby the Scrivener", "The Lightning-Rod Man", "The Encantadas", and "The Bell-Tower" – were collected and published in the spring of 1856 in a volume entitled *The Piazza Tales* along with a sketch called "The Piazza" which Melville wrote especially as an introduction to this volume. Many of Melville's short stories, such as "The Two Temples", are slight, and have nothing to do with pacifism and rebellion. The finest of his tales, "Bartleby the Scrivener" and "Benito Cereno" are concerned with these issues, the one being a humorous yet pathetic and probing study of passive resistance, the other dealing with the bloody native revolt aboard the Spanish slave ship, the *San Dominick*. Perhaps the most important aspect of the short stories in terms of our topic, however, is the emergence of a new attitude, a sort of defiant stoicism (similar to that expressed in the lines quoted from *Prometheus Unbound* at the beginning of this chapter), which, without resolving any of the differences between pacifism and rebellion, lies half-way between these two philosophies, and which foreshadows the thematic conclusion of *Clarel*. Although this attitude is most apparent in the magnificent "The Encantadas," it also appears to a lesser extent in several other of Melville's tales.

"Bartleby the Scrivener"

"Bartleby the Scrivener" is one of the most perplexing of Melville's stories. Though Merlin Bowen in *The Long Encounter* makes the mistake of classifying Bartleby as a modern Prometheus, he does astutely put his finger on one of the central problems of the tale when he writes of the title character that "the exact line between defense and offense is, in this matter as in others, not easy to define".[1] In other words, it is often impossible to determine whether Bartleby represents resistance or resignation. Another puzzling aspect is the question of who is the central figure of the story. If Bartleby is the hero, then comic as the tale may be, it is nevertheless a story of death and despair. If, on the other hand, one believes as I do that the lawyer is the most important character, "Bartleby" is concerned with the gradual growth and understanding on the part of the narrator as a result of his exposure to Bartleby and the latter's passive resistance.

At the beginning of the work, the lawyer, who describes himself as an "eminently safe man"[2] with a "profound conviction that the easiest way of life is the best",[3] is a person whose sole concern is with comfort and reputation, a man who, though in no way cruel, is absolutely selfish and feels not the slightest concern for his fellow humans. Because he has been recently appointed a Master In Chancery by the State of New York, the narrator needs another scrivener in his office, and for this position he hires a pale and earnest young man named Bartleby. Bartleby proves to be an ideal workman for quite a while, until one day the lawyer asks him to

---

[1] Chicago, 1960, p. 134.
[2] In Richard Chase (ed.), *Selected Poems and Tales by Herman Melville* (New York, 1956), p. 93.
[3] *Ibid.*, p. 92.

proofread a copy. Much to the narrator's amazement, Bartleby responds " 'I would prefer not to.' "[4] As the days go by, Bartleby's "I would prefer not to" becomes a more and more frequent response to the lawyer's requests.

Since the barrister's demands are highly reasonable, requesting only the minimum of what should be expected of an employee, and since the lawyer himself is such a stickler for propriety, it would seem that he might fire Bartleby on the spot. But something about the non-belligerency of the latter's refusals prevents the lawyer from doing this.

Nothing so aggravates an earnest person as passive resistance. If the individual so resisted be of a not inhumane temper, and the resisting one perfectly harmless in his passivity, then, in the better moods of the former, he will endeavor charitably to construe to this imagination what proves impossible to be solved by his judgment. Even so, for the most part, I regarded Bartleby and his ways. Poor fellow! thought I, he means no mischief; it is plain he intends no insolence, his aspect sufficiently evinces that his eccentricities are involuntary. He is useful to me. I can get along with him. If I turn him away, the chances are he will fall in with some less-indulgent employer, and then he will be rudely treated, and perhaps driven forth miserably to starve.[5]

Bartleby has other surprises in store for the lawyer. One Sunday the narrator goes for a walk and decides to stop by his office briefly. When he inserts his key into the lock, he is greeted by Bartleby, who has apparently been living in the office for months and who informs the narrator that he would prefer not admitting him at the present. The lawyer is initially seized with "sundry twinges of impotent rebellion against the mild effrontry of this unaccountable scrivener",[6] but his anger swiftly changes to compassion.

Immediately then the thought came sweeping across me, what miserable friendlessness and loneliness are here revealed! His poverty is great; but his solitude, how horrible! Think of it. Of a Sunday, Wall Street is deserted as Petra; and every night of every day it is an emptiness. This building, too, which of weekdays hums with industry

[4] *Ibid.*, p. 101.
[5] *Ibid.*, pp. 104-5.
[6] *Ibid.*, p. 109.

168   THE SHORT STORIES: PARTIAL RECONCILIATION

and life, at nightfall echoes with sheer vacancy, and all through Sunday is forlorn. And here Bartleby makes his home; sole spectator of a solitude which he has seen all populous – a sort of innocent and transformed Marius brooding among the ruins of Carthage! [7]

With the best intentions at heart, the lawyer resolves to discuss the situation with Bartleby the next morning, but Bartleby refuses to be drawn out. When the lawyer pleads with him to be a little more reasonable, Bartleby replies "'At present I would prefer not to be a little reasonable.'"[8] The next day, Bartleby announces that he would prefer not to do any more copying. After a period of time, the lawyer kindly but firmly dismisses Bartleby, giving him some money on which to live. But Bartleby, defying all ultimatums, refuses to leave the office, telling the lawyer that he would prefer not to quit him for the present. Though the lawyer is again angered by Bartleby's behaviour, he has so grown in stature as a result of his exposure to the scrivener and his passive resistance that the former's charitable nature once again triumphs.

But when this old Adam of resentment rose in me and tempted me concerning Bartleby, I grappled him and threw him. How? Why, simply by recalling the divine injunction: "A new commandment give I unto you, that ye love one another." Yes, this it was that saved me.[9]

The lawyer virtually resolves to tolerate Bartleby and his idiosyncracies forever, but he fails, because like many other virtuous men, he is unwilling to go against public opinion. Clients who come into the office ask Bartleby to do some trivial duty, and he refuses. Soon the lawyer begins to fear that his professional reputation will be jeopardized and that people are making fun of him for tolerating Bartleby. Since Bartleby won't leave him, the lawyer resolves that he will leave Bartleby. But the lawyer can not this easily escape his duty, for even after he moves into new quarters, leaving Bartleby behind in the old office, he is approached by the new occupant who insists that Bartleby is the narrator's

[7] *Ibid.*, pp. 109-10.
[8] *Ibid.*, p. 113.
[9] *Ibid.*, p. 120.

responsibility. The lawyer goes back to his old chambers, tells Bartleby that he must leave the premises, and even offers to take Bartleby into his own house, to "remain there till we can conclude upon some convenient arrangement for you at our leisure".[10] When Bartleby refuses, saying that he would at the moment prefer not to move, the lawyer rushes away. Shortly thereafter, the lawyer receives a note saying that the scrivener has been taken to jail. He goes to visit his former employee but Bartleby does not wish to talk to him. When he next visits the jail, Bartleby is dead.

Though it is suggested that at one time Bartleby worked as a subordinate clerk in the Dead Letter Office, we learn little about what motivates Bartleby, and the exact nature of what Bartleby is resisting or quietly protesting against remains at least partially shrouded by mystery. A possible explanation, however, is to be found in the wall symbolism which recurs throughout the story.[11] The tale is sub-titled "A Story of Wall Street", and the double meaning of the word "Wall", referring to a specific street and to walls in general is obvious. The lawyer's office looks out upon two walls, one a "white wall of the interior of a spacious skylight shaft, penetrating the building from top to bottom", and the other, which was pushed within ten feet of the office windows, was "a lofty brick wall, black by age and everlasting shade".[12] When Bartleby comes to work, the lawyer assigns him a place by the corner of the folding doors which separate the two rooms of the office, and which is near a small side window.

Within three feet of the panes was a wall, and the light came down far from above, between two lofty buildings, as from a very small opening in a dome. Still further to a satisfactory arrangement, I procured a high green folding screen, which might entirely isolate Bartleby from my sight, though not remove him from my voice.[13]

This screen, which so effectively isolates Bartleby, is another species of wall. Bartleby spends most of his time behind the screen,

[10] *Ibid.*, p. 127.
[11] For a fuller discussion of wall symbolism in this story, see Leo Marx, "Melville's Parable of the Walls", *SR*, XLI (Autumn, 1953), 602-27.
[12] Chase, p. 93.
[13] *Ibid.*, p. 100.

looking out "upon the dead brick wall".[14] As the tale progresses, the narrator becomes more and more aware of the scrivener's "dead wall reveries".

When the lawyer visits Bartleby in prison, the scrivener is "standing all alone in the quietest of the yards, his face toward a high wall".[15] The lawyer tries to cheer him up by telling him that things aren't too bad.

"And to you, this should not be so vile a place. Nothing reproachful attaches to you by being here. And see, it is not so sad a place as one might think. Look, there is the sky, and here is the grass."
"I know where I am," he replied, but would say nothing more, and so I left him.[16]

Several days later, the lawyer again goes to see Bartleby, who is sleeping in a yard.

The yard was entirely quiet. It was not accessible to the common prisoners. The surrounding walls, of amazing thickness, kept off all sounds behind them. The Egyptian character of the masonry weighed upon me with its gloom. . . .
Strangely huddled at the base of the wall, his knees drawn up, and lying on his side, his head touching the cold stones, I saw the wasted Bartleby.[17]

Even in death, Bartleby is surrounded by the walls which so oppressed him during his life. The emphasis on walls not only in prison but in the lawyer's office as well, indicates that the two places are really alike. Or, as one critic observes, "the difference between Wall Street and the Tombs was an illusion of the lawyer's, not Bartleby's".[18]

Walls in "Bartleby the Scrivener" symbolize the isolation of the individual man and the sterility and hopelessness of human life. The fact that Bartleby is the character in the tale most conscious of walls indicates that he is most aware of the sterility and despair which they imply. The realization that mankind, whether in the

---

[14] *Ibid.*, p. 111.
[15] *Ibid.*, p. 128.
[16] *Ibid.*, pp. 128-9.
[17] *Ibid.*, p. 130.
[18] Leo Marx, *op. cit.*, p. 618.

Tombs or in the "outside" world, is everywhere imprisoned is what eventually destroys the scrivener.

The central irony of the tale is that although the passive resistance practiced by Bartleby does not save him from death and desperation, the exposure on the part of the lawyer to this philosophy eventually leads to his salvation. As we have seen, the narrator makes it clear that the only reason he initially tolerates Bartleby and eventually sympathizes with him is because of the type of resistance Bartleby offers. As a result of his sympathy for Bartleby, the lawyer outgrows his initial position of callousness and lack of concern for his fellows and comes to realize that no man is an island, that to be human means to be involved with the human situation. The final words of the tale, "Ah, Bartleby! Ah, humanity!", indicate to the reader that not only is Bartleby representative of mankind, but that the lawyer has matured in understanding and has, through his relationship with Bartleby, achieved a true perspective of man's fate.

Bartleby is the only one of Melville's' pacifists who is not either religiously oriented – such as Starbuck or Nehemiah – or a man who, though not necessarily an orthodox Christian, is continually described in terms of Christ imagery – such as Billy Budd. The scrivener is also one of the most enigmatic of Melville's characters. Though he is portrayed humorously, Bartleby is a delicate balance between almost schizophrenic withdrawal and surrender and an odd yet definite type of defiance. As the lawyer soon realizes, when Bartleby says he would prefer not to, he means that he *will* not. Though we cannot help but feel that the scrivener dies because he no longer prefers to live, it is also true, as Ronald Mason observes, that "Bartleby's death damns society, not himself".[19]

"Benito Cereno"

"Benito Cereno" is one of Melville's most prefectly constructed and complex works, and also is one of the few creations in which Melville is concerned with actual physical revolt or mutiny. Oddly enough, though "Benito Cereno" contains some of the basic

[19] *The Spirit Above the Dust* (London, 1951), p. 182.

themes which recur in Melville's writings – the discrepancy between appearance and reality, the struggle between the white "civilized" and the colored "primitive" races of the world, and the issue of freedom and slavery – the tale has little to do with the philosophy of rebellion. The reason for this is that though we enter into the mind of Captain Delano, through whose eyes most of the action is seen, and though we are told in retrospect at the close of the story the thoughts of Benito Cereno, we never penetrate into the consciousness of the mutineers.

Yet if one ignores the fact that on its simplest level "Benito Cereno" portrays an uprising of slaves, the story can easily be misunderstood. Many critics speak of Babo in terms of "motiveless malignity" and compare him to Iago. But to do this is to forget that Babo is the leader of a group of slaves who are seeking their freedom through the only possible way. To further the cause of the uprising aboard the *San Dominick*, Babo does some evil things, but this evil is motivated solely by a desire for freedom.[20] Indeed, Babo himself commits no murder, stops the mulatto steward Francesco from poisoning food intended for Captain Delano, and tries to prevent the Spaniards aboard the ship from being tortured by the other natives.

Nevertheless, despite the fact that one commentator observes that although "the mutineers are bloodthirsty and cruel, Melville does not make them into villains; they revolt as mankind has always revolted",[21] this revolt quickly gets out of hand. As I have tried to show elsewhere, much of the imagery and symbolism of the tale is drawn from the Spanish Inquisition.[22] In short, the rebellion aboard the *San Dominick* turns into an Inquisition.

The theme of the Inquisition in "Benito Cereno" is not used by Melville either to condemn the slaves' mutiny in this particular

---

[20] For a further development of this argument see Joseph Schiffman, "Critical Problems in Melville's 'Benito Cereno'," *MLQ*, XI (September, 1950), 317-24.

[21] Sterling Brown, *The Negro Character in American Fiction*, cited by Warren D'Azevedo, "Revolt on the San Dominick", *Phylon*, XVIII (2nd Quarter, 1958), 129-40.

[22] See my article, "*Benito Cereno* and the Spanish Inquisition". *NCF*, 16 (March, 1962), 345-50.

case, or as a comment about the general nature of all violent revolutions, though history would probably show that most bloody rebellions are immediately followed by Inquisition-like periods. Rather, Melville uses the Inquisition motif for structural purposes and to introduce a veiled warning. Much of the complexity and ambiguity of the tale is brought in by means of the Inquisition imagery. Thus, Babo is not merely the leader of a group of slaves and their liberator, but he also emerges as an inquisitor, an almost Torquemada-like figure. Benito Cereno is a weak and corrupt sea captain engaged in the trade of slavery, but he is also the victim of an Inquisition and a man who gains in stature as a result of the ordeal he undergoes. It is through the use of the Spanish Inquisition that Melville destroys any simple distinctions between good and evil, appearance and reality, the past and the present, and that "Benito Cereno" is raised from the level of a well-written adventure story to a tale of the magnitude and complexity of Melville's best works. It is also through this motif that Melville presents the reader with an almost D. H. Lawrence-like threat. What is really happening aboard the *San Dominick* is a modern Inquisition, an Inquisition which the colored races of the world are holding for the white race, and an Inquisition which is brought about as a direct result of the white man's maltreatment of the darker races. A spectator to this Inquisition is Captain Delano, an American, a man who "took to negroes, not philanthropically, but genially, just as other men to Newfoundland dogs",[23] yet a man who can nevertheless remark, "'Ah, this slavery breeds ugly passions in men.'"[24] If we remember that "Benito Cereno" appeared serially in *Putnam's Monthly Magazine* in October, November, and December of 1855, a time at which the slavery controversy was at its zenith, it is perhaps not too extreme to suggest that Melville's tale is a warning to America to either "Keep faith with the blacks" (as each of the Spaniards aboard the *San Dominick* is warned to do in front of the skeleton of Don Aranda, which hangs from the bowsprit of the ship) or to be prepared to

---

[23] Chase, p. 50.
[24] *Ibid.*, p. 55.

follow the leadership of Alexandro Aranda to ultimate destruction.

"The Encantadas"

In the character of Hunilla, the heroine of the eighth sketch of "The Encantadas", we find a partial meeting of pacifism and rebellion. This strain of "defiant stoicism" which Patricia Lacy calls the Agatha theme,[25] appears in a less developed and somewhat different form in numerous of Melville's other short stories. Before discussing "The Encantadas", therefore, I would like to comment briefly on those stories in which the attitude of defiant stoicism or something reasonably akin to this outlook prevails.

Altogether, there are six stories in addition to "The Encantadas" related to this theme. The handling of this motif in two of the tales is humorous. In "The Fiddler", Hautboy, at one time a world renowned violinist, has mysteriously given up his concert career, and is now an unknown. Despite this apparent turn for the worse in his fortunes, he impresses the narrator of the work as a

> boy of twelve; and this too without the slightest abatement of my respect. Because all was so honest and natural, every expression and attitude so graceful with genuine good-nature, that the marvelous juvenility of Hautboy assumed a sort of divine and immortal air, like that of some forever youthful god of Greece.[26]

The hero of "The Happy Failure" is an old man who has devoted the last ten years developing a Hydraulic-Hydrostatic Apparatus for draining swamps. When finally put to the test, however, the machine turns out to be a complete bust. The old man greets his failure with calm, almost with joy. "'Boy, I'm glad I've failed. I say, boy, failure has made a good old man of me. It was horrible at first, but I'm glad I've failed. Praise be to God for the failure!'"[27] A slightly more melancholy tale, though still more or less comic is "Cock-a-Doodle-Doo! *or* The Crowing of the Noble Cock Beneventamo." This concerns a rooster whose clarion crowing is

---

[25] "The Agatha Theme in Melville's Stories", *UTSE*, XXXV (1956), 96-105.
[26] Chase, p. 145.
[27] Herman Melville, *Selected Writings* (New York, 1952), p. 231.

THE SHORT STORIES: PARTIAL RECONCILIATION

so enobling that those who hear him forget their troubles and greet life eagerly. Beneventano is owned by a poor woodcutter named Merrymusk, whose wife and children are dying. The narrator comments to Merrymusk,

> "It must be a doleful life, then, for all concerned. This lonely solitude — this shanty — hard work — hard times."
>
> "Haven't I Trumpet? He's the cheerer. He crows through all; crows at the darkest; Glory to God in the highest! continually he crows it."
>
> "Just the import I ascribed to his crow, Merrymusk, when first I heard it from my hill. I thought some rich nabob owned some costly Shanghai; little weening any such poor man as you owned this lusty cock of a domestic breed."
>
> "*Poor* man like *me*? Why call *me* poor? Don't the cock I own glorify this otherwise inglorious, lean, lantern-jawed land? Didn't *my* cock encourage *you*? And *I* give you all this glorification away gratis. I am a great philanthropist. I am a rich man — a very rich man, and a very happy one. Crow, Trumpet." [28]

The remaining three tales dealing with this theme are out and out tragedies. In "Jimmy Rose" — a work somewhat reminiscent of Shakespeare's *Timon of Athens*, the title character is the wealthiest man in New York City and a gracious host whose generosity seems unbounded. But when Jimmy suddenly goes bankrupt, his former friends abandon him. Adversity does not break Jimmy's spirit nor does it make him bitter or a misanthrope. He continues to live, in tremendous poverty to be sure, but not in despair. Even the roses in his cheek do not fade.

> But the most touching thing of all were those roses in his cheeks; those ruddy roses in his nipping winter. How they bloomed: whether meal and milk, and tea and toast could keep them flourishing; whether he now painted them; by what strange magic they were made to bloom so; no son of man might tell. But there they bloomed. And besides the roses, Jimmy was rich in smiles. He smiled ever. The lordly door which received him to his eleemosynary teas, knew no such smiling guest as Jimmy. In his prosperous days the smile of Jimmy was famous far and wide. It should have been trebly famous now.[29]

The heroines of "Poor Man's Pudding" and "The Piazza" are in

---

[28] *Ibid.*, pp. 143-4.
[29] Chase, p. 140.

their most important characteristics like lesser developed Hunillas. In the former tale, Mrs. Coulter and her husband live in poverty near the house of a rich squire. As the narrator tries to eat the putrid pudding which the good woman has cooked for him, Mrs. Coulter begins to speak of her dead children.

"Ah sir, if those little ones yet to enter the world were the same little ones which so sadly left it; returning friends, not strangers, strangers, always strangers! Yet does a mother soon learn to love them; for certain, sir, they come from where the others have gone. Don't you believe that, sir? Yes, I know all good people must. But, still, still – and I fear it is wicked and very blackhearted, too – still, strive how I may to cheer me with thinking of little William and Martha in heaven, and with reading Dr. Doddridge there – still does dark grief leak in, just like the rain through our roof. I am left so lonesome now; day after day, all the day long, dear William is gone; and all the damp day long grief drizzles and drizzles down my soul. But I pray to God to forgive me for this; and for the rest, manage it as well as I may." [30]

Marianna, the heroine of "The Pizza", lives deep in the woods with her seventeen year old brother, who comes home only to sleep. Being alone continually, not feeling at all in harmony with the beauties of nature, she lives in a continual state of "wakeful weariness".[31] Marianna is the only one of the characters in these tales to surrender to despair, but she nevertheless continues to live with a quiet sort of courage, not unlike that of Hunilla.

Although Hunilla appears only in the eighth section of "The Encantadas", which is entitled "Norfolk Isle and the Chola Widow", some sort of brief analysis of the works as a whole is necessary to understand her full significance, for the ten sketches are united by common imagery, and there is, generally speaking, a careful development from sketch to sketch. In the first sketch, "The Isles at Large", Melville describes the Encantadas, which are "cut by the Equator",[32] as looking as if some one had dumped twenty-five heaps of cinders in an outside city lot. "In no world but a fallen could such lands exist."[33] Continuing his description,

---

[30] *Selected Writings*, p. 175.
[31] *Ibid.*, p. 452.
[32] *Ibid.*, p. 50.
[33] *Ibid.*, p. 51.

Melville adds "Nothing can better suggest the aspect of once living things malignly crumbled from ruddiness into ashes. Apples of Sodom, after touching, seem these isles."[34] Thus the Galapagos are pictured as a sort of hell on earth, and in conjunction with this, the world of nature is here described as being basically hostile to man. The second sketch, "Two Sides of a Tortoise", discusses the turtles which inhabit these isles, and continues the hemisphere imagery which is introduced in "The Isles at Large". The tortoise of the Encantadas, "dark and melancholy as it is upon the back, still possesses a bright side, its calipee or breastplate being sometimes of a faint yellowish or golden tinge".[35] It becomes even more obvious that Melville is here writing about the dual aspect of human existence when he adds "Enjoy the bright, keep it turned up perpetually if you can, but be honest, and don't deny the black."[36] In a strange way, the turtles of the Galapagos foreshadow Hunilla. One day, three of these tortoises are captured and taken aboard a passing ship.

> As I lay in my hammock that night, overhead I heard the slow weary draggings of the three ponderous strangers along the encumbered deck. Their stupidity or their resolution was so great, that they never went aside for any impediment. One ceased his movements altogether just before the mid-watch. At sunrise I found him butted like a battering-ram against the immovable foot of the foremast, and still striving, tooth and nail, to force the impossible passage. That these tortoises are the victims of a penal, or malignant, or perhaps a downright diabolic enchanter, seems in nothing more likely than in that strange infatuation of hopeless toil which so often possesses them. I have known them in their journeyings ram themselves heroically against rocks, and long abide there, nudging, wriggling, wedging, in order to displace them, and so hold on their inflexible path. Their crowning curse is their drudging impulse to straightforwardness in a belittered world.[37]

[34] *Ibid.,* p. 53.
[35] *Ibid.,* p. 55.
[36] *Ibid.,* p. 56. At the risk of being super-subtle, however, it should be pointed out that the bright side of a turtle can be seen only if it is turned on its back, and if a turtle is turned on its back, the creature is completely helpless.
[37] *Ibid.,* pp. 57-8.

The courage, suffering, and steadfastness of the turtles is later reflected in the courage, suffering, and steadfastness of Hunilla. In sketches three through seven, Melville writes of the individual islands of the Encantadas group and of their histories, and gradually, the sketches begin to include vignettes of the people who have touched at or inhabited these isles. The cruel and misanthropic hermit Oberlus, who is the protagonist of the ninth sketch, is in sharp contrast to Hunilla, and this contrast might almost be said to further the hemisphere imagery and to develop the implications of the two sides of the tortoise.

"Norfolk Isle and the Chola Widow" is the most moving part of "The Encantadas", indeed, one of the most moving things Melville ever wrote. Hunilla, a half-breed Indian, along with her young new-wedded husband Felipe and her only brother Truxhill are landed on Norfolk Isle by a French whaler, which is to return and pick them up in three months time. The purpose of their stay is to procure the valuable tortoise oil. Seven weeks after their arrival, tragedy strikes. Before Hunilla's eyes, Felipe and Truxhill drown. Felipe's body is later washed ashore, and Hunilla buries him with her hands, but Truxhill's corpse is never recovered. Hunilla now awaits the return of the French whaler, marking the days off on a hollow reed. But after many weeks it becomes obvious that the whaler will never return. "Time was her labyrinth, in which Hunilla was entirely lost."[38] Though some vessels pass near the island, the only thing that probably happens is that their crews rape the young widow. Alone, without hope, at the mercy of the elements, Hunilla still continues her courageous struggle for life.

She seemed as one who, having experienced the sharpest of mortal pangs, was henceforth content to have all lesser heart-strings riven, one by one. To Hunilla, pain seemed so necessary, that pain in other beings, though by love and sympathy made her own, was unrepiningly to be borne. A heart of yearning in a frame of steel. A heart of earthly yearning, frozen by the frost which falleth from the sky.[39]

When a friendly ship at last arrives at Norfolk Isle and rescues

[38] *Ibid.*, p. 93.
[39] *Ibid.*, p. 101.

Hunilla, her last action is to visit the grave of her husband. But no tears fall from her eyes. "Pride's height in vain abased to proneness on the rack; nature's pride subduing nature's torture."[40]

Though Hunilla, isolated in the hell-like Encantadas, never complains about her lot, the narrator of her story see in it a paean for humanity – "see here Hunilla, this lone shipwrecked soul, out of treachery invoking trust. Humanity, thou strong thing, I worship thee, not in the laureled victor, but in this vanquished one"[41] – and a condemnation of God – "Ah, Heaven, when man thus keeps his faith, wilt Thou be faithless who created the faithful one? But they cannot break faith who never plighted it."[42]

Representative of all humanity, Hunilla, as Ronald Mason suggests, is the victim of the elements and the cruelties of man.[43] Her reaction to tragedy lies somewhere between pacifism and rebellion. She has the pride of an Ahab, the faith of a Starbuck. There is something defiant even in her submission, something that seems to say to the universe, "Do what you can to break me, but you will never succeed, for I am human, and therefore better and stronger than you are."

---

[40] *Ibid.*, p. 100.
[41] *Ibid.*, p. 94.
[42] *Ibid.*, p. 91.
[43] *Op. cit.*

CHAPTER IX

THE POETRY:
A WORKABLE PHILOSOPHY
OF REBELLION

> What is a rebel? A man who says no, but whose refusal does not imply a renunciation. He is also a man who says yes, from the moment he makes his first gesture of rebellion.
>
> *The Rebel*, Albert Camus

No general study of Melville would be complete without at least brief discussion of his transition from novelist and writer of short stories to poet. Two generalizations often made about Melville's writing after *The Confidence Man* are that the last thirty years of his life were "silent years" and that his switch to poetry represents an abrupt break with his earlier work. I would disagree with both of these hypotheses. First, in the Constable Edition of Melville's works, the collected poems total almost 1200 pages, which is considerable, far more, for example, than T. S. Eliot has produced in a lifetime of writing verse. Next, Melville's poetry contains much of the same imagery and deals with many of the same themes as does his prose. More important, much of Melville's prose writing can legitimately be regarded as poetry. One example of this is the following passage about whales feeding on brit from *Moby-Dick*.

As morning mowers, who side by side slowly and seethingly advance their scythes through the long wet grass of marshy meads; even so these monsters swam, making a strange, grassy, cutting sound; and leaving behind them endless swaths of blue upon the yellow sea.[1]

---

[1] *Moby-Dick* (New York, 1930), p. 396.

Or, as F. O. Matthiessen shows, some of Melville's prose can be written as blank verse. The following is a speech of Captain Ahab.

"But look ye, Starbuck, what is said in heat,
That things unsays itself. There are men
From whom warm words are small indignity.
I mean not to incense thee. Let it go.
Look! see yonder Turkish cheeks of spotted tawn –
Living, breathing pictures painted by the sun.
The pagan leopards – the unrecking and
Unworshipping things that live; and seek, and give
No reasons for the torrid life they feel."[2]

In the light of the above instances, it would seem much more accurate to describe Melville's poetry as representing a transition rather than an abrupt break with his earlier writings.

Given Melville's unique and penetrating mind, his previous career as a novelist, and his interest in experimenting with verse forms, it is to be expected that his poems would be strongly individualistic. The following are what seem to me to be the most distinctive elements of his poetry. (1) An overwhelming amount of Melville's best imagery is drawn from the sea. An excellent example of this are the following lines from *Clarel*.

> But lo – as when off Tamura
> The splash of north-lights on the sea
> Crimsons the bergs – so here start out
> Some crags aloft how vividly.[3]

The actual description of the crags which "here start out ... how vividly" is hackneyed. But the sea simile is so magnificent that all four lines appear to be great verse. In conjunction with this first point, it should be added that whenever Melville wishes to express a complex philosophical point in concrete physical terms, he also turns to the sea for imagery.

[2] *American Renaissance* (New York, 1941), p. 426.
[3] *Clarel*, Standard Edition (London, 1924), Vol. I, Part 1, chap. 14, p. 56, lines 11-4.

182   THE POETRY: PHILOSOPHY OF REBELLION

> Blue-lights sent up by ship forlorn
> Are answered oft but by the glare
> Of rockets from another, torn
> In the same gale's inclusive snare.[4]

(2) Melville's verse contains a highly characteristic transformation of nouns into verbs. (All italics in this paragraph my own.)

> a) Since *hearsed* was Pan[5]

A description of Judas kissing Christ:

> b) The fulsome serpent on the cheek
> *Sliming*.[6]

(3) Repetition of the same word in the same line. Note the frequency of this in the first 8 lines of "Camoens".

> *Restless, restless,* craving rest,
> Forever must I fan this fire,
> Forever in *flame* on *flame* aspire?
> Yea, for the God demands thy best
> The world with endless beauty teems
> And thought evokes new worlds of dreams;
> Then hunt the flying herds of themes.
> And *fan*, yet *fan*, the fervid fire.[7]

(4) Melville is continually experimenting with rhythm and metre. He seldom writes more than 3 or 4 consecutive lines in the same metre. The opening lines of "The Maldive Shark", for instance, read:

> About the Shark, phlegmatic one,
> Pale sot of the Maldive sea
> The sleek little pilot-fish, azure and slim.
> How alert in attendance be.[8]

---

[4] *Ibid.*, Vol. I, Part 1, chap. 13, p. 51, lines 1-4.
[5] "When Forth the Shepherd Leads his Flock", in *Poems*, Standard Edition (London, 1924), p. 308, line 16. Hereafter called *Poems*.
[6] *Clarel*, Vol. I, Part 1, chap. 30, p. 118, lines 21-2.
[7] In *The Viking Portable Melville* (New York, 1952), p. 740. The standard edition has a bad text for this poem.
[8] *Poems*, p. 237.

Moreover, we find that much of Melville's verse, which ostensibly seems to be in conventional iambic or trochaic tetrameter or pentameter, breaks into different patterns when examined closely, as is the case with the following four lines from *Clarel*.

> A wizened blue fruit drops from them
> Nipped harvest of Jerusalem.
> *Wistful here Clarel turned toward Vine,*
> And would have spoken; but as well.[9]

It is this continual break in rhythm and metre that gives Melville's verse the taut, moving quality which is probably its most distinguishing feature.

It is apparent that Melville was a powerful, original poet who was continually experimenting with his verse, but it is also equally apparent that he never became a completely finished poet. Nevertheless, he shows a progressively greater control of poetic diction and technique, and his last poems have far fewer bad lines in them than does his earlier verse. Though Melville was no Keats, his verse has a philosophical depth which is lacking in the lines of far more "perfect" poets. Melville's poetry, flaws or no, certainly ranks with the very best verse ever produced in America.

Melville's verse includes the poems published in the novels, *Battle-Pieces and Aspects of the War* (1866), *Clarel* (1876), *John Marr and Other Sailors* (1881), *Timoleon* (1891), *Weeds and Wildings, Marquis De Grandvin*, and miscellaneous and uncollected poems. With the exception of *Battle-Pieces* and *Clarel*, pacifism and rebellion play a small part in Melville's poetry. *Battle-Pieces* deals directly with pacifism, and in *Clarel* we find a subtle and complex treatment of both pacifism and rebellion.

Though *Battle-Pieces* is a collection of individual poems, there is unity in the book because all of these verses are concerned with some aspect of the Civil War. The first poem in the volume, "The Portent", is about the hanging of John Brown, and the following poems in the collection deal in rough chronological order with some of the major events of the war – "The March Into Virginia", the "Battle of Stone River". The Surrender at Appomattox", etc.

---

[9] *Clarel*, Vol. I, Part 1, chap. 30, p. 118, lines 1-4.

184   THE POETRY: PHILOSOPHY OF REBELLION

The final poems in the volume are reflections at the close of the Civil War, and the last work in the collection is entitled "A Meditation".

Though Melville had attacked many aspects of the philosophy of pacifism, his writings – even a work such as *Israel Potter* – had continually condemned war in no uncertain terms. In *White-Jacket*, it may be remembered, Melville had written:

> the whole matter of war is a thing that smites common sense and Christianity in the face; so everything connected with it is utterly foolish, unchristian, barbarous, brutal, and savouring of the Feejee Islands, cannibalism, saltpetre, and the devil.[10]

The issue of the Civil War skewered Melville as firmly as it did more doctrinaire pacifists such as John Greenleaf Whittier, for though Melville may have been inexorably opposed to war, he was also inexorably opposed to slavery, regarding it as the worst of human evils.

> I muse upon my country's ills –
> The tempest bursting from the waste of Time
> On the worlds's fairest hope linked with man's foulest crime.[11]

If the destruction of slavery could be brought about only by armed conflict, then a war was necessary.

> strong Necessity
> Surges, and heaps Time's strand with wrecks.[12]

The Civil War becomes a tool of righteousness, and thus it is in *Battle-Pieces* that we find perhaps the only instance in Melville's work where he is willing to justify the means by the ends.

Melville was drawn to the Civil War because he at first viewed the conflict in terms of absolutes. In most of his works, the nets of good and evil are so tightly intermeshed that they are inseparable. In *Clarel*, for instance, Melville writes

---

[10] *White-Jacket* (New York, 1952), p. 299.
[11] "Misgivings", *Poems*, p. 7, lines 5-7.
[12] "The Conflict of Convictions", *Poems*, p. 9, lines 4-5.

> Evil and good they braided play
> Into one cord.[13]

But such was not the case with the Civil War. It presented Melville with subject material in which, initially at least, good and evil appeared in simple terms, easily isolated from each other, and hence easily definable. Though the individual northern soldier was no more noble or ethical than his Confederate counterpart, the Union cause was RIGHT and the Southern cause was WRONG. This point of view is made explicit in a poem entitled "Stonewell Jackson."

> Dead is the Man whose Cause is dead
> Vainly he died and set his seal –
> Stonewall!
> Earnest in error, as we feel;
> True to the thing he deemed was due,
> True as John Brown or steel.[14]

Melville's wholehearted endorsement of the Civil War as a battle of necessity and as a tool for justice was not to last for long, however. This is indicated by the very title of one of the earliest poems in the volume, "Misgivings". And Melville's skeptical comments about the justifiability of the Civil War increase in frequency towards the close of the collection. In "The March into Virginia", Melville writes

> All wars are boyish and are fought by boys.
> The champions and enthusiasts of the state.[15]

War is no longer something potentially glorious, an instrument of good, but a trade or science.

> Hail to victory without gaud
>   Of glory; zeal that needs no fans
> Of banners; plain mechanic power
> Plied cogently in War now placed –
>   Where War belongs –
> Among the trades and artisans.[16]

---

[13] *Clarel*, Vol. II, Part 4, chap. 4, p. 174, lines 1-2.
[14] *Poems*, p. 59, stanza 2.
[15] *Poems*, p. 13, lines 6-7.
[16] "A Utilitarian View of the Monitor's Fight", *Poems*, p. 44, stanza 2.

186 THE POETRY: PHILOSOPHY OF REBELLION

Probably the strongest anti-war sentiment of *Battle-Pieces* is found in the chorus-like italicized stanzas of "The Armies of the Wilderness."

>   The tribes swarm up to war
>   As in ages long ago,
>   Ere in the palm of promise leaved
>   And the lily of Christ did blow.
>
>   Turned adrift into war
>   Man runs wild on the plain,
>   Like the jennets let loose
>   On the Pampas – zebras again.
>
>   At the height of their madness
>   The night winds pause,
>   Recollecting themselves;
>   But no lull in these wars.[17]

A somewhat different outlook upon the war is found in "Shiloh", perhaps the finest poem in the collection.

>   Skimming lightly, wheeling still,
>   The swallows fly low
>   Over the field in clouded days,
>   The forest-field of Shiloh –
>   Over the fields where April rain
>   Solaced the parched one stretched in pain
>   Through the pause of night
>   That followed the Sunday fight
>   Around the church of Shiloh –
>   The church so lone, the long-built one,
>   That echoed so many a parting groan
>   And natural prayer
>   Of dying foemen mingled there –
>   Foemen at morn, but friends at eve –
>   Fame or country least their care:
>   (What like a bullet can undeceive!)
>   But now they lie low,
>   While over them the swallows skim,
>   And all is hushed at Shiloh.[18]

[17] *Poems*, pp. 68-75, italicized stanzas 4, 9, and 15.
[18] *Poems*, p. 46.

In terms of our topic, "Shiloh" is more important for what it doesn't say than for any overt statement which it makes. The poem is neither a bitter condemnation of the slaughter at Shiloh, nor a eulogy in praise of the men who died while trying to make a better world by abolishing slavery. It is concerned not with war as an abstract and impersonal phenomenon, nor with the issues involved in the war, but with the individual men who fought and died in the struggle. The indifferent skimming motions of the swallows are contrasted to the silent and unmoving soldiers who have fallen in battle. The war for them is finished, and the issues which separated them during life vanish with death — "Fame or country least their care." For them, death, not right or wrong, is the ultimate reality. The bullet which undeceives Shiloh's slaughtered may also be said to be that force which destroys Melville's belief in the idea of a just war. If war is thought of in terms of issues, it can be justified. But if war is judged in the light of the individuals who fight and die in it, there can be no justification.

Less than halfway through *Battle-Pieces*, it becomes apparent that Melville is no longer able to think of the Civil War in absolute terms. If judged as a whole, *Battle-Pieces* is an almost schizophrenic work, for its two major themes are a championing of the Union's cause and a strongly developed anti-war sentiment, and they work at cross purposes throughout the volume. This uneasy alliance between pacifism and pro-Unionism injects a thematic and artistic complexity into Melville's war verse. Generally speaking, the poems which are most enthusiastically pro-Union are those poems which are philosophically the simplest and which contain the most conventional imagery. But in the poems which show at least a partial "return to pacifism", Melville is forced to use more complex imagery to convey his ambivalent and more profound feelings.

An excellent example of this ambivalence is found in the final stanza of "Commemorative of a Naval Victory". These lines provide a striking contrast to the previously quoted stanza from "Stonewall Jackson", which not only lacks subtlety, but which is also poor poetry.

> But seldom the laurel wreath is seen
>   Unmixed with pensive pansies dark;
> There's a light and a shadow on every man
>   Who at last attains his lifted mark –
>   Nursing through night the ethereal spark.
> Elate he never can be;
> He feels that spirits which glad had hailed his worth
>   Sleep in oblivion – The shark
> Glides white through the phosphorous sea.[19]

On the phosphorous sea of life, the evil and destructive forces are symbolized by the shark. Yet, like Moby-Dick, this shark is white, the color usually representative of human goodness and purity. Melville is here obviously making a profound observation about the dual nature of both man and of reality. But since this stanza appears in a poem which deals specifically with the War between the States, the passage is also a comment upon the Civil War itself, a war which has both good and bad aspects. Melville's initial reaction to the war had been that it was a clear-cut struggle between right and wrong, and that this conflict was necessary to implement a just cause. But as evidenced in "Commemorative of a Naval Victory", these simple distinctions have vanished, the absolute has become the relative, and once again, good and evil are braided into one cord.

As might be expected, Melville deals more directly with pacifism in those works whose subject matter is founded upon some aspect of war or war-making, as is the case in *White-Jacket* and *Battle-Pieces*. In these works, pacifism is presented in its most specific form, and is not necessarily placed in opposition to the theme of rebellion. As a rule, pacifism and rebellion appear as polarities only in Melville's most complex works, such as *Moby-Dick* and *Billy Budd*. This is true also of *Clarel*, Melville's 630-page narrative poem.

Clarel, the protagonist of the work, is a young American divinity student who suddenly finds himself in a state of mental and spiritual apathy – he neither believes nor rejects anything. He comes to the Holy Land in hope of once again being able to find a purpose in life, to become involved rather than to be a spectator.

[19] *Poems*, p. 130.

> Yes, I am young, but Asia old
> The books, the books not all have told.[20]

While in Jerusalem, he falls in love with Ruth, a Jewish girl. But just as their romance is beginning to blossom, Ruth's father is killed, and because of Jewish tradition, Clarel is forbidden to see her for a certain period of time. To pass away this interim, Clarel decides to go on a short pilgrimage through the Holy Land. When he returns to Jerusalem, Clarel finds out that Ruth has died of a combination of fever and grief.

Throughout *Clarel*, the following two lines in slightly varying forms function almost as a leitmotif.

> If Luther's day expand to Darwin's year
> Shall that exclude the hope – foreclose the fear?[21]

Melville attempts to answer this question in *Clarel*, and the poem, therefore, is concerned with man's search for faith and a system of values in the modern world, a world in which the old faiths and ancient beliefs are no longer sufficient. The urgency and drama of this search for a new faith is heightened by the tension existing between the setting and the characters of the poem. With few exceptions, the major figures are Westerners, either Americans or Europeans, products of a modern, unsettled, science-oriented culture. The setting is the Holy Land, a world both ancient and mystical, and the cradle of three great religions, Christianity, Mohammedanism, and Judaism. This contrast between setting and characters symbolizes the schism between the actualities of present existence and the outdated religious beliefs of the past.

The supreme irony of the poem is that the Holy Land, no matter what the pilgrims may think, is the worst possible place to look for meaning in the modern world. Though Melville never states this explicitly, it is implicit in his imagery. The greatest part of *Clarel* is set against the dry and sterile desert, where the pilgrims' path is strewn with stones. Even Jerusalem itself is described, not as a place where religion flowered forth, but

---

[20] *Clarel*, Vol. I, Part 1, chap. 1, p. 5, lines 21-2.
[21] *Ibid.*, Vol. II, Part 4, chap. 35, p. 297, lines 1-2.

>   where long ago
> Dull fires of refuse, shot below,
> The city's litter smouldering burned,
> Clouding the glen with smoke impure,
> And griming the foul shapes obscure
> Of dismal chain-gangs in their shame
> Raking the garbage thither spurned:
> Tophet the place – transferred, in name,
> To penal Hell.[22]

The landscape comes to play an active rather than a passive role in *Clarel*, at once shaping the actions of the pilgrims and at the same time reflecting their dilemma.

There is little physical action in *Clarel*, and to a large extent, the pilgrimage is more of an intellectual than a physical journey. The pilgrims and the other major figures in the poem – Rolfe, whom most critics regard as the intellectual hero of the poem; Vine, a character perhaps based on Hawthorne;[23] Djalea, the Moslem guide; Glaucon and his father, figures of modern commercialism; Margoth, the Jewish geologist who has made a religion out of science; the jolly Lesbian priest; the young Lyonese traveller, who is a foil to Clarel; the saintly Nehemia; Mortmain; Celio; Derwent; and Ungar – are all representative of definite and contradictory philosophies of life. The force which gives *Clarel* its movement is to be found in the conversations between two or more of these characters, for their discussions bring together not only different individuals, but also conflicting sets of values. Clarel provides the necessary perspective, for he is the only one of the major figures who is not initially committed to a specific philosophy of life, and hence is able to provide an objective commentary on the credos of the others. Clarel functions somewhat like a modern Everyman in pursuit of a satisfactory way of life.

The extreme poles represented within the diverse group of pilgrims are pacifism and rebellion, and it is between these two philosophies that Clarel is ultimately forced to choose. In some ways, *Clarel* represents Melville's most intensive exploration of

---

[22] *Ibid.*, Vol. I, Part 1, chap. 26, p. 104, lines 10-18.
[23] For example, see Newton Arvin, *Herman Melville* (New York, 1957), p. 274.

these two polarities because the poem contains *two* pacifists
– Nehemiah and Derwent – and *three* rebels – Celio, Mortmain,
and Ungar. Thus, not only are pacifism and rebellion placed in
opposition to one another, but different attitudes of pacifism are
contrasted to each other, as are conflicting approaches to rebellion.

The "saintly" Nehemiah is perhaps the most completely pacifistic of all of Melville's pacifist-heroes. He radiates love in the
highest possible degree. The Bible is his sole guide to life. He
converses with sinners and lepers, people who are scorned even
by their own kin. While the other pilgrims rest, the old man even
removes stones from the paths of the horses.

> Latin, Armenian, Greek, and Jew
> Full well the harmless vagrant kenned,
> The small meek face, the habit gray:
> In him they owned our human clay.
> The Turk went further, let him wend:
> Him Allah cares for, holy one:
> A *Santon* held him; and was none
> Bigot enough scorn's shaft to send.
> For, say what cynic will or can,
> Man sinless is revered by man
> Thro' all the forms which creed may lend.[24]

One night on the pilgrimage, Nehemiah has a vision of heaven,
and the next morning, the others find his corpse. Nehemiah, a
Christ-like figure, had lived and died like a saint.

Nehemiah was loved by all who knew him, but even Clarel,
who was closest to the old man, rejects his way of life. Nehemiah's
saintliness is founded, not upon the concept of man's innate value
and dignity, but upon his weakness. When Clarel first meets the
saint, the latter identifies himself as "'The sinner Nehemiah'".[25]
This answer not only reflects Nehemiah's humility, but also reveals
his outlook upon mankind as a whole. For Nehemiah, man is a
weak and miserable creature, redeemed only by the love of God.
In addition, Clarel finds Nehemiah's asceticism devoid of any

---

[24] *Clarel*, Vol. I, Part 1, chap. 8, p. 36, lines 3-13.
[25] *Ibid.*, Vol. I, Part 1, chap. 7, p. 33, line 32.

intellectual content. The old man is usually described as being on the verge of falling asleep, and his doddering physical appearance reflects the doddering nature of his intellect. Nehemiah's past is a mystery, but Rolfe says he once knew a man like Nehemiah,

> Yes, one whom grim
> Disaster made as meek as he.[26]

Disaster did not make Nehemiah bitter. Rather it crushed everything out except his goodness. But in this case, goodness without intellect is futile, Melville suggests. Nehemiah, for all his kindness, does little to relieve human misery or to elevate his fellow men. This is symbolized by his attempt to remove the stones from the path of the pilgrims.

> The saint it was with busy care
> Flinging aside stone after stone
> Yet feebly, nathless, as he wrought
> In charge imposed though not unloved:
> While every stone that he removed
> Laid bare but more.[27]

Clarel's other pacifist is the English parson Derwent, a man whose joie-de-vivre is in sharp contrast to Nehemiah's asceticism.

> A priest he was – though but in part;
> For as the Templar old combined
> The cavalier and monk in one;
> In Derwent likewise might you find
> The secular and cleric tone.
> Imported or domestic mode
> Thought's last adopted style he showed;
> Abreast kept with the age, the year,
> And each bright optimistic mind,
> Nor lagged with Solomon in rear,
> And Job, the furthermost behind – [28]

---

[26] *Ibid.*, Vol. I, Part 1, chap. 37, p. 146, lines 13-4.
[27] *Ibid.*, Vol. I, Part 2, chap. 10, p. 212, line 34; p. 213, lines 1-5.
[28] *Ibid.*, Vol. I, Part 2, chap. 1, p. 172, lines 2-12. This passage clearly indicates Melville's debt to Chaucer's *Canterbury Tales*. In the above quotation, Melville is making a parody on the Knight's description.
  A Knyght ther was, and that a worthy man,

Derwent is thoroughly damned in the above quotation because he has no room in his makeup for Job, for Melville's writings reveal a greater sympathy with Job than any other Biblical character, even Christ. (Later on in the poem, Derwent is attacked by Clarel on these very grounds.) Derwent has no capacity for suffering because he thinks that this is the best of all possible worlds. Nor is anything worth rebelling against, because nothing can be improved upon. Pacifism deteriorates into passivism in the case of Derwent because he not only is opposed to physical conflict, but to intellectual, emotional, and artistic struggle as well. This aversion to any form of unpleasantness becomes a type of intellectual dishonesty with Derwent. His attitude is typified when the pilgrims meet a Dominican Friar, who begins to argue with them vehemently about the merits of Catholicism. Though Derwent hardly enters into the discussion, it is he who terminates the conversation.

> "Brother," said Derwent, friendly here,
> "I'm glad to know ye, glad to meet,
> Even though, in part, your Rome seeks ends
> Not mine. But see, there pass your friends:
> Call they your name?"[29]

It is probable that Melville had the German meaning of Derwent's name in mind when he created this character, for the Englishman, with his mastery of rationalization, is as hard to come to grips with as his namesake, the wind.

It is fitting that both of the characters who represent pacifism in *Clarel* should be religious figures, for pacifism is traditionally associated with some form of religious value. But it is somewhat surprising that one of the poem's rebels, Celio, should be a Catho-

---

Melville pays more formal homage to Chaucer in the following lines:
> Not from brave Chaucer's Tabard Inn
> They pictured wend; scarce shall they win
> Fair Kent, and Canterbury ken;
> Nor franklin, squire, nor morris dance
> Of wit and story good as then:
> Another age, and other men,
> And life an unfulfilled romance.

[29] *Ibid.*, Vol. I, Part 2, chap. 25, p. 274, lines 30-4.

lic monk. Celio, whose name means the heavenly one, represents a sort of transitional and only partially-realized stage of rebellion. He does not become an active revolutionist as do Mortmain and Ungar, but his philosophical revolt is much the same as is theirs.

While living in Rome, Celio gradually comes to dispute some of the basic canons of Catholicism. He realizes that to reject some aspects of Catholicism is to reject all of it.

> At sea, in brig which swings no boat,
> To founder is to sink.[30]

Celio accepts the consequences of his founderings and looks for a new philosophy.

> This world clean fails me: Still I yearn
> Me then it surely does concern
> Some other world to find. But where?
> In creed? I do not find it there.
> That said, and is the emprise o'er?
> Negation, is there nothing more?
> This side the dark and hollow bound
> Lies there no unexplored rich ground?
> *Some other world:* well, there's the *New*
> Ah, joyless and ironic too![31]

Having spurned the present as a source of faith, Celio carries his search to the Holy Land, saying "'The Past, the Past is half of time'".[32]

Though Celio's philosophical rebellion is admirable, his search into the past for a new faith is misdirected. For Melville, much of the evil of the modern world is a result of the past. If there is any hope for man, it is to be found in the future. The most explicit statement of this viewpoint is in *White-Jacket*.

The world has arrived at a period which renders it the part of Wisdom to pay homage to the prospective precedents of the Future in preference to those of the Past. The Past is dead, and has no resurrection; but the Future is endowed with such a life, that it lives to us even in anticipation. The Past is, in many things, the foe of mankind; the

---

[30] *Ibid.*, Vol. I, Part 1, chap. 12, p. 48, lines 8-9.
[31] *Ibid.*, Vol. I, Part 1, chap. 12, p. 49, lines 1-10.
[32] *Ibid.*, Vol. I, Part 1, chap. 12, p. 49, line 18.

Future is, in all things, our friend. In the Past is no hope; the Future is both hope and fruition. The past is the text-book of tyrants; the Future the Bible of the Free.[33]

Thus Celio's seach is doomed before it starts. Unable to find a new belief which he so desperately needs, Celio dies and is buried even before the beginning of the actual physical pilgrimage.

Mortmain and Ungar, the other two rebels in *Clarel*, are rebels both in theory and in practice. Like Celio, they both have intellectually rebelled against the evil they have found in the world. But unlike the Roman monk, they realize that if man rejects traditional and religious beliefs, he himself must assume the responsibility of introducing new and suitable values into the world. Both Ungar and Mortmain accept the obligation of re-shaping the world, the former by becoming a professional soldier, the latter by being an active revolutionist.

Ungar and Mortmain are alike in many ways. Both are born outcasts into a hostile world. The Swede was an illegitimate child, and Ungar was the son of an Indian guide and a Maryland Catholic. Both men have at one time had faith in democracy, in the future, and in man's ability to successfully shape his own destiny, and both men become bitterly disillusioned. Indeed, Ungar delivers the most scathing attack upon democracy to be found in Melville's works, calling her a

> Harlot on horseback, riding down
> The very Ephesians who acclaim
> This great Diana of ill fame![34]

When Mortmain loses his faith in the beneficent efficacy of revolution, he becomes a broken man.

> He, under ban
> Of strange repentance and last dearth,
> Roved the gray places of earth
> And what seemed most his heart to wring
> Was some unrenderable thing:[35]

[33] *White-Jacket, op. cit.*, p. 150.
[34] *Clarel*, Vol. II, Part 4, chap. 19, p. 240, lines 12-14.
[35] *Ibid.*, Vol. I, Part 2, chap. 4, p. 190, line 34; p. 191, lines 1-4.

The Swede's ultimate reaction to life is symbolized when he scoops up a handful of water from the Dead Sea and tries to drink it. As his name indicates, Mortmain has surrendered the battle of life, and has become a "dead-hand". Shortly before he commits suicide, Mortmain screams at the universe that man can be saved neither by his own actions nor by God.

> "*Knowledge is power*: tell that to knaves;
> 'Tis knavish knowledge: the true lore
> Is impotent for earth: '*Thyself*
> *Thou canst not save; come down from the cross!*'
> They cast it in His teeth; trim Pelf
> Stood by, and jeered, *Is gold then dross?* –
> Cling to His tree, and there find hope:
> Me it but makes a misanthrope." [36]

Ungar, "A wandering Ishmael from the West",[37] joins the pilgrims almost immediately after the Swede's suicide. Since Celio, Nehemiah, and Mortmain all die well before the close of the poem, the ultimate struggle of rebellion against pacifism in *Clarel* is between Derwent and Ungar. This conflict comes to a head in the chapter entitled, appropriately enough, "Derwent and Ungar". The two men discuss the nature of reform and the improvement of man's state in this world. Derwent argues that the world naturally improves in the course of time.

> "Through all methinks I see
> The object clear: belief revised,
> Men liberated – equalized
> In happiness. No mystery
> Just none at all; plain sailing." [38]

To this argument, Ungar replies:

> "Now the world cannot save the world:
> And Christ renounces it. His faith
> Breaking with every mundane path,
> Aims straight at heaven. To founded thrones
> He says: Trust not to earthly stanchions;

---

[36] *Ibid.*, Vol. II, Part 3, Chap. 28, p. 135, lines 7-14.
[37] *Ibid.*, Vol. II, Part 4, chap. 10, p. 199, line 22.
[38] *Ibid.*, Vol. II, Part 4, chap. 20, p. 242, lines 28-9; p. 243, lines 1-3.

> And unto poor and houseless ones –
> My Father's house has many mansions.
> Warning and solace be but this;
> No thought to mend a world amiss.[39]

Ungar's reply is a restatement of Mortmain's tirade about Christ not being able to save himself from the cross, and Derwent is unable to answer, murmuring only "'Ah now, ah, now!'"[40]

But Ungar's response also reflects the inconsistency of his own position. Ungar admits that religion offers little hope for this world – "No thought to mend a world amiss." He has also found from his own experiences, as has Mortmain, that man himself is unable to better the human condition either. Once Ungar has reached these conclusions, there are two logical courses of action. One of them is to commit suicide, which is what Mortmain does. The other is to adopt a code of amorality, a chameleon-like type of behaviour, such as that of Melville's Confidence Man. Meaningless and inconsistent though it may be, however, Ungar rebels against life by continuing to live.

> Now was he the self-exiled one.
> Too steadfast! Wherefore should be lent
> The profitless high sentiment?
> Renounce conviction in defeat:
> Pass over, share the spoiler's seat
> And thrive. Behooves thee else turn cheek
> To fate with wisdom of the meek.
> Wilt not? Unblest then with the store
> Of heaven, and spurning wordly lore
> Astute, eat thou thy cake of pride,
> And henceforth live on unallied.[41]

Ungar possesses an Ahab-like pride, a pride which is at once his greatest strength and his chief weakness. Earlier in *Clarel*, it is suggested that most men learn to accept evil but that there are a few individuals who never do. Nehemiah is one of the many who accept evil. Derwent tries to ignore it. When Celio becomes aware of the evil in the universe, this discovery kills him. Mortmain

[39] *Ibid.*, Vol. II, Part 4, chap. 20, p. 243, lines 7-15.
[40] *Ibid.*, Vol. II, Part 4, chap. 20, p. 243, line 16.
[41] *Ibid.*, Vol. II, Part 4, chap. 5, p. 179, lines 125-35.

gives up the battle against evil when he comes to realize that man is unable to vanquish it. Ungar not only is unwilling to accept the existence of evil in the world, but, because of his pride, he is the sole figure in *Clarel* who continues to struggle against it.

For the greater part of the pilgrimage, Clarel has merely been an interested listener to the various philosophical debates, which have taken place during the journey. But he is eventually drawn into the discussions, and it is Clarel, not Mortmain or Ungar, who most thoroughly routs the Englishman in a discussion. Clarel admits to Derwent that

>"Yes, all was dim.
>He saw no one secure retreat;
>Of late so much had shaken him." [42]

Derwent replies:

>"Have Faith, which, even from the myth
>Draws something to be useful with:
>In any forms some truths will hold . . ." [43]

When Clarel expresses doubt at this philosophy, Derwent continues.

>"Be not extreme. Midway is best.
>. . . . .
>Byron's storm-cloud away has rolled —
>Joined Werter's; Shelley's drowned; and why,
>Perverse were now e'ven Hamlet's sigh:
>Perverse? — indecorous indeed!" [44]

But this drives Clarel to a passionate outbreak.

>"Forbear!
>Ah, wherefore not at once name Job.
>In whom these Hamlets all conglobe
>Own, own with me, and spare to feign,
>Doubt bleeds, nor Faith is free from pain!" [45]

---

[42] *Ibid.*, Vol. II, Part 3, chap. 21, p. 103, lines 25-7.
[43] *Ibid.*, Vol. II, Part 3, chap. 21, p. 105, lines 22-4.
[44] *Ibid.*, Vol. II, Part 3, chap. 21, p. 108, lines 15, and 30-3.
[45] *Ibid.*, Vol. II, Part 3, chap. 21, p. 109, lines 2-6.

For the only time in the poem, Derwent admits defeat.

> Derwent averted here his face —
> With his own heart he seemed to strive;
> Then said: "Alas, too deep you dive."[46]

Clarel is unable to find the faith for which he has searched on the pilgrimage through the Holy Land. He comes to believe that all meaning in life is to be found in the relationship between man and woman, as represented by his love for Ruth. Shortly after he reaches this conclusion, the pilgrims return to Jerusalem, and are greeted by the sight of a funeral procession at the outskirts of the city. When Clarel is informed that the victim is Ruth, he screams

> "O blind, blind, barren universe!
> Now I am a bough torn down,
> And I must wither, cloud or sun!"[47]

With these words, Clarel has rejected the pacifistic philosophies of Derwent and the saintly Nehemiah, and has aligned himself with the rebels Celio, Mortmain, and Ungar. For the ultimate division between pacifism and rebellion with *Clarel* as with *Moby-Dick* and *Pierre* is the question of whether or not value is structured into the universe. Though Nehemiah and Derwent differ on many points, both believe in a benevolent and powerful God, in whom the ultimate meaning of man's life is to be found. Nehemiah is a pacifist because he feels that every living creature — even the most miserable sinner — is a product of God. To use violence against one of God's creatures is in reality to use violence against God himself. Derwent is a pacifist because he believes that any form of rebellion is an attack upon God's order, which is wellnigh perfect to begin with. Mortmain and Ungar, men virtually born into exile, do not think that man is what God makes him, but that he himself is responsible for his own destiny. Everywhere in the world, vast majorities of men are subjected to tyranny and injustice. It is man's duty to drive forth this tyranny and injustice and to bring dignity and meaning into the lives of all mankind.

[46] *Ibid.*, Vol. II, Part 3, chap. 21, p. 109, lines 7-9.
[47] *Ibid.*, Vol. II, Part 4, chap. 30, p. 285, lines 3-5.

And the only way to do this is through revolution, as the "blind, blind, barren universe" has no concern with man's welfare, nor will the evil in the world right itself in the course of time, as Derwent suggests. Mortmain and Ungar become rebels because they are concerned with man and this world. *Clarel*'s pacifists are interested primarily in God and the next world.

Not surprisingly, Melville's sympathies lie clearly with the rebels. Neither Derwent nor Nehemiah can answer the arguments brought forth by Mortmain and Ungar. And Clarel, the lone uncommitted character in the poem, eventually rejects the universe on the same grounds as do the rebels. It is Clarel who gives utterance to the manifesto of the disillusioned rebels, a declaration of idealism in the face of disaster which is probably the poem's intellectual credo.

> "Conviction is not gone
> Though faith's gone: that which shall not be
> Still *ought* to be!" [48]

Clarel is one of the most complex of Melville's generally complex works. The various philosophies represented in the poem are systematically torn into shreds. The characters themselves are inconsistent in both their beliefs and their actions. The imagery and symbolism are as difficult and ambivalent as in *Moby-Dick*. But the most puzzling aspect of *Clarel* is the epilogue. The narrative section of the poem ends with Clarel entirely alone, bereft of friends, faith, hope, and Ruth, asking himself

> "Where, where now He who helpeth us,
> The Comforter?" [49]

Nothing seems left but the complete negation which Celio so greatly feared. Yet the last few lines of the epilogue read:

> Then keep thy heart, though yet but ill–resigned –
> Clarel, thy heart, the issues there but mind;
> That like the crocus budding through the snow –
> That like a swimmer rising from the deep –

---

[48] *Ibid.,* Vol. II, Part 4, chap. 30. p. 285, lines 29-31.
[49] *Ibid.,* Vol. II, Part 4, chap. 32, p. 291, lines 11-2.

> That like a burning secret which doth go
> Even from the bosom that would hoard and keep;
> Emerge thou mayst from the last whelming sea,
> And prove that death but routs life into victory.[50]

There are two possible interpretations of this ending. Either Melville was unwilling to accept the logical philosophical and artistic outcome of his own creation, and tried to sugar over the bitterness found throughout the body proper of the poem by offering a faint and unrelated ray of hope at the end of the work, or there is an underlying philosophy which does not become fully apparent until the very last line of *Clarel*.

I would tend to accept the latter possibility. The emphasis in the last lines is on the word *mayst*, not *willst*. There is some chance – and in light of the tragical strain permeating *Clarel*, a very small chance – that meaning may still exist in the world. Ungar continues his rebellion against the universe, though by his own admission the struggle is useless, and in a similar vein, Melville appeals to Clarel and to all men not to surrender the battle of life. It is perhaps that irrational quality in man which enables him to fight blindly against overwhelming odds which will be his salvation. In the struggle against life, we may find life.

This philosophy, that man's ultimate expression of defiance against the universe is to continue to live, was foreshadowed in the courageous stoicism of Hunilla in "The Encantadas," and is the most mature phase of rebellion as it appears in Melville's writings. Noble as the revolt of a Pierre, Ahab, or Mortmain might be, it is somewhat Gotterdammerungish and self-defeating, for its logical conclusion is suicide. But Ungar and Clarel, without in any way compromising their principles, can continue their struggle without necessarily surrendering their lives.

---

[50] *Ibid.*, Vol. II, Part 4, chap. 35, p. 298, lines 5-12.

CHAPTER X

BULLY BUDD:
THE TESTAMENT OF REBELLION

> "That's rebellion," murmured Alyosha, looking down. "Rebellion? I am sorry you call it that," said Ivan earnestly. "One can hardly live in rebellion. and I want to live. Tell me yourself, I challenge you – answer. Imagine that you are creating a fabric of human destiny with the object of making men happy in the end, giving them peace and rest at last, but that it was essential and inevitable to torture to death only one tiny creature – that baby beating its breast with its fist, for instance – and to found that edifice upon its unavenged tears, would you consent to be the architect on those conditions? Tell me, and tell the truth." "No, I wouldn't consent," said Alyosha softly.
> Dostoyevsky, *The Brothers Karamazov*

Virtually all criticism of *Billy Budd* falls into two camps: those who see in Melville's last work a "Testament of Acceptance" or those who view it as a "Final Irony". Wendall Glick, a member of the first camp, argues that *Billy Budd* illustrates that "The ultimate allegiance of the individual, in other words, is not to an absolute moral code, interpreted by conscience and enlivened by his human sympathies, but to the utilitarian principle of social expediency."[1] This viewpoint is attacked vigorously by Leonard Caspar in his fine article "The Case Against Captain Vere".

Billy Budd has often been considered Herman Melville's "Testament of Acceptance" because of Billy's unrebellious nature and because of the final blessing which he bestows on the officer who has condemned him to hang. Such an argument depends on the assumption that

---

[1] "Expediency and Absolute Morality in 'Billy Budd'," *PMLA*, LXVIII (March, 1953), p. 104.

Melville can be completely identified with Billy. Similarly, it demands the conclusion that the man who rebelled against orthodox religious and political thought all of his life and who, despite his unending interest, found no resolution to the tensions of good and evil, finally succumbed and accepted moral expediency and horological law. Because such a startling concession is unprepared for by any of Melville's writings – his novels, poetry, journals, or letters – one is inevitably led to question the validity of such an interpretation and to review again the case against Captain Vere.[2]

In this chapter I will attempt to develop this latter interpretation of the novel, and try to show that in *Billy Budd* Melville continues his championing of chronometrical time over horological time, that he condemns not only Claggart, but Captain Vere and perhaps even Billy as well, and that though the work is strongly anti-war, the ultimate message, first stated in the Preface, is a call to rebellion, not only philosophical rebellion but violent revolution if necessary.

The seeds for the tragedy of *Billy Budd* are sown when the hero is seized aboard the merchant ship, the *Right-of-Man*, and impressed into service on the British warship, the *H. M. S. Indomitable*. Billy's transfer represents more than a mere change of scenery, for the differences between the two ships are the differences between two worlds with conflicting sets of values, and the young sailor is destroyed because he is unable to adjust to the more complex and sinister life on the *Indomitable*.

The *Rights-of-Man*, as the name indicates, is a place in which the rights of every individual are respected. It symbolizes at once an unfallen world in which inherent evil does not exist, and also a primitive world, such as the Valley of the Typees, where man is governed not by a codified set of laws, but by natural law. Billy, who "in the nude might have posed for a statue of young Adam before the Fall"[3] and who is "a sort of upright barbarian, much such perhaps as Adam presumably might have been ere the urbane serpent wriggled himself into his company",[4] is eminently suited

---

[2] "The Case Against Captain Vere", *Perspective,* V (1952), p. 146.
[3] *Selected Writings of Herman Melville* (New York, Modern Library, 1952), p. 863.
[4] *Ibid.,* p. 817.

for life aboard such a ship as the *Rights-of-Man*. Because of his physical beauty and moral purity, Billy emerges as a natural leader among the crew of this vessel. "Ashore he was the champion; afloat the spokesman; on every suitable occasion always foremost."[5] And, as Captain Graveling remarks to Lieutenant Ratcliffe,[6] the officer who impresses young Budd, Billy is the peacemaker aboard the *Rights-of-Man*.

The world represented by the *H. M. S. Indomitable* is antithetical to Billy's former ship. To begin with, the *Indomitable* is not a vessel of commerce but a ship of war, and as such, is subjected to much the same sort of condemnation as is the *Neversink* in *White-Jacket*. Once again, we find that the presence of a chaplain on a battleship infuriates Melville. Discoursing upon the clergyman's attitude towards the doomed Billy, Melville writes:

Marvel not that having been acquainted with the young sailor's essential innocence (an irruption of heretic thought hard to suppress) the worthy man lifted not a finger to avert the doom of such a martyr to martial discipline. So to do would not only have been as idle as invoking the desert, but would also have been an audacious transgression of the bounds of his function, one as exactly prescribed to him by military law as that of the boatswain or any other naval officer. Bluntly put, a chaplain is the minister of the Prince of Peace serving in the host of the God of War – Mars. As such, he is as incongruous as that musket of Blücher etc. at Christmas. Why then is he there? Because he indirectly subserves the purpose attested by the cannon; because too he lends the sanction of the religion of the meek to that which practically is the abrogation of everything but brute Force.[7]

Life on the merchant vessel was governed by the rights of man. Aboard the *Indomitable,* the Articles of War, which have no concern with right or wrong but merely with expediency and which are highly arbitrary, prevail. Under these Articles, the individual has few rights, as Billy's impressment demonstrates, and man is

---

[5] *Ibid.*, p. 808.
[6] Even the Lieutenant's name – *Rat*-cliffe – condemns him and the duty he is performing.
[7] *Selected Tales*, p. 892.

regarded not as a free and thinking being, but merely as a pawn of the King's.

Most important of all, however, there exists a type of evil on the warship which was lacking aboard the *Rights-of-Man*. This is embodied in Claggart, the Master-at-Arms, "in whom was the mania of an evil nature, not engendered by vicious training or corrupting books or licentious living, but born with him and innate, in short, 'a depravity according to nature' ".[8] As we have seen, Billy is described as being similar to Adam before the Fall. This Biblical imagery is further developed by Claggart, who assumes the role of the Serpent in the Garden of Eden. (The Master-at-Arms looks at Billy with "serpent fascination",[9] and when Billy and Captain Vere attempt to lift Claggert's corpse, "it was like handling a dead snake".[10]

The Adam-like Billy is an easy victim for the serpent-like Claggert. The young man is so innocent and naive that he is unable to perceive evil, much less to cope with it. Billy's dilemma is instantly recognized by the aged Dansker, who speculates "as to what might eventually befall a nature like that, dropped into a world not without some man-traps and against whose subtleties courage lacking experience and address without any touch of defensive ugliness, is of little avail".[11] When small things start going wrong for Billy — something awry with his hammock or the storage of his gear — he appeals to the oracular Dansker for advice. The old man comments that *"Jemmy Legs"* (a nickname for Claggart), is down on him. Such sinister subtlety completely eludes the young sailor. "*'Jemmy Legs!'* ejaculated Billy his welkin eyes expanding; 'what for? Why he calls me *the sweet and pleasant young fellow,* they tell me.'"[12]

But *Jemmy Legs* is indeed down on Billy, so much so that the Master-at-Arms concocts an elaborate plot and accuses young Budd of planning mutiny. This is a particularly serious charge in the year 1797, the time in which the story is set, for England

[8] *Ibid.*, p. 843.
[9] *Ibid.*, p. 867.
[10] *Ibid.*, p. 868.
[11] *Ibid.*, p. 836.
[12] *Ibid.*, p. 837.

is not only at war with France, but the British Navy has been rocked with a series of mutinies. When Captain Vere hears this accusation, he summons Billy to this cabin in order for the youth to hear Claggart's charges face to face. Now Billy has one flaw in his otherwise flawless make-up: he stutters. When Claggart repeats his slander, Captain Vere urges Billy to speak in his own defense. But Billy, unable to protect himself in the face of evil, cannot speak. Captain Vere, realizing the problem, tells Billy to take as much time to reply as he needs. But the usually pacifistic Billy still can't utter a word. "The next instant, quick as the flame from a discharged cannon at night, his right arm shot out, and Claggart dropped to the deck."[13] After Captain Vere affirms that the Master-at-Arms has been killed by this blow, he exclaims "'Struck dead by an angel of God. Yet the angel must hang.'"[14]

This rapid evaluation by the *Indomitable*'s captain not only neatly summarizes the basic tension of *Billy Budd*, but sheds a great deal of light on the character of Vere himself. What kind of a man is this who can so quickly size up a situation and so quickly pass judgment? Is he, as F. Barron Freeman suggests, "the author's mouthpiece who resolves the plot and points the moral",[15] or is his role somewhat more equivocal? The character of Vere must be carefully analyzed, for he is far more complex than Billy Budd, who symbolizes goodness and innocence, or Claggart, who represents out and out evil. It is Vere who is the most important figure in the novel, not Billy, for his is the crucial moral decision which forms the crux of the novel.

Captain Vere is a wise man, "mindful of the welfare of his men, but never tolerating an infraction of discipline".[16] Vere's wisdom springs from three sources – from his own personal experience, from his vast reading ("books treating of actual men and events no matter what era – history, biography, and unconventional writers, who, free from cant and convention, like Montaigne, honestly and in the spirit of common sense philosophize

[13] *Ibid.*, p. 868.
[14] *Ibid.*, p. 869.
[15] *Billy Budd* (Cambridge, Mass., 1948), p. 92.
[16] *Selected Writings of Herman Melville, op. cit.*, p. 826.

upon realities"[17]), and occasionally from an almost intuitive perception of truth. One of the numerous examples of "Starry" Vere's empirical understanding is shown when Billy is unable to speak in the face of Claggart's accusations. Though Vere is until that moment unaware of Billy's vocal impediment, he "now immediately divined it" because he recalls the case of one of his schoolmates "whom he had seen struck by much the same startling impotence in the act of eagerly rising in class to be foremost in the response to a testing question put by the master".[18] Unlike Billy, who has no knowledge of his fellow men, there is "something exceptional in the moral quality of Captain Vere [which] made him, in earnest encounter with a fellow-man, a veritable touch-stone of that man's essential nature".[19] Thus, though Claggart has done nothing to antagonize his Captain, he "first provokes a vaguely repellent distaste"[20] in Vere, who intuitively realizes that the Master-at-Arms' charges against Billy are lies.

Vere's wisdom is coupled with goodness. Throughout Billy's ordeal, he shows a consummate kindness to the young sailor, so much so, that, during the trial when Billy becomes confused, he turns "an appealing glance towards Captain Vere as deeming him his best friend and helper".[21] After Billy has been sentenced, Vere makes an unprecedented visit to the compartment of the condemned foretopman, and exists from this interview in a greater state of suffering than the prisoner himself.

The first to encounter Captain Vere in act of leaving the compartment was the senior Lieutenant. The face he beheld, for the moment one expressive of the agony of the strong, was to that officer, though a man of fifty, a startling revelation. That the condemned one suffered less than he who mainly had effected the condemnation was apparently indicated by the former's exclamation in the scene soon perforce to be touched upon.[22]

[17] *Ibid.*, p. 828.
[18] *Ibid.*, p. 867.
[19] *Ibid.*, pp. 864-5.
[20] *Ibid.*, pp. 859-60.
[21] *Ibid.*, p. 876.
[22] *Ibid.*, p. 885.

Despite Captain Vere's kindly and paternal feelings towards Billy (Melville likens the older man's attitude toward the condemned youth to Abraham's compassion for Isaac), he nevertheless believes that the young seaman must hang, for since the British Navy is not only involved in a war, but threatened by rebellion from within, to allow the killing of an officer to go unpunished would encourage mutiny among the British sailors and might eventually lead to an overthrow of the entire English system. Moreover, such punishment must be immediate. Thus Vere's sense of duty wins out over his sense of compassion, and he argues to the hastily summoned drumhead court that Billy must be sentenced to death. Chronometrical law must be ignored if the law of man is to survive, as Vere attempts to make clear to the confused and unphilosophical members of the court.

"How can we adjudge to summary and shameful death a fellow-creature innocent before God, and whom we feel to be so? — Does that state it aright? You sign sad assent. Well, I too feel that, the full force of that. It is Nature. But do these buttons that we wear attest that our allegiance is to Nature? No, to the King. . . . Would it be so much we ourselves that would condemn as it would be martial law operating through us? For that law and the rigor of it, we are not responsible. Our vowed responsibility is in this: That however pitilessly that law may operate, we nevertheless adhere to it and administer it."[23]

To the officer of the marines, who, aware of Billy's innate goodness and Claggart's inherent depravity, argues that Budd intended neither mutiny nor homicide, the *Indomitable's* Captain replies

"Surely not, my good man. And before a court less arbitrary and more merciful than a martial one that plea would largely extenuate. At the last Assizes it shall acquit. But how here? We proceed under the law of the Mutiny Act. . . . And the Mutiny Act, War's child, takes after the father. Budd's intent or non-intent is nothing to the purpose."[24]

The drumhead court shortly thereafter accepts Vere's arguments, not because they are convinced of the necessity for hanging Billy,

[23] *Ibid.*, pp. 879-80.
[24] *Ibid.*, p. 881.

but because they realize that the issues involved are too large for them to comprehend and they have faith in their Captain's judgment.

Though compassionate and kindly as Vere may be, though his plea for Billy's execution is honest, painful, and carefully thought out, the Captain advocates an evil and wrong verdict. Melville is no more able to accept a system founded upon the sacrifice of an innocent babe than is Ivan Karamazov, the intellectual hero of Dostoyevsky's monumental novel, *The Brothers Karamazov,* a work which deals with virtually the same theme as does *Billy Budd* and which comes to somewhat the same conclusions. If a system can exist only if its most innocent and just members must be sacrificed, then this system is not worth preserving. Though white civilized man might be appalled at the conclusion that it is better for an innocent man to be spared and society to collapse completely with all the resulting anarchy then it is for society and its institutions to be preserved at the cost of one of its members, this is nonetheless the direction towards which Melville is inexorably pointing in *Billy Budd*.

Though there is no criticism of Vere's integrity, his decision as to the necessity of sacrificing Billy to preserve the law is sharply attacked by Melville. When the Surgeon is summoned into Vere's cabin to ascertain whether Claggart is dead, something in the Captain's attitude makes him wonder if Vere's mind has suddenly become affected. The Surgeon's doubts are echoed and re-echoed in the succeeding pages. "Whether Captain Vere, as the Surgeon professionally and primarily surmised, was really the sudden victim of any degree of aberration, one must determine for himself by such light as the narrative may afford."[25] Even Vere's fellow officers question his wisdom in these proceedings. "Certain it is however that subsequently in the confidential talk of more than one or two gun-rooms and cabins he was not a little criticized by some officers."[26] Nevertheless, it must be emphasized – as the Captain himself stresses – that Vere is acting not though his own volition but as an agent of martial law. The fact that Vere is such

[25] *Ibid.,* p. 871.
[26] *Ibid.,* p. 872.

a good man makes it even more clear that the responsibility for Billy's death lies with such arbitrary codes as the Articles of War and the Mutiny Act rather than with any specific individual.

I have earlier suggested that Melville takes not only Captain Vere to task, but Billy Budd as well. Moreover, in his criticism of Billy, we find perhaps Melville's most subtle attack on Christ. There is little doubt that by the end of the novel, Billy has acquired Christ-like characteristics. Claggart's accusations bring to Billy's face "an expression which was as a crucifixion to behold".[27] At the moment that Billy is hanged,

> it chanced that the vapory fleece hanging low in the East, was shot through with a soft glory as of the fleece of the Lamb of God seen in mystical vision and simultaneously therewith, watched by the wedged mass of upturned faces, Billy ascended, and ascending, took the full rose of the dawn.[28]

After Billy's execution, the spar from which he was hanged was in great demand among common sailors, for "To them a chip of it was as a piece of the cross."[29]

As we have seen, Billy was a natural leader aboard the *Rights-of-Man*, a peacemaker and a spokesman among the crew. In an unfallen world, Billy is a tower of nobility and strength, a righter of wrongs. But in a fallen world, a world of innate evil and Claggarts, the philosophy represented by Billy is ineffective. This is indicated immediately when Billy is impressed by Lieutenant Ratcliffe. The Handsome Sailor does not resist this injustice, he seems almost to welcome it. "To the surprise of the ship's company, though much to the Lieutenant's satisfaction, Billy made no demur. ... Noting this uncomplaining acquiescense, all but cheerful one might say, the shipmates turned a surprised glance of silent reproach at the sailor."[30] When Billy is questioned by the drumhead court as to whether he would participate in a mutiny, he replies, " 'I have eaten the King's bread and I am

---

[27] *Ibid.*, p. 868.
[28] *Ibid.*, p. 294.
[29] *Ibid.*, p. 902.
[30] *Ibid.*, p. 809.

true to the King.'"[31] This answer indicates that Billy seems completely unaware that not only he, but a large part of the crew which has also been impressed, are unquestionably the victims of injustice, and that the King is ultimately one of the chief sources of this injustice. When shortly before his execution Billy calls out "'God bless Captain Vere!'"[32] and this shout is echoed by the crew, Billy in one sense is again furthering the system of injustice which has doomed him and others. It is one thing to bless Captain Vere as an individual, and it is another thing to accept so quietly the decisions of the inherently evil authority invested in Captain Vere. In his calm acceptance of what befalls him and others, Billy himself becomes an unconscious tool of injustice, for he is a natural leader, yet he does nothing to help free the mass of mankind from their fetters. Billy's life – as is Billy's death – is meaningless and wasteful, and offers not hope to mankind, but despair. In the character of Billy Budd, whose "smooth face all but feminine in purity"[33] recalls descriptions in the author's earlier writings about the feminine nature of Christ, Melville is making his final and most profound observation on the character of Jesus and the nature of Christianity. To be Christ-like in a Christ-like and unfallen world is well and good. But a Jesus-like meekness in a fallen world does nothing to rectify the evil that exists therein. A more vigorous attitude is necessary if injustice is to be crushed out.

The ultimate message of *Billy Budd* is an appeal to revolution, and the work is Melville's most complete statement on rebellion, both political and spiritual. Though critics comment upon the marvelous craftsmanship of *Billy Budd*, most of them ignore the implications of the Preface of the novel, which indicate the course of the action to follow and suggest the moral to be drawn.

The year 1797, the year of this narrative, belongs to a period which as every thinker now feels, involved a crisis for Christendom not exceeded by its undetermined momentousness at the time by any other era whereof there is record. *The opening proposition made by*

---

[31] *Ibid.*, p. 875.
[32] *Ibid.*, p. 894.
[33] *Ibid.*, p. 815.

the Spirit of that Age, involved the rectification of the Old World's hereditary wrongs. In France to some extent this was bloodily effected. But what then? Straightway the Revolution itself became a wrongdoer, one more oppressive than the kings. Under Napoleon it enthroned upstart kings, and initiated that prolonged agony of continual war whose final throe was Waterloo. *During those years not the wisest could have foreseen that the outcome of all would be what to some thinkers apparently it has turned out to be, a political advance along nearly the whole line for Europeans.*

Now, as elsewhere hinted, it was something caught from the Revolutionary Spirit that at Spithead emboldened the man-of-war's men to rise against real abuses, long-standing ones, and afterwards at the Nore to make inordinate and aggressive demands, successful resistance to which was confirmed only when the ringleaders were hung for an admonitory spectacle to the anchored fleet. *Yet in a way analogous to the operation of the Revolution at large the Great Mutiny, though by Englishmen naturally deemed monstrous at the time, doubtless gave the first latent promptings to most important reforms in the British Navy.*[34] [Italics my own.]

Thus, the Preface implies that though rebellions such as the French Revolution often initially result in confusion and wrongdoing, they eventually may lead to important reforms and political advancement.

The theme of rebellion is further developed throughout *Billy Budd*. There are continual reference to such important leaders of the French Revolution as Anacharsis Cloots and General Murat. The owner of the *Rights-of-Man* "was a staunch admirer of Thomas Paine whose book in rejoinder to Burke's arraignment of the French Revolution had then been published for some time and had gone everywhere".[35] Indeed, two entire section of *Billy Budd* in addition to the Preface – Sections Three and Five – are devoted entirely to an analysis of revolution and mutiny.

Billy Budd, therefore, is a struggle between the forces of rebellion and those who are opposed to rebellion, such as Admiral Nelson, who is continually cited throughout the novel, and Captain Vere, a man who opposes revolutions not because he was a member of the aristocracy but because "they seemed to him in-

[34] *Ibid.,* p. 805.
[35] *Ibid.,* p. 813.

capable of embodiment in lasting institutions, but at war with the peace of the world and the true welfare of mankind".[36] But the fate of Billy Budd, who is often likened to Adam and who on one level is representative of Everyman, condemns the system and the authority represented by men like Vere and Nelson. Such authority can only be effectively opposed by active rebellion. Captain Vere is eventually slain in a combat with the French ship, the *Athéiste*, whose name obviously symbolizes the forces of the French Revolution, which, as may be remembered, Melville suggests led to "a political advance along nearly the whole line for Europeans".

A restatement of the central problem of *Billy Budd* is as follows. Throughout the world, men are supressed and victimized by systems of authority such as the Articles of War. Though good men such as Captain Vere often administer these codes, there can be no justice under a system which is inherently wrong. Nor can the cause of justice for all be furthered by a Christ-like resignation to the authorities who represent this system. Freedom and justice can be gained only by vigorously striking out against the offending system and its authorities. This rebellion, as evidenced by the French Revolution, may itself for a time become perverted and act as a tool of injustice. But in the long run, the force of rebellion, which is a combination of social and, in a sense, spiritual protest, is that power which eventually liberates mankind.

---

[36] *Ibid.*, p. 828.

CHAPTER XI

SUMMARY AND CONCLUSION

> ZEUS: But the disease can't be deeply rooted yet; it began only yesterday. Come back to the fold. Think of your loneliness; even your sister is forsaking you. Your eyes are big with anguish, your face is pale and drawn. The disease you're suffering from is inhuman, foreign to my nature, foreign to yourself. Come back. I am forgetfulness, I am peace.
> ORESTES: Foreign to myself – I know it. Outside nature, against nature, without excuse, beyond remedy, except what remedy I find within myself. But I shall not return under your law; I am doomed to have no other law but mine. Nor shall I come back to Nature, the Nature you found good; in it are a thousand beaten paths all leading up to you – but I must blaze my trail. For I, Zeus, am a man, and every man must find out his own way. Nature abhors man, and you too, god of gods, abhor mankind.
>
> Jean-Paul Sartre, *The Flies*

In this study, I have tried to show that pacifism or rebellion appear in virtually all of Melville's works, that they emerge as polarities in *Moby-Dick* and the major works following this novel, and that these two themes are tightly interwoven with Melville's concept of natural law and natural man, with his attitude towards Christ and Christianity, and with the enigma of evil, both human and metaphysical.

In *Typee*, Melville's first novel, Tommo escapes from the world of the white man to a primitive and unfallen society inhabited by people remarkably similar to Rousseau's concept of the noble savage. The Typees possess far more dignity and honor than does the white man because they live closer to the earth, because they are governed by natural law, rather than by some more artificial and arbitrary code. Despite the fact that he finds undreamed of happiness among the Typees, Tommo flees back to the white man's world in order to fight against the injustice and evil which he knows is an inescapable part of the life of civilized man. But in the act of fleeing from the Typees, he maims a savage chief who is pursuing him, and in this incident we have the first conflict between pacifism and rebellion in Melville's writing. This scene appears in somewhat different form in the author's following works – when Taji slays the old priest in order to save the beautiful Yillah in *Mardi* and when Starbuck meditates the murder of the sleeping Ahab in order to save the crew from the old captain's tyranny.

Omoo, which is a sequel to *Typee*, concerns the further adventures of Tommo and his new friend, Long Ghost, among the Tahitians, a primitive race corrupted by their contact with the white man, and who consequently lack the goodness and dignity of the Typees. Both *Typee* and *Omoo* deal with pacifism and rebellion in their most embryonic form, but both novels develop some of the attitudes crucial to an understanding of the conflict between these two themes. Nature is portrayed in these two works as being sympathetic to man, and evil is shown not as an inherent part of the scheme of things, but as the fault of man himself – particularly the fault of white and civilized man. Though missionaries and some of the trappings of institutionalized Christianity are roundly flayed, the basis of Christianity itself is not questioned.

Mardi, Melville's third novel, presents a view of life which is in direct opposition to that found in the earlier books. Man and nature are no longer seen as being in harmony. As the philosopher Babbalanja says, "'If not against us, nature is not for us.'" Though Babbalanja expresses skepticism about many popular religious and political beliefs, he eventually finds peace on the isle of Serenia, which symbolizes the spirit of true Christianity. Serenia is not perfect, but it is the best that man can hope for in this world. In other words, Babbalanja accepts Christianity as a form of ethical compromise, a way of life which, while not explaining the existence of evil, offers man meaning and hope. Babbalanja's compromise is rejected by Taji, the first of Melville's rebel-heroes, who spurns Serenia and sails out into the uncharted and deadly oceans in pursuit of the unattainable Yillah – symbol of the absolute, the perfect, and the beautiful. Taji's hopeless quest for Yillah typifies the outlook for Melville's future rebel-heroes. They are unable to accept the existence of evil and would rather pursue an unattainable good than compromise by agreeing to a workable but not perfect modus vivendi.

Redburn is the story of a young boy and his gradual awareness of and reaction to evil. Wellingborough Redburn sets out on a voyage to England in order to follow the footsteps of his deceased father. But as the result of his getting lost while using his dead parent's fifty year old guide book and of his exposure to social evil in the slums of Liverpool and to a more metaphysical type of evil symbolized by the Satanic sailor Jackson, Redburn comes to realize that not only is his earthly father lost forever, but that there is no spiritual father to look after the welfare of mankind either. With this understanding comes the added knowledge that to be a man, one must fight against the evil he finds in the world. By the end of the novel, Redburn is able to cope with social injustice, but he has not yet developed to a stage where he is able to combat the type of evil represented by Jackson.

White-Jacket is Melville's testament of pacifism. The viewpoint expressed in this work differs sharply from the skepticism of *Mardi* and *Redburn*. *White-Jacket* champions orthodox Christianity and natural law. Evil is shown as a man-made creation, and the cure to all injustice is to be found in a strict adherence to democracy and Christianity, two ways of life which are inexorably bound together. The major aspect which differentiates Christianity from all other religions, Melville suggests, is the "turn the other cheek" attitude of Christ.

The philosophy of pacifism developed in *White-Jacket* is carried over into *Moby-Dick,* where it is embodied in Starbuck, the Quaker first mate. Though Starbuck is a gentle and kindly man, there is steel in his make-up; he is the only man aboard the *Pequod* who has the courage to stand firm against Captain Ahab.

But, as Starbuck himself admits, he is more than overmanned, for nothing can sway Ahab – neither an appeal to his reason nor to his humanities – from his pursuit of the White Whale. On a previous whaling cruise, Ahab's leg was shorn away by Moby-Dick. Ahab universalizes this incident and sees in it the fate of innocent mankind plagued by the hostile forces which permeate the universe. The old man thinks that by killing the White Whale, he will be able to free humanity from these forces which torment man. At the close of the novel, after Moby-Dick has destroyed the *Pequod* and is posing no danger to the captain's whale-boat, Ahab at last realizes that he will never be able to kill the great whale, that Moby-Dick is immortal. Nevertheless, with one final oath, Ahab flings himself at the whale, knowing that his own destruction is inevitable. Rebellion emerges as a philosophy of life with this final courageous but foredoomed act of Ahab's. Another climactic moment of the novel is when the pacifistic Starbuck debates whether or not he should shoot Ahab as the latter lies sleeping in his cabin. Starbuck knows that the only way he can save himself and the crew of the *Pequod* from annihilation is by destroying the old man. But the Quaker mate realizes that if he kills Ahab, he will move towards the philosophical position held by his captain, and he concludes that it would be better to be doomed and retain his principles than to kill Ahab and surrender his commitment to pacifism as a way of life.

The irony of *Pierre*, Melville's next work, is that the more intensely its hero pursues virtue and truth, the more destruction and horror he brings into the lives of those he loves. The philosophical center of the book is found in the chapters dealing with a pamphlet by one Plotinus Plinlimmon. In this pamphlet, the author discusses two types of time, chronometrical (the time of God) and horological (the time of man). Plinlimmon suggests that it is impossible to be God-like in the world of man, that to do so would lead an individual to commit "strange, *unique* follies and sins, unimagined before." The highest attainable excellence in this world is a virtuous expediency, Plinlimmom concludes. The way of virtuous expediency is followed by Reverend Falsgrave who represents a watered-down form of pacifism. Pierre, as is typical of all of Melville's rebels, refuses to compromise. He attempts to follow chronometrical time in the world of man, and as a result, destroys not only himself but his mother, his cousin, and the two women he loves. The more Pierre strives to be God-like, the more he finds himself at war with God. Pierre's plight is reflected in what might well be the secret motto of the novel – *Nemo contra Deum nisi Deus ipse* (No one against God if not God himself).

The Confidence Man is the most pessimistic of Melville's works. Not only does the author continue to picture nature as being hostile to man, but in this novel we find Melville's only sustained attack upon mankind as a whole. The human race, Melville argues, can be divided into two classes, knaves and fools. Since Melville's rebels base their position on the belief that man is a far nobler thing than the elements which surround him, the attack on human nature found in *The Confidence Man* undercuts much of the basis for a philosophy of rebellion. Melville, however, returns to a more optimistic outlook of humanity in his later writings.

The short stories are varied in content and theme, and with the exception of *Moby-Dick* and *Billy Budd*, include Melville's most successful achievement in prose. "Bartleby the Scrivener" is a humorous, moving, and puzzling account of pacifism. The hero is the only one of Melville's pacifists who is not associated with some form of religious values. Bartleby's quiet "I would prefer not to" in reality is a firm refusal to do things which he finds distasteful. Bartleby dies probably because he prefers to live no longer, but it is difficult to figure out if his death is surrender or protest, for Bartleby's demise condemns not himself but the society in which he lives. "Benito Cereno", though is portrays an actual physical mutiny, nevertheless tells us little about the nature of rebellion, for we never penetrate deeply into the minds of the revolting slaves.

The philosophy developed in most of Melville's short stories is a kind of defiant stoicism, an outlook upon life which lies halfway between the extremes of pacifism and rebellion, though reconciling none of the differences that exist between these two antitheses. This attitude of defiant stoicism is found in such diverse tales as "Jimmy Rose" and "The Piazza", but it is most fully matured in the person of Hunilla, the heroine of the eighth sketch of "The Encantadas". Shortly after Hunilla, her husband, and her brother have been stranded on one of the Galapagos isles, the two men drown before her eyes. During the course of the following years, Hunilla is exposed to all the horror that both man and nature can create. But nothing can break her spirit. She endures all with pride and without complaint. Symbolic of all mankind, Hunilla represents the indomitable courage of humanity in the face of the most overwhelming obstacles.

Battle-Pieces and *Clarel* are those works of Melville's poetry in which pacifism and rebellion are most fully explored. *Battle-Pieces*, a collection of poems about the Civil War, is an almost schizophrenic work. On the one hand, Melville views the war as a battle of necessity, a means to liberate America from slavery, the greatest of human evils. But throughout the collection, there is a strong current of anti-war feeling. Though most of the poetry in this work is poor, the uneasy balance between pro-Unionism and pacifism gives a few of the poems the type of profundity and complexity which is found in Melville's best works. *Clarel* concerns man's search for values in the modern world, a world which can no longer accept the traditional religious beliefs. In some ways, *Clarel* represents Melville's most penetrating treatment of pacifism and rebellion, for the poem has three rebels – Celio, Mortmain, and Ungar – and two pacifists – Nehemiah and Derwent. Clarel the protagonist, initially does not choose sides between these two groups. But when he returns to Jerusalem and hears that Ruth is dead, Clarel curses the blindness and barrenness of the universe, and ultimately moves to a philosophical position similar to that of Ungar, the intellectual hero of the poem. The philosophy of rebellion developed in *Clarel* has two basic tenets: that the supreme protest which man can make against life is to continue to live, and that since the universe is at best amoral and chaotic, it is the duty of humanity to structure some sort of man-made value into the cosmos.

Billy Budd is Melville's testament of rebellion. The novel's primary concern is with the problem of justice. Captain Vere argues that it is necessary to sacrifice the innocent Billy in order to preserve society, but Vere's position is condemned by Melville. Even Billy Budd's way of life is questioned. Melville suggests that it is fine to be Christ-like in an unfallen and primitive world, but that to submit with Christian resignation to the harshness and cruelty of such arbitrary codes as the Articles of War is to betray the cause of justice. Injustice must be fought against actively, not merely endured. At the close of the novel, Captain Vere is killed by a shot from the French warship, the *Athéiste*. This ship, obviously symbolic of the French Revolution, is the only force in the book to openly combat tyranny. Melville's ultimate position is that rebellion, a combination of social and spiritual protest, is the only power which may eventually liberate mankind and bring dignity into the lives of all men.

In an age and a country which was, for the most part, content to ask orthodox questions and give orthodox answers, Melville dived deep into the meaning of existence and was not afraid to face the consequences of his findings. In all of his major works, we find an unflagging search for truth and a refusal to accept anything which might be considered unjust or shoddy. Moreover, there is as much idealism and defiance of conventional attitudes in his more mature work as in his earlier writings. Jay Leyda has noted that "Glued on the inside of the writing box on which *Billy Budd* and the last poems were composed was found a tiny clipping – Melville's own motto – 'Keep true to the dreams of thy youth'."[1] Melville's intellectual wanderings led him to condemn God and to challenge the basis of Christianity. Though in this sense Melville might be considered the phenomenologist of relativism, he was an absolutist in his refusal to compromise his principles. For Melville, the universe was basically hostile to the human race, but like Albert Camus he felt that "there are more things to admire in man than to despise".[2] And, what is perhaps the keynote to Melville as a writer and as a thinker, is his insistence that mankind

---

[1] Jay Leyda (ed.), *The Viking Portable Melville* (New York, 1952), pp. 739-40.

[2] Albert Camus, *The Plague*, Translated by Stuart Gilbert (New York, 1952), p. 278.

is never more noble than in this struggle against injustice, both human and universal, that by rebelling against evil, man can wrest meaning from the cosmos and in this struggle find some sort of salvation.

BIBLIOGRAPHY

Texts

Billy Budd. Ed. F. Barron Freeman (Cambridge, Mass., Harvard Press, 1948).
The Confidence Man. Ed. Elizabeth Foster (New York, Hendricks House, 1954).
The Confidence Man (New York, Grove Press, 1955).
Moby-Dick (New York, Modern Library Giant, 1930).
Pierre. Ed. Henry Murray (New York, Hendricks House, 1949).
Pierre (New York, Grove Press, 1957).
Redburn (New York, Doubleday Anchor, 1957).
The Romances of Herman Melville (New York, Tudor, 1931).
Selected Tales and Poems. Ed. Richard Chase (New York, Rinehart, 1956).
Selected Writings of Herman Melville (New York, Modern Library Giant, 1952).
Typee and Billy Budd. Ed. Milton Stern (New York, Dutton Everyman, 1958).
The Portable Melville. Ed. Jay Leyda (New York, Viking Press, 1952).
White Jacket (New York, Grove Press, 1956).
The Works of Herman Melville. Standard Edition. 16 vols. (London Constable, 1922-24).

I have followed the *MLA* style of abbreviations for names of journals, as given in the annual bibliographical volume of *PMLA*.

Abele, Rudolph von, "Melville and the Problem of Evil", *Am Merc*, LXV, No. V (1947), 592-8.
Ament, W. S., "Bowdler and the Whale", *AL*, IV (March, 1932), 39-46.
Anderson, Charles, "Contemporary American Opinions of *Typee* and *Omoo*", *AL*, IX (March, 1937), 329-46.
———, "The Genesis of *Billy Budd*", *AL*, XII (Nov., 1940), 329-46.
———, *Melville in the South Seas* (New York, 1939).
———, "A Reply to Melville's *White-Jacket*", *AL*, VII (May, 1935), 123-44.

Arms, George, "Moby-Dick and the Village Blacksmith", *N&Q*, CLXXXXII (3 May 1947), 187-8.
Arvin, Newton, *Herman Melville* (New York, 1957).
——, "Melville and the Gothic Novel", *NEQ*, XXII (March, 1949), 33-48.
Auden, W. H., "The Christian Tragic Hero", *NYT BR*, L (16 Dec., 1945), 1, 21.
——, *The Enchafèd Flood* (New York, 1950).
Babcock, C. Merton, "The Language of Melville's 'Isolatoes'", *WF*, X (October, 1951), 285-9.
Baird, James, *Ishmael* (Baltimore, 1946).
Barrett, Laurance, "The Differences in Melville's Poetry", *PMLA*, LXX (Sept., 1955), 602-23.
Battenfeld, David H., "The Source for the Hymn in *Moby-Dick*", *AL*, XXVII (Nov., 1955), 393-6.
Belgion, Montgomery, "Heterodoxy on *Moby-Dick*", *SR*, LV (Jan.-March, 1947), 108-25.
Bell, Milicent, "Melville and Hawthorne at the Grave of St. John (A Debt of Pierre Bayle)", *MLN*, LXVII (Feb., 1952), 116-8.
Bewley, Marius, "A Truce of God for Melville", *SR*, LXI (Autumn, 1953), 682-700.
Bezanson, Walter, "Melville's Reading of Arnold's Poetry", *PMLA*, LXIX (June, 1954), 365-91.
Birss, John H., "Another, but Later Redburn", *AN&Q*, VI (Jan., 1947), 150.
——, "Herman Melville and Blake", *N&Q*, CLXVI (5 May 1934), 311.
——, "'Moby-Dick' under Another Name", *N&Q*, CLXIV (25 March, 1933), 206.
——, "The Story of Toby, A Sequel to *Typee*", *HLB*, I (Winter, 1947), 118-9.
Blackmur, R. P., "The Craft of Herman Melville", *VQR*, XIV (Spring, 1938), 266-82.
Bowen, Merlin, *The Long Encounter. Self and Experience in the Writings of Herman Melville* (Chicago, 1960).
Braswell, William, "The Early Love Scenes of Melville's *Pierre*", *AL*, XXII (Nov., 1950), 283-9.
——, "Melville's *Billy Budd* as an Inside Narrative", *AL*, XXIX (May, 1957), 133-46.
——. *Melville's Religious Thought* (Durham, 1943).
——. "Melville's Use of Seneca", *AL*, XII (March, 1940), 98-104.
——. "The Satirical Temper of Melville's *Pierre*", *AL*, VII (Jan., 1936), 424-38.
Brown, E. K., "Hawthorne, Melville and 'Ethan Brand'", *AL*, III (March, 1931), 72-5.
Burnam, Tom, "Tennyson's 'Ringing Grooves' and Captain Ahab's Grooved Soul", *MLN*, LXVII (June, 1952), 423-4.
Campbell, H. M., "The Hanging Scene in Melville's *Billy Budd, Foretopman*", *MLN*, LXVI (June, 1951), 378-81.
Canfield, F. X., "*Moby-Dick* and the Book of Job", *CathW*, CLXXIV (Jan., 1952), 254-60.

Carpenter, F. I., "Melville: The World in a Man-of-War", *UKCR*, XIX (Summer, 1953), 257-64.

———, "Puritans Preferred Blondes: The Heroines of Melville and Hawthorne", *NEQ*, IX (June, 1936), 253-72.

Casper, Leonard, "The Case Against Captain Vere", *Per*, V (1952), 146-52.

Cawelti, John G., "Some Notes on the Structure of *The Confidence Man*", *AL*, XXIX (Nov., 1957), 278-88.

Chase, Richard, *The American Novel and Its Tradition* (New York, 1957).

———, "An Approach to Melville", *PR*, XVI (May-June, 1947), 285-95.

———, "Dissent on *Billy Budd*", *PR*, XV (Nov., 1948), 1212-8.

———, *Herman Melville* (New York, 1949).

———, "Melville's *Confidence Man*", *KR*, XI (Winter, 1949), 122-40.

Collin, Richard and Rita, "Justice in an Earlier Treatment of the Billy Budd Theme", *AL*, XXVIII (Jan., 1957), 513-5.

Collins, Carvel, "Melville's *Mardi*", *Expl.*, XII (May, 1954), item 42.

Connolly, Thomas E., "A Note on Name Symbolism in Melville", *AL*, XXV (Jan., 1954), 489-90.

Cook, Charles, "Ahab's Intolerable Allegory", *BUSE*, I (Spring-Summer, 1955), 45-52.

Crowley, William, "Melville's Chimney", *ESQ*, XIV (1st Quarter, 1959), 2-6.

Dahl, Curtis, "Moby Dick's Cousin Behemoth", *AL*, XXXI (March, 1959), 21-9.

Damon, S. Foster, "Why Ishmael Went to Sea", *AL*, II (Nov., 1930), 281-3.

Davidson, Frank, "Melville, Thoreau, and 'The Apple-Tree Table'", *AL*, XXV (Jan., 1954), 479-88.

Davis, Merrell, "The Flower Symbolism in *Mardi*", *MLQ*, II (Dec., 1941), 625-38.

———, *Melville's Mardi: A Chartless Voyage* (New Haven, 1952).

D'Azevedo, Warren, "Revolt on the San Dominick", *Phylon*, XVIII (2nd Quarter, 1956), 129-40.

Duffy, Charles, "A Source for the Conclusion of Melville's *Moby-Dick*", *N&Q*, CLXXXI (Nov. 15, 1941), 278-9.

Eliot, Alexander, "Melville and Bartleby", *Furioso*, III (Fall, 1947), 11-21.

Farnsworth, Robert, "*Israel Potter*: Pathetic Comedy", *BNYPL*, LXV (Feb., 1961), 125-32.

Feltenstein, Rosalie, "Melville's 'Benito Cereno'", *AL*, XIX (Nov., 1947), 245-55.

Fenton, Charles, "'The Bell-Tower': Melville and Technology", *AL*, XXIII (May, 1951), 219-32.

Fiedelson, Charles, Jr., *Symbolism and American Literature* (Chicago, 1953).

Fiess, Edward, "Melville as a Reader and Student of Byron", *AL*, XXIV (May, 1952), 186-94.

Firebaugh, Joseph, "Humorist as Rebel: The Melville of *Typee*", *NCF*, IX (Sept., 1954), 108-20.

Fogle, Richard, "Billy Budd – Acceptance or Irony?", *TSE*, VIII (1958), 107-13.

———, "The Monk and the Bachelor: Melville's *Benito Cereno*", *TSE*, III (1953), 155-78.
Forsythe, R. S., "Herman Melville's Father Murphy", *N&Q*, CLXXII (10 April 1937), 254-8.
———, "Herman Melville in the Marquesas", *PQ*, XV (Jan., 1936), 1-15.
———, "Herman Melville's 'The Town-Ho's Story' ", *N&Q*, CLXVIII (4 May 1935), 314.
Foster, Elizabeth, "Melville and Cetology", *AL*, XVII (March, 1945), 50-65.
Freeman, F. Barron, "The Enigma of Melville's 'Daniel Orme' ", *AL*, XVI (Nov., 1944), 208-11.
Friedrich, Gerhard, *In Pursuit of Moby Dick* (Pendle Hill, 1958).
Gary, L. M., "Rich Colors and Ominous Shadows", *SAQ*, XXXVII (Jan., 1938), 41-5.
Geiger, Don, "Melville's Black God: Contrary Evidence in 'The Town-Ho's Story' ", *AL*, XXV (Jan., 1954), 464-71.
Gilman, William, *Melville's Early Life and Redburn* (New York, 1951).
Giovannini, G., "The Hanging Scene in Melville's *Billy Budd*", *MLN*, LXX (Nov., 1955), 491-7.
———, "Melville and Dante", *PMLA*, LXV (March, 1950), 329.
———, "Melville's *Pierre* and Dante's *Inferno*", *PMLA*, LXIV (March, 1949), 70-8.
Gleim, W. S., *The Meaning of Moby-Dick* (New York, 1938).
———, "A Theory of *Moby-Dick*", *NEQ*, II (July, 1929), 402-19.
Glick, Wendell, "Expediency and Absolute Morality in 'Billy Budd' ", *PMLA*, LXVIII (March, 1953), 103-10.
Grdseloff, Dorothee, "A Note on the Origin of Fedallah in *Moby-Dick*", *AL*, XXVII (Nov., 1955), 396-403.
Gross, John, "Melville's *The Confidence Man:* The Problem of Source and Meaning", *NM*, LX (Sept., 1959), 299-310.
Haber, Tom, "A Note on Melville's 'Benito Cereno' ", *NCF*, VI (Sept., 1951), 146-7.
Hall, James B., "*Moby-Dick*: Parable of a Dying System", *WHR*. XIV (Spring, 1950), 223-36.
Harding, Walter, "A Note on the Title 'Moby-Dick' ", *AL*, XXII (Jan., 1951), 500-1.
Hayford, Harrison, "Melville's Usable or Visible Truth", *MLN*, LXXIV (Dec., 1951), 702-5.
———, "Poe in *The Confidence Man*", *NCF*, XIV (Dec., 1959), 207-18.
———, "The Sailor Poet of *White-Jacket*", *BPLQ*, III (July, 1951), 221-8.
Heflin, Wilson, "The Source of Ahab's Lordship over the Level Loadstone", *AL*, XX (Nov., 1948), 323-7.
Hillway, Tyrus, "Billy Budd: Melville's Human Sacrifice", *Pacific S*, VI (Summer, 1952), 242-8.
———, "Melville's *Billy Budd*", *Expl.*, IV (Nov., 1945). item 12.
———, "Pierre, the Fool of Virtue", *AL*, XXI (May, 1949), 201-11.
———, "Taji's Abdication in Herman Melville's *Mardi*", *AL*, XVI (Nov., 1944), 204-7.
———, "Taji's Quest for Certainly", *AL*, XVIII (March, 1946). 27-34.

Hillway, Tyrus, and Mansfield, Luther, eds., *Moby-Dick Centennial Essays* (Dallas, 1953).
Hoffman, Charles, "The Shorter Fiction of Herman Melville", *SAQ*, LII (July, 1953), 414-30.
Hoffman, Dan, "Melville's 'Story of China Aster' ", *AL*, XXXII (May, 1950), 185-91.
Holman, C. Hugh, "The Reconciliation of Ishmael. *Moby-Dick* and the Book of Job", *SAQ*, LVII (Autumn, 1958), 477-90.
Homans, G. C., "The Dark Angel: The Tragedy of Herman Melville", *NEQ*, V (Oct., 1932), 699-730.
Horsford, Howard, "Evidence of Melville's Plans for a Sequel to *The Confidence Man*", *AL*, XXIV (March, 1952), 85-8.
Howard, Leon, *Herman Melville* (Berkeley and Los Angeles, 1958).
Hull, William, "*Moby-Dick*: An Interpretation", *Etc.*, V (Autumn, 1947), 8-21.
Huntress, Keith, "Melville's Use of a Source for *White-Jacket*", *AL*, XVII (March, 1945), 66-74.
———, "A Note on Melville's *Redburn*", *NEQ*, XVIII (June, 1945), 259-60.
Hutchinson, William, "A Definitive Edition of *Moby-Dick*", *AL*, XXV (Jan., 1954), 472-8.
Hyman, Stanley, "Melville the Scrivener", *NMQ*, XXIII (Winter, 1953), 381-415.
Jaffé, David, "Some Sources of Melville's *Mardi*", *AL*, IX (March, 1937), 56-69.
Jones, Joseph, "Ahab's 'Blood Quench': Theater or Metallurgy?", *AL*, XVII (March, 1946), 35-7.
Kazin, Alfred, "The Inmost Leaf", *NRp*, CXI (18 Dec. 1944), 840-1.
———, "Ishmael and Ahab", *Atl.*, CXCVIII (Nov., 1956), 81-5.
———, "On Melville as Scripture", *PR*, XVII (Jan., 1950), 67-75.
Lacy, Patricia, "The Agatha Theme in Melville's Stories", *UTSE*, XXXV (1956), 96-105.
Larrabee, S. A., "Melville Against the World", *SAQ*, XXXIV (Oct., 1935), 410-8.
Lawrence, D. H., *Studies in Classic American Literature* (New York, 1955).
Leiter, Louis, "The Wake of the White Whale", *NCF*, XIII (Dec., 1958), 249-54.
Lewis, R. W. B., *The American Adam* (Chicago, 1955).
Leyda, Jay, *The Melville Log* (New York, 1951).
Lueders, E. G., "The Melville-Hawthorne Relationship in *Pierre* and *The Blithedale Romance*", *WHR*, IV (Aug., 1950), 323-34.
Mabbott, T. O., "Melville's *Moby-Dick*", *Expl.*, VIII (Nov., 1949), item 15.
Marx, Leo, "Melville's Parable of the Walls", *SR*, LXI (Autumn, 1953), 602-27.
Mason, Ronald, *The Spirit Above the Dust* (London, 1951).
Matthiessen, F. O., *American Renaissance* (New York, 1941).
Maugham, W. Somerset, "*Moby-Dick*", *Atl.*, CLXXXI (June, 1949), 98-104.
Mayoux, Jean-Jacques, *Melville*. Translated by John Ashbery (New York, 1960).

McCutcheon, Roger, "The Technique of Melville's *Israel Potter*", *SAQ*, XXVII (April, 1928), 161-74.

Metcalf, Eleanor, *Herman Melville: Cycle and Epicycle* (Cambridge, Mass., 1953).

Milhauser, Milton, "The Form of *Moby-Dick*", *JAAC*, XIII (June, 1955), 527-32.

Miller, James, "The Confidence Man: His Guises", *PMLA*, LXXIV (March, 1959), 102-11.

——, "The Many Masks of Mardi", *JEGP*, LXIII (July, 1959), 400-13.

——, "*Redburn* and *White-Jacket*: Initiation and Baptism", *NCF*, XIII (March, 1959), 277-93.

Miller, Paul, "Sun and Fire in Melville's *Moby-Dick*", *NCF*, XII (Sept., 1958), 139-44.

Miller, Perry, "Melville and Transcendentalism", *VQR*, XXIX (Autumn, 1953), 556-75.

Mills, Gordon, "The Castaway in *Moby-Dick*", *UTSE*, XXIX (1950), 231-48.

——, "The Significance of 'Arcturus' in *Mardi*", *AL*, XIV (May, 1942), 158-61.

Montague, Gene, "Melville's *Battle-Pieces*", *UTSE*, XXXV (1956), 106-15.

Moorman, Charles, "Melville's *Pierre* and the Fortunate Fall", *AL*, XXV (March, 1953), 13-30.

Mumford, Lewis, *Herman Melville* (New York, 1929).

Murray, Henry, "In Nomine Diaboli", *NEQ*, XXIII (Dec., 1951), 435-52.

Myers, H. A., "Captain Ahab's Discovery: The Tragic Meaning of *Moby-Dick*", *NEQ*, XV (March, 1942), 15-34.

Oliver, Egbert, " 'Cock-A-Doodle-Doo!' and Transcendental Hocus Pocus", *NEQ*, XXI (June, 1948), 204-16.

——, "Herman Melville's Lightning Rod Man", *Philadelphia Forum*, XXXV (June, 1956), 4-5, 17.

——, "Melville's Picture of Emerson and Thoreau in *The Confidence Man*", *CE*, VIII (Nov., 1946), 61-72.

——, "A Second Look at Bartleby", *CE*, VI (May, 1945), 431-9.

Olson, Charles, *Call Me Ishmael* (New York, 1947).

——, "Lear and *Moby-Dick*", *Twice a Year* (Fall-Winter, 1938), 165-89.

Osbourn, R. V., "The White Whale and the Absolute", *EIC*, VI (April, 1956), 160-70.

Parke, John, "Seven Moby Dicks", *NEQ*, XXVII (Sept., 1955), 319-38.

Parks, A. W., "Leviathan: An Essay in Interpretation", *SR*, XLVII (Winter, 1939), 130-2.

Paul, Sherman, "Melville's 'The Town-Ho's Story' ", *AL*, XXI (May, 1949), 212-21.

Pearce, Roy Harvey, "Melville's Indian Hater: A Note on the Meaning of *The Confidence Man*", *PMLA*, LXVII (Dec., 1952), 942-8.

Pearson, Norman Holmes, "Billy Budd: 'The King's Yarn' ", *AQ*, III (Summer, 1951), 99-114.

Percival, M. O., *A Reading of Moby-Dick* (Chicago, 1950).

Philbrick, Thomas, "Another Source for *White-Jacket*", *AL*, XXIX (Jan., 1958), 431-9.

Pommer, Henry, "Herman Melville and the Wake of the *Essex*", *AL*, XX (Nov., 1948), 290-304.

———, *Milton and Melville* (Chicago, 1950).

Proctor, Page, "A Source for the Flogging Incident in *White-Jacket*", *AL*, XXII (May, 1950), 176-82.

Reed, Herbert, "*Billy Budd*", *NS and S*, XXXIII (31 May 1947), 397.

Riegel, O. W., "The Anatomy of Melville's Fame", *AL*, III (May, 1931), 195-203.

Rizzardi, Alfredo, "La Poesia de Herman Melville", *SA*, I (1955), 159-203.

Rosenberry, Edward, *Melville and the Comic Spirit* (Cambridge, Mass., 1955).

Roudiez, Leon, "Strangers in Melville and Camus", *FR*, XXX (Jan., 1958), 217-26.

Sackman, Douglas, "The Original of Melville's 'Apple-Tree Table'", *AL*, XI (Jan., 1940), 448-51.

Satterfield, John, "Perth: An Organic Digression in *Moby-Dick*", *MLN*, LXXIV (Feb., 1959), 106-7.

Schiffman, Joseph, "Critical Problems in Melville's 'Benito Cereno'", *MLQ*, XI (Sept., 1950), 317-24.

———, "Melville's Final Stage, Irony: A Re-examination of *Billy Budd* Criticism", *AL*, XXII (May, 1950), 128-36.

Schroeder, J. W., "Sources and Symbols for Melville's *Confidence Man*", *PMLA*, LXVI (June, 1951), 363-80.

Scott, Sumner, "Some Implications of the Typhoon Scene in *Moby-Dick*", *AL*, XII (March, 1940), 91-8.

Scudder, H. H., "Melville's *Benito Cereno* and Captain Delano's Voyages", *PMLA*, XLIII (June, 1928), 502-32.

Sealts, Merton, "Herman Melville's 'I and My Chimney'", *AL*, XIII (May, 1941), 142-54.

———, *Melville as Lecturer* (Cambridge, Mass., 1957).

———, "Melville's Reading: A Check List of Books Owned and Borrowed." *HLB*, II (Spring, 1948), 141-63; (Autumn, 1948), 378-92; III (Winter, 1949), 119-30; (Spring, 1949), 268-77; (Autumn, 1949), 407-21; IV (Winter, 1950), 98-109; VI (Spring, 1952), 239-47.

Sedgwick, William, *Herman Melville: The Tragedy of Mind* (Cambridge, Mass., 1944).

Sherbo, Arthur, "Melville's Portuguese Catholic Priest", *AL*, XXVI (Jan., 1955), 563-4.

Slochower, Harry, "Freudian Motifs in *Moby-Dick*", *Complex*, III (Fall, 1950), 16-25.

———, "*Moby-Dick*", *AQ*, II (Fall, 1950), 259-69.

Snyder, Oliver, "A Note on *Billy Budd*", *Accent*, XI (Winter, 1951), 58-60.

Spiller, Robert E., *The Cycle of American Literature* (New York, Mentor, 1957).

———, et al., eds., *A Literary History of the United States* (New York, 1948).

Stanton, Robert, "*Typee* and Milton: Paradise Well-Lost", *MLN*, LXXIV (May, 1959), 407-11.

Stein, William, "Melville Roasts Thoreau's Cock", *MLN*, LXXIV (March, 1959), 218-9.

———, "The Moral Axis of *Benito Cereno*", *Accent*, XV (Summer, 1955), 221-33.

Stern, Milton, *The Fine Hammered Steel of Herman Melville* (Urbana, 1957).

Stewart, George, "The Two Moby-Dicks", *AL*, XXV (Jan., 1954), 417-48.

Stone, Geoffrey, *Melville* (New York, 1949).

Thomas, Russell, "Melville's Use of Some Sources in *The Encantadas*", *AL*, III (Jan., 1932), 432-56.

———, "Yarn for Melville's *Typee*", *PQ*, XV (Jan., 1936), 16-29.

Thompson, Lawrance, *Melville's Quarrel with God* (Princeton, 1952).

Thorp, Willard, ed., *Herman Melville: Representative Selections, with Introduction, Bibliography, and Notes* (New York, 1938).

———, "Redburn's Prosy Old Guide Book", *PMLA*, LIII (Dec., 1938), 1146-56.

Vincent, Howard P., *The Trying Out of Moby-Dick* (Boston, 1949).

———, "*White-Jacket*: An Essay in Interpretation", *NEQ*, XXII (Sept., 1949), 304-15.

Vogelback, Arthur, "Shakespeare and Melville's 'Benito Cereno'", *MLN*, LXVII (Feb., 1952), 113-6.

Walcutt, Charles, "The Fire Symbolism in *Moby-Dick*", MLN, LIX (May, 1944), 304-10.

Warren, Robert Penn, "Melville the Poet", *KR*, VIII (Spring, 1946), 208-23.

Watson, E., "Melville's Testament of Acceptance", *NEQ*, VI (June, 1933), 319-27.

Watters, R. E., "The Meanings of the White Whale", *UTQ*, XX (Jan., 1951), 155-68.

———, "Melville's 'Isolatoes'", *PMLA*, LX (Dec., 1945), 1113-48.

———, "Melville's Metaphysics of Evil", *UTQ*, IX (Jan., 1940), 170-82.

———, "Melville's Sociality", *AL*, XVII (March, 1945), 33-49.

Weaver, Raymond, *Herman Melville, Mariner and Mystic* (New York, 1921).

Weeks, Donald, "Two Uses of *Moby-Dick*", *AQ*, II (Summer, 1950), 165-76.

Weir, Charles, "Malice Reconciled: A Note on Melville's *Billy Budd*", *UTQ*, XIII (April, 1944), 276-85.

West, Ray, "The Unity of *Billy Budd*", *HudR.*, V (Spring, 1952), 120-8.

White, E. W., "*Billy Budd*", *Adelphi*, XXVIII (First Quarter, 1952), 492-8.

Williams, Stanley, "'Follow Your Leader': Melville's 'Benito Cereno'", *VQR*, XXIII (Winter, 1947), 61-76.

———, "Spanish Influence on American Fiction: Melville and Others", *NMQ*, XXII (Spring, 1952), 5-14.

Winters, Yvor, *Maule's Curse* (Norfolk, Conn., 1938).

Withim, Phil, "*Billy Budd*: Testament of Resistance", *MLQ*, XX (June, 1959), 115-7.

Wright, Nathalia, "Biblical Allusions in Melville's Prose", *AL*, XII (May, 1940), 185-99.

——, "The Confidence Men of Melville and Cooper: An American Indictment", *AQ*, IV (Fall, 1952), 266-8.
——, "The Head and the Heart in Melville's *Mardi*", *PMLA*, LXVI (June, 1951), 351-62.
——, *Melville's Use of the Bible* (Durham, 1949).
——, "A Note on Melville's Use of Spenser: Hautia and the Bower of Bliss", *AL*, XXIV (March, 1952), 83-4.
——, "Pierre: Herman Melville's Inferno", *AL*, XXXII (May, 1960), 167-81.
Young, James Dean, "The Nine Gams of the *Pequod*", *AL*, XXV (Jan., 1954), 449-63.
Zink, Karl, "Herman Melville and the Forms – Irony and Social Criticism in *Billy Budd*", *Accent*, XII (Summer, 1952), 131-9.

INDEX

Acushnet, the, 15
"Armies of the Wilderness, The", 186

"Bartleby the Scrivener" 13, 14, 127, 165, 166-171, 218
"Battle of Stone River", 183
Battle-Pieces, 11, 49, 183-188, 219
Beethoven, Ludwig, 15
"Bell Tower, The", 165
"Benito Cereno", 13, 21, 165, 171-174, 218
Billy Budd, 11-12, 13, 18, 47, 127, 165, 171, 188, 202-213, 219-220
Blake, William, 48n, 57, 82

"Camoens", 182
Camus, Albert, 180, 220
Chaucer, Geoffrey, 191-192 n
Christ 11, 12-13, 31, 50, 69, 80, 81, 123-124, 137-138, 140-141, 155-156, 160, 171, 186, 191, 193, 196, 197, 210-211, 213, 214, 216, 220
Clarel, 11, 12, 21, 38, 166, 171, 181, 182, 183, 185, 188-201, 219
"Cock-A-Doodle-Doo!", 174-175
"Commemorative of a Naval Victory", 187-188
Confidence Man, The, 146, 147-164, 180, 197, 218
"Conflict of Convictions, The", 184
Conrad, Joseph, 31

Dostoyevsky, Fyodor, 202, 209

"Encantadas, The", 36, 165, 166, 174-179, 201, 219
Epicurus, 41, 52

"Fiddler, The", 174

Gandhi, Mohandas, 11, 12, 68, 80, 107
Gulliver's Travels, 32

Haggard, Henry R., 16
"Happy Failure, The", 174
Hemingway, Ernest, 31
Housman, A. E., 126
Hume, David, 32, 41 n

Israel Potter, 146-147, 184

"Jimmy Rose", 175, 219
John Marr and Other Sailors, 183

Lawrence, D. H., 21, 22-23, 24, 83 n, 105, 173
"Lightning Rod Man, The", 165
Lucy Ann, the, 15

"Maldive Shark, The" 182
Mann, Thomas, 54-55
"March Into Virginia, The", 183, 185
Mardi, 24, 31 56, 67, 69, 81, 82, 149, 161, 215, 216

Marquis de Grandvin, 183
"Meditation, A", 184
"Misgivings", 184, 185
Moby-Dick, 11, 12, 13, 14, 21, 24, 30, 33 n, 36, 38, 39, 52, 54, 55, 56, 69, 71, 82-125, 126-127, 144, 145, 148, 163, 165, 171, 179, 180-181, 188, 197, 199, 200, 201, 211, 214, 215, 216-217

Oedipus Rex, 30
Omoo, 12, 15, 16, 25-30, 32, 39, 55, 215

Paton, Alan, 27
"Piazza, The", 165, 175-176, 219
Pierre, 126-145, 147, 149, 155, 161, 163, 199, 201, 217-218
Plato, 32
"Poor Man's Pudding", 175-176
"Portent, The", 183
Prometheus, 14, 82, 101-103, 108, 114, 163

Redburn, 29, 57-67, 69, 81, 127, 135, 216

Rousseau, Jean-Jacques, 16, 19, 214

Sartre, Jean-Paul, 214
Shakespeare, William, 31, 108, 143, 146, 172, 175, 198
Shelley, Percy B., 32, 85, 165, 198
"Shiloh", 11, 186-187
"Stonewall Jackson", 11, 185, 187
"Surrender at Appomattox, The", 183

Timoleon, 183
"Two Temples, The", 165
Typee, 12, 15-24, 27, 29-30, 31, 39, 55, 77-78, 214-215

United States, the, 68
"Utilitarian View of the Monitor's Flight, A", 185

Weeds and Wildings, 183
White-Jacket, 11, 17, 25, 29, 56, 68-81, 84, 123, 141, 144, 147, 148, 163, 184, 188, 194-195, 204, 216
Whittier, John Greenleaf, 184